GREEN MEAT?

GREEN MEAT?

Sustaining Eaters, Animals, and the Planet

Edited by

Ryan M. Katz-Rosene
and Sarah J. Martin

McGill-Queen's University Press
Montreal & Kingston • London • Chicago

ISBN 978-0-2280-0133-1 (cloth)
ISBN 978-0-2280-0271-0 (ePDF)
ISBN 978-0-2280-0272-7 (ePUB)

Legal deposit second quarter 2020
Bibliothèque nationale du Québec

Printed in Canada on acid-free paper that is 100% ancient forest free
(100% post-consumer recycled), processed chlorine free

This book has been published with the help of a grant from the Canadian Federation
for the Humanities and Social Sciences, through the Awards to Scholarly Publications
Program, using funds provided by the Social Sciences and Humanities Research Council
of Canada.

Funded by the   Financé par le
Government   gouvernement
of Canada   du Canada

Canadä

Canada Council   Conseil des arts
for the Arts   du Canada

We acknowledge the support of the Canada Council for the Arts.

Nous remercions le Conseil des arts du Canada de son soutien.

Library and Archives Canada Cataloguing in Publication

Title: Green meat? : sustaining eaters, animals, and the planet / edited by Ryan M.
    Katz-Rosene and Sarah J. Martin.

Names: Katz-Rosene, Ryan, editor. | Martin, Sarah J., 1961- editor.

Description: Includes bibliographical references and index.

Identifiers: Canadiana (print) 20200155318 | Canadiana (ebook) 20200155385 |
    ISBN 9780228001331 (cloth) | ISBN 9780228002710 (ePDF) | ISBN 9780228002727 (ePUB)

Subjects: LCSH: Animal industry–Environmental aspects. | LCSH: Meat industry
    and trade–Environmental aspects. | LCSH: Animal culture. | LCSH: Livestock. |
    LCSH: Sustainable agriculture.

Classification: LCC HD9410.5 .G74 2020 | DDC 338.1/76–DC23

This book was designed and typeset by Peggy & Co. Design in 10.5/13 Sabon.

Ryan would like to dedicate this book to Fanny, a fine Jersey cow, who may or may not know how much she's contributed to his thinking on the relationship between animals, humans, and their shared environment.

Sarah would like to dedicate this book to all the students who have taught her so much.

Contents

The Future of "Green Meat"

9   The Promise and Peril of "Cultured Meat"   169
    Lenore Newman

10 The Structural Constraints on Green Meat   185
    Abra Brynne

11 Which Way(s) Forward?   206
    Ryan M. Katz-Rosene and Sarah J. Martin

    Contributors   229
    Index   233

Tables, Figures, and Maps

Tables

Figures

Maps

Preface

Ryan M. Katz-Rosene and Sarah J. Martin

Let us be clear from the outset: This book is not intended in any way as an apology for carefree meat consumption, nor is it intended as a condemnation of eating animals. For any hardline carnivores or vegans out there seeking to find material that bolsters their claims of superior dietary practices – look elsewhere! If anything, our foremost intention as editors – and that of our contributors – is to reiterate the importance of thinking carefully about *what* you eat, *where* it comes from, and *how* it was produced. What are the impacts of your diet on you, your community/communities, and your planet? This critical thinking about food and diet is a responsibility that we believe we have as editors, who are part of a consumption-driven class of settlers in what is presently known as Canada, all while living in a particularly challenging epoch in terms of global environmental change – and the social, political, and economic changes that come along with it.

From this starting point, however, each of the contributors to this volume travels in a different direction. Some of us have arrived at "no-meat" or "low-meat" diets after embarking upon this careful dietary calculus; others of us have been less concerned with the material presence of meat on our plates and more with the *qualitative* aspects of its production (which, in turn, usually has *quantitative* implications). In bringing together this variety of perspectives on what constitutes "green meat," and in considering whether the practice of "eco-carnivorism" is even *possible* in the first place, we hope to provide fodder (sorry, this is the first of many puns, intended or otherwise, that result from a book themed around food and animal agriculture) for the various debating voices in your head as they reach a synthesis regarding dietary practices that work for you and your attempt to limit your dietary footprint.

As this book makes clear, the environmental impact of food production, and in particular meat production, is a very hot topic these days. As you will read in the ensuing chapters, a range of new agricultural practices, new agricultural thinkers and practitioners, and even new non-meat protein alternatives have emerged in recent years, raising the pitch of discussion around this subject. In preparing this book we have also noted considerable interest in the theme of "meat-environment relations," dating back to some scholarly panels we held in 2016 at the annual meetings of the Environmental Studies Association of Canada, the Canadian Political Science Association, and the Canadian Association for the Study of Food – panels which preceded this book and served as an early "launch pad" for some of our contributors to fine-tune their arguments. Those panels solicited considerable interest from the audience, and some heated (though respectful) debate. We mention this here in part to remind the reader that this book is part of a larger dialogue taking place in society, and it should be viewed not as an effort to portray a definitive theory of meat-environment relations, but rather a contributing partner in the broader canon on this complicated theme.

Acknowledgments

Of course, as the early panels we held suggest, this book has been a multi-year effort, and the result of numerous contributing minds. As such, we have many people to thank (though it goes without saying that these helpful individuals bear no responsibility for any of the book's limitations – for those you can thank us editors). In particular, we want to thank Jonathan Crago from McGill-Queen's University Press, who was excited by this idea from the very start, along with Khadija Coxon and Kathleen Fraser of MQUP who guided us through this project thereafter, and Scott Howard, whose copyediting was world-class. We would also like to thank Christopher Kelly-Bisson, Laura O'Brien, and Jose Augusto Costa for helping us enormously with editing, formatting, indexing, and all the other fun nuts and bolts of putting an edited collection together – without them this project would have been delayed even further! Of course, we thank all of our contributors, not just to the present volume, but also those who contributed to the panel sessions we held, and all those who provided excellent questions and feedback at those early roundtable sessions. Last, but not least, we thank our friends and family for laying a foundation of support necessary for carrying out a long-term project of this nature.

PART ONE

Problematizing "the Problem"

Introduction

Sarah J. Martin and Ryan M. Katz-Rosene

In recent years, it has seemingly become an irrefutable truth: *The production of animals for meat is unsustainable*. Land is being eroded and destroyed, water resources overdrawn, greenhouse gases over-emitted, and energy and grains unnecessarily diverted – all to satiate a growing, unhealthy, and inequitable global pattern of meat overconsumption. For many concerned about this unsustainable relationship between meat and environment, the logical way to reduce one's "ecological hoof-print" is to dramatically reduce or reject the consumption of meat and animal-based products, as well as diets characterized by "meatification" (see Weis, chapter 2). Hence recent headlines from widely read media outlets warning of the ecological devastation associated with one of our species's most common culinary practices – the consumption of animal products: "Eat less meat to avoid dangerous global warming, scientists say" (Harvey 2016); "Avoiding meat and dairy is 'single biggest way' to reduce your impact on Earth" (Carrington 2018); and perhaps most blunt of all, "Meat is horrible" (Premack 2016). As these headlines suggest, the notion that "animal agriculture" is one of the main culprits in the earth's environmental predicament – an argument further popularized in the recent documentary film *Cowspiracy* (Anderson 2014) – is becoming increasingly commonplace in popular culture and academia.

But does it have to be so? Is *all* meat unsustainable? And is cutting out meat and dairy really the "best way to save the planet" (as George Monbiot 2018 recently mused in his weekly column in *The Guardian*)? The suggestion strikes the "critical thinker" in (some of) us as perhaps too simplistic a claim, an ostensibly singular truth that masks a vast, complex array of competing truths. Many political ecologists and political economists studying the environment, for instance, have emphasized a wide array of biases underlying various claims to what *is* or *is not* "sustainable," such that any claim about what is "good" or "bad" for the environment ultimately must be interpreted as a political statement (Swyngedouw 2007; Harvey 1993). When people make claims about the "sustainability" of the meat-environment *problematique*, what implicit assumptions are they making about the welfare of farm and wild animals, the nutritional profile and health impacts of different diets, the global development and food security of people in industrializing economies and poor nations – and how does this impact their mode of analysis? As editors, we believe that sustainable food *systems* are multiple and varied, and represent the diversity and complexity we see in the world. In turn, there is a range of socio-ecological and political-economic challenges and solutions related to the question of whether sustainable meat consumption exists. This book teases out some of that complexity in order to consider what role(s) animals and their products might play in the future as our global society works towards more sustainable ways of living. It brings together a dozen leading thinkers on the relationship between food and environment to offer an in-depth, multi-dimensional exploration of the meat-environment relationship.

We differentiate between various *forms* and *scales* of animal agriculture and different *practices* of meat consumption – an important nuance which seems to be absent from the popular literature on the subject. As such, this book asks what it is precisely about some forms of existing meat production and consumption practices that are unsustainable; and more importantly, whether there are ways to envision more sustainable human-animal relations that include eating meat. Is there a fundamental problem with "animal agriculture," or do we need to engage in a discussion about the way that various political-economic forces at work within the food system have (re)shaped and universalized contemporary livestock production and meat consumption relations? In short, if indeed we can start to think of "sustainable meat" or "green meat," what might such a thing look like?

What Is Green Meat?

We posit from the outset that there is no singular definition of green meat, but rather there are a multitude of ways to sustain animals and the humans who consume them. As Mason and Lang (2017) note in *Sustainable Diets*, a sustainable food system is one that takes into account a wide variety of criteria – including health and nutrition, environmental impacts, social values, overall quality, economic outcomes, and effective governance. In a food system that has been defined by distance rather than connection (Clapp 2012), people are increasingly asking where their food is coming from, and how is it being produced. Consumers want to know how the animals who provide food were treated. The question of whether they were treated humanely leads to or includes others, such as whether or not they were injected with antibiotics and hormones which could filter their way into the food system (Animal Welfare Institute 2016; Bohne and Halloran 2012; Doane 2001). This growing interest and concern about meat production and consumption will likely only continue to grow as the pressures of anthropogenic climate change, growing global population, and diet-based health epidemics (in both "developed" and "developing" economies, albeit in very different ways) – along with the fast pace of technological change and innovation – all pose challenges to societies confronting questions of development, inequality, well-being, prosperity, health, and human security. In short, concerned eaters are thinking more about their own consumption habits, their ecological footprints, their "contributions" to society, and the well-being of other living beings (of both present and future generations).

In industrialized countries, this shift in public interest in animal welfare, human health, and the environmental implications surrounding meat is manifested in popular culture and the media. This is perhaps most notable in the corporate world's response to changing consumer demand: for instance, fast food chain A&W has catered its entire marketing strategy around the notion that its hamburger patties are free of hormones and steroids, and it has been rewarded handsomely with a major boost in sales for being an industry "leader" in this regard (Blair 2015).[1] Their competitors have followed suit. For its part, McDonald's Canada has embarked on what it calls a "sustainable beef" pilot project, a new verification system for improved production practices. Maple Leaf Foods is – according to a recent headline – "Pursuing Ambition to Be the Most Sustainable Protein Company on Earth" (Maple Leaf Foods 2017). And let us not forget the "Earls debacle," when the Canadian restaurant chain caused a major social backlash after announcing that it would have to start sourcing its beef from an American distributor because there was not enough Canadian-produced beef verified as "humane, hormone-free and antibiotic-free" – a decision it later overturned and which caused it to issue an open apology to Canadian beef producers (Bakx 2016).

At the same time, we approach the above examples cautiously. While they demonstrate positive shifts in the consumer demand for a more sustainable product, as well as in suppliers' attempts to meet those changing demands, they represent just a tiny crack in the serious environmental and animal welfare impacts of industrial scale meat production. Further, there is always the risk that – as with so many other areas of corporate-framed sustainability – it becomes primarily a matter of re-branding and re-marketing, rather than a reflection of genuine material transformations in production methods and consumption practices. As such, we want to problematize these recent corporate efforts to define and co-opt the notion of "sustainable meat" while recognizing that these efforts are part of a larger cultural shift in attitudes around meat.

Again, there is no clear-cut universal definition of sustainable meat. How could there be, really, given the eternal complexity of factors that determine whether or not a practice can "meet the needs of the present without compromising the ability of future generations to meet their own needs" (as the famed Brundtland report defined "sustainability" three decades ago; see World Commission on Environment and Development 1987)? How do we know what the needs of the future are, or how large or small those needs will be, or how they will be shaped by new technologies and shifting cultural tastes and different regimes of production and regulation, to say nothing of drastically changing agricultural settings and practices!?

To belabour the earlier point, *context* really does matter. Admittedly, this seems to contradict the claim made by some leading commentators on meat-environment relations about messaging – that the message to consumers about meat ought to be simple (Wellesley, Froggatt, and Happer 2015). While there is some wisdom in simple messaging from a communications point of view, it nevertheless makes some unkind assumptions about the public's ability to distill information, and simple messages have the unfortunate character of hiding a broader complexity. Further, people tend not to respond favourably to simple messages when such messages ask them to change long-held aspects of their identity. As an example, when acclaimed environmentalist David Suzuki wrote an editorial about meat and the environment under the headline "Eat Less Meat to Reduce Earth's Heat!" (Suzuki 2016), some of the reactionary (and unnecessarily vicious) responses on social media highlighted the challenges of signalling to people that their very consumption habits may be unsustainable. One commenter wrote, "I added an extra patty to my double baconator today for lunch in honor of this tripe," while another tweeted, "beef is delicious. You should breathe less." In point of fact, Suzuki was not advocating an end to animal agriculture; those who actually read the article would have noted that he addressed the complexity involved in this relationship and made note of the "benefits of animal consumption and agriculture" (ibid). Yet unreflective responses highlight how the message of "don't eat meat" – or even "eat less meat," a message most of the contributors herein would generally support in principle – is a tough one to swallow for a large number of people whose food consumption practices help define who they are. Arguably, a more fruitful message would be one that gets people thinking about the social, health, and environmental implications of all their dietary choices – not just those of one or two food groups. In fact, one psychological study about messaging regarding meat-eating and climate change came to this very conclusion: "The results support the notion that the meat-free meal idea may serve as a counterproductive message. From the perspective of motivation, it is preferable not to isolate the meat-climate issue but to develop an approach that combines multiple values regarding food choices, including health and nature-related values" (de Boer, Schösler and Boersema 2013, 1). To put this in different terms, however, what disservice might we do to the planet and to various communities and groups of people if the result of our campaigning is merely a shift from one form of environmentally damaging protein (for instance, factory-farmed meat) to another (for instance, industrially grown soy; see Hall, 2012)?

Substitution: Alternatives to Meat?

The issue of swapping out meat for an alternative protein is one way to address the problems of industrial agriculture and factory farming. We need to think seriously about this in all its various dimensions – and we note a variety of approaches in this book. Any discussion of reducing or changing meat's place within the food system must keep in mind at least the following four key problems. First, for better or worse (and it's probably the latter), global meat consumption is growing, with per capita consumption doubling since 1961 (Bittman 2008) – though much of this growth is concentrated in Asia, South America, and Africa (whereas meat consumption, in particular red meat, has held fairly steady if not declined in Europe and North America) (see figures 1.1 and 1.2). Second, the vast majority of the world's people (around 95 per cent) eat meat, although for a majority it is a rare foodstuff (Smil 2013; Heinrich Böll Stiftung and Friends of the Earth Europe 2014, 55). Third, economic development is almost always correlated to growth in animal protein consumption (which suggests that as incomes rise people are choosing to include meat in their diets; see Sans and Combris 2015). Finally, the research shows that a majority of people who attempt vegetarianism eventually return to eating meat in some capacity (Herzog 2014), and that many surveys overstate the number of

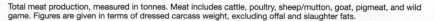

Total meat production, measured in tonnes. Meat includes cattle, poultry, sheep/mutton, goat, pigmeat, and wild game. Figures are given in terms of dressed carcass weight, excluding offal and slaughter fats.

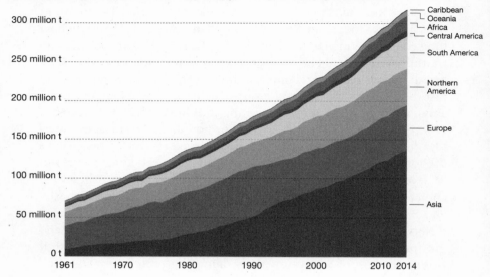

Figure 1.1   Global meat production by region (in tonnes)

Source: UN Food and Agricultural Organization, ourworldindata.org/meat-and-seafood-production-consumption/.

true vegans and vegetarians. In fact, a recent study on food preferences made the remarkable discovery that "one third of those who identified as vegetarians and more than half of those who identified as vegans *ate meat relatively regularly*" (Weersink, von Massow, and Gallant 2019). We mention these points not to discount the merits and possibility of successfully fulfilling a vegetarian or vegan diet (the virtues of which are many; Craig and Mangels 2009), but rather to be realistic about what types of messages and policies will actually translate into substantive change in meat consumption practices. In Canada, only some 4 per cent of the population adheres to a genuine vegetarian diet (Graham 2012). As Taylor writes, "eating meat is an essential and established part of human physiology, human nature and human history. It is not going to drop off the menu any time soon" (2010).

Some inevitable questions follow from this: Is there a way to achieve a balance between the "no meat" and "yes meat" camps? Should we even bother to try to make meat production and consumption more sustainable, or is the whole idea of "green meat" a lost cause? If it is *not* a lost cause, should the focus then be on changing demand (say, through a "meat tax"), or through changing production methods (say, through innovations in methane management), or both? If, from a policy perspective, it is decided that we ought to reduce meat

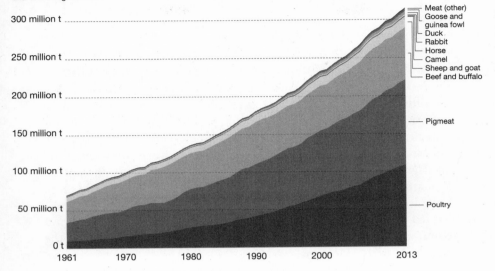

Meat production by commodity or product type, measured in tonnes per year. All data shown relate to total meat production, from both commercial and farm slaughter. Data are given in terms of dressed carcass weight, excluding offal and slaughter fats.

Figure 1.2   Global meat production by livestock type (in tonnes)

Source: UN Food and Agricultural Organization, ourworldindata.org/meat-and-seafood-production-consumption/.

consumption, what policies are likely to work, which are likely to fail, and what will be their range of consequences (intended and otherwise)?

Presumably, the message to eat *less* meat, if successfully taken up by those in industrialized countries where per capita consumption is high – for instance through the successful mobilization of the "Meatless Monday" campaign (Kramberger 2016) – could reduce a portion of the ecological pressures from meat production. But again, "eat less meat," on its own, does not really get to the heart of the matter, and the campaign could have unintended consequences. Namely, it could result in people merely eating less of what is still a polluting product (e.g., factory farmed meat) or more of another (e.g., factory farmed soy), all while justifying their continued detrimental consumption habits during the rest of the week on the false belief that they have "done their part" to protect the planet (see Katz-Rosene 2016).

The "eat less meat" message may also hold detrimental consequences for countless people involved in animal agriculture (of both the large business and small business variety). In Canada, for instance, there are some 205,000 family farms, just over half of which focus specifically on animal livestock (Beaulieu 2014; Statistics Canada 2007), but the overall trend in North America has been one of a smaller number of farms concurrent with their increasing size, mechanization, and corporatization. In our view, this trend toward industrialization has come alongside a number of unsustainable practices – including overall growth in per capita food consumption, the so-called efficient Concentrated Animal Feeding Operations (CAFOs), and the diversion of food crops for the production of transport fuel, and so on. As McDonald notes, the recent "norm" in North America has turned primarily to "two monoculture crops, corn and soy, grown on ever-larger sterile fields, too often owned by remote landowners, and, subsidized by taxpayers." She goes on: "These two crops are being produced to turn into feed for industrial livestock, or, into ethanol and biodiesel which is shipped by rail across the country to be burned in urban cars and SUVs under the label 'green'. The land use changes involved ... have led to a threatened Monarch butterfly, scarce bird populations, depleted soil microbes, and other losses of biodiversity ... Sterile fields growing monoculture crops has led to contaminated and depleted ground water in rural areas and communities, tons upon tons of topsoil loss, and the Dead Zone in the Gulf of Mexico" (McDonald 2016).

At the same time, we are cognizant of the argument that *more intensive* livestock operations offer the promise of improved efficiency thanks to greater productivity (for instance, Nijdam, Rood, and Westhoek 2012; Jones, Jones, and Cross 2014; Avery and Avery 2008). But whether or not these efficiency gains cancel out the losses from the requirement for larger scales of inputs and transport is a question that is bound to result in controversy and debate (an excellent critique is offered up by Weis in chapter 2; see also Smil 2013 for a thorough discussion).

Thus, while there is no doubt something to the idea of reducing global meat consumption, there are some evident limitations and qualifications which need to be considered. One we have not yet considered above, but which enters the discussion later in the book, relates to the vast amount of agricultural land that is presently unfit for vegetable production by virtue of its being too hilly, rocky, or forested – land which may be ideally suited to animal pastures, and often where pastoralists build their livelihoods (Eisler et al. 2014). Does it not make sense to maintain these types of marginal lands in the service of ecological food production? And if not, what are the consequences for the people who live on such lands, and presently depend on it and animals to sustain themselves?

A related challenge has to do with the significant quantity of phytomass, or plant material, found in grasslands and croplands that is simply not digestible by humans, but is perfectly suited for animal consumption (Smil 2013). These factors suggest that livestock can play an important role within the food system and ecosystems, and that while some shifting in the *proportion* of animal to non-animal protein may be in order to yield more sustainable global food systems, there is much to lose from phasing out the former entirely (we take up this discussion further in our concluding chapter).

Green Meat Debates

Meat production and consumption has been examined from a variety of critical positions, from political economists who have examined the industrialization of livestock production and its environmental effects (see Weis, chapter 2) to critical animal studies scholars who have taken an ethical position aiming to dismantle the unequal power relations between animals and humans (Potts 2016). Industrial *livestock* production is embedded in broader structures of industrial *agriculture*, founded on surplus grain used as feed (Friedmann 1992; 1993), a model that is increasingly being adopted in new sites around the world where production is growing quickly, such as China (Schneider 2015). The industrial model of agriculture has been shown to be environmentally destructive, leading to greenhouse gases, biodiversity loss, and water pollution and depletion (Clapp and Martin 2013). In turn, industrial livestock production not only relies on this model for feed, but further generates manure and GHGs (in the form of methane and nitrous oxide), and draws heavily on fossil fuels (Grain 2017).

Critics of meat consumption in human-animal studies problematize "carnism" as "an invisible belief system that propagates meat consumption as a given" (Potts 2016, 21) and as "natural, normal and necessary" (Joy 2011) – a list which recently received a fourth "N," "nice" (Piazza et al. 2015). Meat consumption is often central to these studies because it exemplifies the unequal power relations between animals, humans, and the environment. Many in the field seek to liberate sentient animals from their violent lives in industrial livestock systems (Singer 1990). In short, carnism has been argued to be a form of violence against animals and the environment. At the same time, animals are also rendered invisible in discussions of food security and the environment (Arcari 2017). Both these sets of scholarship are crucial for understanding industrial livestock and the often-unthinking meat-eating that accompanies mass consumption. In this volume, we acknowledge both these positions and agree with their premises. Yet, as editors, we have experienced different relationships with animal agriculture and meat consumption. In drawing from the various contributions herein, we aim to challenge both these depictions of production and consumption, and to set out a vision that makes animal agriculture visible and asks eaters to be reflexive about their meat consumption in political, economic, and environmental terms.

The following collection is designed to engage the reader with a multifaceted exploration and critique of what we are calling a new ecological subject – the "eco-carnivore" – a socially and environmentally conscious consumer seeking to promote sustainable animal agriculture. That is, the following chapters examine whether the historic, cultural, and culinary importance of meat can be reconciled with contemporary efforts to regenerate the environment. In one sense the eco-carnivore has emerged along with the rise of reclaimed small-scale organic agriculture in North America, the exponential growth of farmer's markets, and the concurrent cultural manifestation of the "foodie" movement (Pollan 2010). To many of these conscientious consumers, if done right, animal agriculture can and should play an important role in the food system. For them, size matters and place matters; in short, context matters.

That is, the animal-human relations that produce meat in CAFOs are qualitatively different from those that produce meat on a farm practising regenerative agriculture through (for example) managed grazing and pasturing (Shepard 2013). In addition, grasslands and pasturelands have been identified as key sites to sequester carbon through animal management practices (Gerber et al. 2013, 89; Toensmeier 2016), in contrast to monocrop practices that produce grain-fed meat and often require extensive tillage which releases carbon back into the atmosphere (though this is slowly changing). The very notions of "green meat" and "eco-carnivorism" help us to ask a variety of questions that complicate how we understand and consume meat in the context of sustainable landscapes.

In short, the book before you critically examines the multifaceted dimensions of "green meat" – questioning the idea that we might be able to eat animal flesh, not only in ways that do not damage the landscape, the climate, and water systems, but in a way that plays a role in generating and regenerating such ecosystems. In this sense *Green Meat* aims to add to some recent assessments of the sustainability potential of meat by journalists and food producers – like Judith Schwartz's *Cows Save the Planet* (2013), Nicolette Hahn Niman's *Defending Beef* (2014), Simon Fairlie's *Meat: A Benign Extravagance* (2010), Sheldon Frith's *Letter to a Vegetarian Nation* (2016), and Vaclav Smil's *Should We Eat Meat?* (2013). Dawkins and Bonney (2008) in the *Future of Animal Agriculture: Renewing the Ancient Contract* provide a particular focus on animal welfare and how to improve care for domesticated animals, but they are less focused on environmental sustainability even though they see the two issues linked. While we, as editors, take a somewhat similar approach as that taken by Fairlie (2010, 2) in asking "whether farming animals for meat is sustainable" as a central research question, we nevertheless confront the topic from a plurality of views (thanks to our diverse contributors), and our own approach focuses on the question of *possibilities*. We ask: *Can* meat-eating be sustainable? *Can* the present trends be reversed? While some of the contributors in this volume are unequivocal, answering with either a resounding "yes" or a resounding "no," others offer more nuanced explications for how and why the context matters. As to whether meat-eating *is* or *is not* or *can be* sustainable, we leave that up to the reader to decide, based on which arguments and angles they find most compelling.

Pathways to Green Meat

If the preceding discussion seems riddled with contradictory premises, it is because it is – there are clearly a range of responses to the meat-environment *problematique*, ranging from proposals calling for the end of animal agriculture (Monbiot 2018), to the further "sustainable intensi-fication" of livestock production using new technologies to increase yield per animal, to more "mindful" individual or communitarian approaches to animal consumption based on subsistence hunting or trapping (Cerulli 2013; Gray 2017). As we identify in the concluding chapter, we see the world simultaneously headed in three different directions (or "pathways") when it comes to the future of meat-society-environment relations. We call these pathways "modernizing meat," "replacing meat," and "restoring meat." While we elaborate more on these pathways (and their inherent limitations) in chapter 11, we briefly introduce them here for the reader to keep in mind as they dive into the book.

The first pathway – "modernizing meat" – applies an ecological modernization approach to the topic. For such proponents the problem is not that meat is necessarily "bad" for the environment, but rather that old antiquated ways of producing meat are highly inefficient; as such, through the adoption of new technologies and innovations, we will be able to produce meat in much more efficient (and thus sustainable) ways (Capper 2011). This solution leans heavily towards industrial forms of production, emphasizing the efficiency gains that have been made in terms of the volume of inputs required to produce a given amount of meat in highly industrialized countries. If there is one pathway that presently dominates the policy-making community across the indus-trialized and industrializing world, this is likely it – given the high value that this subsector of agriculture generates in the way of economic growth (Bansback 2014).

While the "replacing meat" pathway rejects the central premise of the other pathways (claiming that meat production generally marks an inefficient use of resources and that sustainable food systems ought to greatly reduce – if not entirely remove – meat from the menu; see Poore and Nemecek 2018), it nevertheless shares some implicit commonalities with the eco-modernist presuppositions of the "modernizing meat" pathway. That is, the replacing meat pathway typically requires some openness to industrial methods of protein production, in part because the critique is based on a concern for using crops to feed *animals* when there is a need to feed a growing *human population* instead, and similarly because in substituting animal protein for plant-based proteins, more food is typically required to satiate the same amino acid content of plant-based protein sources (as an example, one would typically have to eat about twice as much soy tofu as they would beef to acquire the same total amount of protein). The production of "meat analogues" has been on the upswing and are developed from plant or animal cells cultured in laboratories or bioreactors (Froggatt and Wellesley 2019). In a recent report from Chatham House, Froggatt and Wellesley (2019) identify two categories of meat analogues, advanced plant-based "meat" and cultured meat. The first category is designed to replicate the experience of meat, such as the Impossible™ Burger, which has a texture like ground beef, but which uses plant-derived ingredients. The second category is cultured meat, sometimes known as in vitro animal meat or "lab meat," which is grown from animal-derived stem cells using a growth medium, but is not harvested from a living animal. It uses techniques from regenerative medicine to grow meat, sometimes called "cellular agriculture" (ibid., 51). Both are industrial because products are designed to align with mass production and consumption systems already in place. This is not to say that all advocates of "replacing meat" support industrialized forms of food production; there has been growing support in particular for "agro-ecological" forms of food production (of both animal and plant-based foods) that reject hyper-industrialization in general, and which generally require a downscaling of meat production given the inability to use industrially produced grains for livestock feed. Interestingly, this agro-ecological approach has recently found support in global governance circles (most notably in the Food and Agriculture Organization of the UN).

Along these lines, there is some overlap between those in the "replacing meat" category who support more agro-ecological methods of production, and proponents of the third pathway – "restoring meat." In general, proponents of the latter pathway view agri-food systems

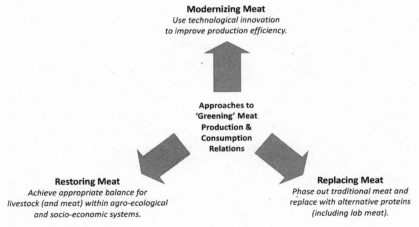

Modernizing Meat
*Use technological innovation
to improve production efficiency.*

**Approaches to
'Greening' Meat
Production &
Consumption
Relations**

Restoring Meat
*Achieve appropriate balance for
livestock (and meat) within agro-ecological
and socio-economic systems.*

Replacing Meat
*Phase out traditional meat and
replace with alternative proteins
(including lab meat).*

Figure 1.3   Pathways to green meat

as ecosystems and ask what roles or niches different types of animals might play in the system, and consequently what functions may be lost in the absence of animals. As with the other pathways, there is a range of proponents within the "restoring meat" category – with some calling for major *upscaling* of meat production globally (Savory 2013) and others calling for modest *reductions* in meat consumption as part of a major transition towards more "restorative" methods of animal husbandry centred on integrating animals within mixed agricultural systems (Shepard 2013; Fairlie 2010). As figure 1.3 notes, these three pathways mark a fluid typology, with nuanced differences within each pathway and some crossover with other pathways.

As readers will note, the contributions in this book tend to lean either towards "restoring meat" or "replacing meat" – or some combination thereof. That is, while there are significant differences between us, most authors in this book approach this topic with skepticism toward the efficiency claims made by the "modernizing meat" crowd, and call for a return to more "natural" ways of producing food and managing animals. This critique is partly situated in an ethical framework that sees industrially managed animals being deprived of the natural conditions to which their species are best suited; an environmental critique based on exposing the "externalities" associated with industrial agriculture; and a political economic critique of the corporate agglomeration and control of food which has been facilitated by the industrial food system.

Who Benefits, and Who Loses?

A final theme that we feel is important to consider is the dual question of "who benefits and who loses?" Who would benefit from the greening of meat, and who would lose from it? And similarly, who would benefit or lose from policies aiming to phase out animal agriculture? Strong arguments have been made about "future generations" benefitting from both the greening of meat and the elimination of it, but in what ways do present-day producers and consumers of meat gain from these proposals? For some, it is this question that ultimately tips the balance in favour of greening meat, as opposed to eliminating it. For one, countless farmers and pastoralists around the world benefit from producing meat alongside crops ("mixed systems"), and thus stand to lose more from centralized policies that aim to bring an end to animal agriculture than from policies that aim to help them reduce their footprint (Herrero et al. 2010). At a global level, despite the fast pace of urbanization throughout the industrial revolution, today just under half of humanity still lives in a rural setting. *Livestock's Long Shadow*, the very report by the FAO which helped launch the meat-environment debate into the mainstream, notes that for a significant portion of humanity, meat production is the primary source of income and an "insurance policy" for pastoralists to boot, particularly in landscapes where large crops may not be suitable. In their words, "raising livestock is often the only economic activity available to poor people in developing countries" (Steinfeld et al. 2006). This, along with other admissions, leads commentators like Fairlie to conclude that policies such as taxing biospheric emissions from livestock (methane and nitrous oxide) or forcing dietary shifts would ultimately hurt poor nations and poor farmers the most (despite their smaller net footprint), and thus reflects a form of "carbon colonialism" (Fairlie 2010, 175–84).

A second issue here has to do with the role that animal agriculture and meat consumption plays in various cultures. In addition to the above complicating factors, there is the deeply challenging question of how a shift away from animal agriculture would influence practices in cuisine and human-animal relations in those cultures which give an important role to the consumption of animal flesh. This of course forms part of the "social" dimension of sustainability, since practices of livestock raising and meat consumption have been sustained by humans since the origins of sedentary societies – some argue that these practices have helped define *homo sapiens'* place amongst all the other animals on earth. Of course, there are also many cultural examples of selected meat *omissions*, particularly in various religions – observant Jews eat neither pork nor shellfish, observant Muslims do not eat pork, Hindus do not eat beef, and many Buddhists do not eat animal products (though it is a myth that Buddhists are by creed vegetarians; see Liusuwan 2016). There are also, of course, other cultural manifestations – some ancient – of vegetarianism (Osborne 1995). Yet as noted above, for the vast majority of people in the world, meat consumption is quite simply a part of life, and while many may be willing to give up meat, others simply are not (Zaraska 2016).

There can be no doubt that cultures evolve – diets in particular quickly go in and out of fashion, especially in industrialized economies – but the "staying power" of various cultural adaptations or shifts will likely be commensurate with the scale of change required. While it would be naïve to conclude that the world could *never* go meat-free, perhaps it is just as naïve to suggest that humanity will voluntarily accept an entirely meat-free diet within the next few decades (the window of time we now appear to have to decarbonize global society in order to meet international climate objectives). Again, these realities suggest to us that a more pragmatic approach is likelier to generate more sustainable meat-society-environment relations (which at least according to us as editors includes eating *less* meat overall, and changing how it is produced); from a strategic perspective, that is preferable to trying to move forward without meat at all and with no change to the underlying industrial character of food production.

This relates to another potential (albeit highly contested) benefit of the greening meat option – that of human nutrition. Taylor argues for the important role of meat in the global diet: "Meat is a necessary component of the global diet, comprising approximately one-third of all protein consumed. Meat is also a vitally important supply of micronutrients. This is particularly so in less-developed countries. Adding even small amounts of meat to the diet of those who are malnourished can provide a tremendous health benefit" (Taylor 2010). There may be health benefits to *reducing* meat consumption, particularly in industrialized economies where meat consumption is clearly excessive (Popkin 2009). But aggressively phasing out animal agriculture might have serious nutritional implications (even within industrialized economies, where there is a risk of certain types of nutritional deficiencies; Haider et al. 2018). *Reducing* global meat consumption (particularly in certain contexts) could offer significant health benefits according to the literature, but *eliminating* meat consumption (in certain contexts) could be detrimental as well.[2]

Finally, there is the ironic point about livestock animals *benefitting* from the greening of meat rather than from the elimination of meat, which would theoretically entail the removal in some way of countless livestock animals – ironic, of course, because producing meat requires the death of sentient beings. Obviously, one could rationally argue from an animal rights perspective (Foer 2010) that livestock thus stand to lose from a greening meat situation, but the same applies to a policy of quickly ending animal husbandry (what does one do with all the animals already here?). Thinking through who benefits and who loses from green meat is complex and multifaceted, and requires us to delve into the complicated interactions between animals, humans and the environment.

Overview and Chapter Summary

The chapters in this book are divided into three parts. The first, "Problematizing 'the Problem,'" is so titled to emphasize the importance of nuance in the discussion surrounding meat and environment. Not all forms of livestock production are the same, notes our first contributor, Tony Weis, in chapter 2. Industrial systems of production exact an enormous (if often hidden) toll on the environment, what he terms its "ecological hoofprint": the toll on resources, the enormous pollution loads, and the public health risks as our diets become increasingly weighted towards meat consumption. The biophysical problems of industrial livestock production are complicated by poor animal welfare. Weis argues that the "meatification" of diets is not merely a *reflection* of global inequalities, but is actually worsening them by engendering greater food insecurity and the unsettling effects of climate change on the world's poorest people.

In chapter 3, Ryan Katz-Rosene problematizes the hot button issue of livestock's contribution to anthropogenic climate change. He aims to complicate the idea of "undifferentiated livestock" and the emergent "common-sense" narrative on meat and climate change. He argues that the common-sense wisdom that the production and consumption of meat is "*bad* for the climate" is a problematic oversimplification. On the one hand many of these critiques erase the complexity and variety of livestock practices, and on the other hand livestock is taken out of context and animals emerge as merely GHG-emitting machines. Katz-Rosene interrogates these portrayals and underscores the differentiation between "agro-ecological" models of livestock production, and "industrial" models of livestock production, primarily around the different types of emissions that they produce (biospheric and fossil fuel emissions, notably).

Chapter 4 wraps up the first section of the book. Caitlin M. Scott demonstrates how recent efforts to define sustainable diets have put meat consumption at the centre of a number of key debates surrounding human health and environmental sustainability. At the same time, as Scott demonstrates, these debates are being shaped by powerful actors to align with their own interests. As such, Scott asks us to reflect on the discourse of sustainability, and to examine the actors who are shaping the debates and what their underlying motivations and interests may be.

The second part of the book – "Getting It Right: Case Studies and Specific Practices" – highlights examples that our contributors felt already qualified as "green meat" or signalled successful cases of truly engaging with the idea of more sustainable meat production or consumptive relations. In chapter 5, Sheldon Frith comes to the defense of practitioners of holistic planned grazing (a label which he would apply to himself given his current work as a holistic management supervisor and consultant at the Northern Farm Training Institute in Hay River, Northwest Territories). Despite some criticisms about holistic management being "unscientific," Frith points out that in fact there is plenty of evidence (both scientific and anecdotal) showing that carefully planned grazing techniques *can* help prevent soil erosion and boost soil fertility and water retention capacity, all while helping to sequester carbon dioxide. In short, Frith makes the case for why meat produced through Holistically Planned Grazing methods is sustainable, and offers great hope for the restoration of agro-ecological systems.

Chapter 6 offers another example of existing sustainable meat consumption practices – eco-carnivorism in Canada's Northern Indigenous communities, as exemplified through the case study of the Garden Hill First Nation in Manitoba. Shirley Thompson, Pepper Pritty, and Keshab Thapa discuss a post-colonial foodshed in the context of the poverty and health disparities witnessed in many Indigenous Canadian communities. They argue that reclaiming a diet that has sustained Indigenous populations prior to colonization, and a diet based on Indigenous knowledge systems, has the restorative power to heal the root cause of many Indigenous communities' ill-health and food insecurity. As they argue, wild-trapped meat can play an integral role in this restorative process.

In chapter 7, Alexandra Kenefick tackles the question of "responsible meat consumption" through a "praxis-based" approach, expanding upon lessons learned in her own lived experience as a vegan-turned-carnivore seeking to feed herself while supporting more ethical forms of food production. Kenefick makes the critical point that it is not just "meat" consumption, but specifically the eating of *varied meat sources* (which includes eggs, offal, fish, and insects, in addition to the muscle tissue that North Americans typically consume), that ensures that this food category provides literally *all* the essential nutrients to sustain and nurture human life. This broader framework of thinking about the nutritional value of meat as being tied to a more diverse inclusion of meats within our diets (beyond a steak) lends itself to more sustainable forms of consumption, since it prompts both a diversification in the production of different species of animals and a more holistic notion of eating the whole animal (thereby minimizing waste).

As Gwendolyn Blue points out in chapter 8, thinking about eco-carnivorism through the prism of different frames changes what we see in this complex process. Taking on a feminist multi-species approach (inspired by Haraway 2008; 2015), Blue challenges the dominant frame of "only a vegan diet is a climate friendly diet." She does this by reminding us that the practice of ecological food consumption is complicated by three inescapable realities – first, that all organisms must eat to survive; second, that diets are not limited to just human diets, but are entangled within multi-species relations, and in some instances conflicting; and third, that the process of consuming food is "intimately entangled" with killing, life, and death. In the end, a feminist multi-species approach reminds us to avoid reductionist and universalizing solutions to the problem of agriculture-related climate change, since while these may help simplify action in the short term, they "may also prove to be ecologically and politically wrongheaded in the long run."

We conclude the book with a final three-chapter part, "The Future of 'Green Meat.'" In chapter 9, Lenore Newman offers up a vision of the future in which "meat" is derived not from animals, but from new lab-based technologies centreed on growing cell cultures.[3] Newman expands on this emerging market (of cellular agriculture) and argues that it holds tremendous potential to destabilize the existing dominance of animal agriculture in global food systems. While Newman admits that the complete replacement of animal products with such cultured meat analogues is far away, she identifies how many meat-replacement or meat-alternative proteins are being developed and already consumed. For Newman, green meat inevitably means cultured meat analogues which can benefit from efficiencies found in growing only the requisite "muscle tissues" destined for human consumption.

In chapter 10, Abra Brynne's contribution to the discussion of green meat's future centres on an analysis of its past. That is, Brynne confronts the evolution of the North American meat processing industry through-out modern capitalism, showing how the combination of wealth, power, and politics have yielded a market and regulatory structure that largely favours large industrial-scale meat producers (at the expense of smaller-scale producers who are practising ecological methods of meat production). Brynne focuses on the case study of the re-regulation of abattoirs in British Columbia in recent years, demonstrating the layers of politics involved in either hindering or supporting those livestock producers who rear animals in a sustainable manner.

In the concluding chapter (chapter 11), we sum up what we see as the three main pathways along which the discussion of green meat appears to be headed (pathways identified above as modernizing, replacing, and restoring meat). We suggest that green meat is not so much a singular end goal as much as a multifaceted process continually in flux. We argue that green meat requires us to be more reflective about food *needs*, and further requires us to produce meat in a way that is equitable to animals and humans alike, taking into consideration the complex socio-environmental relations that bring people and animals together, whether across field fences or on our dinner plates. In the end, this likely means that "green meat" is not just about the production methods, but also the consumption relations and geographical spaces involved. As we see it, green meat *does* mean eating *less* meat – particularly for most of us within industrialized economies – but it must be more than that. It means embracing modest dietary shifts to allow for a proportional replacement of animal-based proteins with non-animal proteins in industrial societies; and, in other contexts where livestock are an integral component of food security, it means embracing the consumption of high-quality meat proteins. Further, green meat, for us, means pursuing a post-industrial food system centred in community well-being and nourishment, as well as ecologically oriented production systems which view animals as part of a larger farm ecosystem.

Conclusion: Beyond "Slippery Slopes" and "Grey Zones"

As we can see from the various approaches taken by the contributors in this book, the relationship between meat and environment is compli-cated. If all of the above strikes you as an attempt on our behalf to be "fence-sitters" – cowardly hiding in the grey zone between clear positions for or against meat – keep in mind that all of the contributors in this volume are in some way concerned about the possible slippery slopes that could arise if their arguments are taken out of context. For instance, we would be concerned if this book was used by those aiming to justify the status-quo continuation of the industrial livestock industry. As noted above, even with per capita meat consumption in Canada declining in recent years (Atkins 2015), it is still at very high levels. At the same time, the black and white rhetoric about meat's ecological impact has given rise to another slippery slope, on which some have called for the elimination of all "animal agriculture," which strikes (at least some of) us as equally untenable a solution for yielding a sustainable agro-ecological model. As editors, we are inclined to believe that animals have a crucial role to play in the future of agriculture, albeit one which is drastically redefined from their role at present. Our hope is that this compilation of contributions will further the discussion about whether "green meat" is possible, and if so, what it might look like, while also complicating the notion of a singular "green meat" or a meatless world.

A few final caveats: Our aim with this book is to contextualize green meat within a rapidly changing socio-ecological environment, where meat consumption is frequently held up as a significant contributor to environmental degradation and climate change, and increasingly labelled as "unnecessary" given plant-based and cell-cultured alternatives, not to mention novel proteins like cricket powder. This discussion is bound to take shape in very different ways depending on where in the world it is taking place. In some of the poorest communities around the globe, to have such a discussion would be considered a luxury. That said, we are primarily focused on North American foodways in the context of the global food system, and the book mostly focuses on settler systems of agriculture (chapter 6 is an exception). One drawback relating to this is that we do not fully explore the fisheries or seafood meat – an evident gap, if one considers how humanity now consumes more seafood (about 150 million tonnes per year) than any other type of farmed meat. Similarly, much of the book's focus is on ruminants, such as cattle, since they are typically the most commonly accused culprits, and since they also offer the most potential for regenerative grass-based forms of agriculture thanks to their ability to "upcycle" human-inedible plant matter. This imbalance largely captures the imbalance in popular discourses about the (un)sustainability of animal agriculture. We believe more work should be focused on Indigenous food sovereignty, fisheries, and other kinds of foodways, but as editors, and as settlers in Canada, the book has a point of view that is strengthened and limited by our training and experiences.

Notes

1   More recently, the fast food chain has also added the vegan "Beyond Burger" produced by California-based firm Beyond Meat to their menu, and included this as an important part of their marketing strategy (Sagan 2018).
2   The debate on the health risks and benefits of meat consumption is exceptionally complex and hotly contested. It is no easy task to try to

reconcile the benefits offered by the protein, iron, zinc, and vitamin B12, and various types of fats found in meat, with the associated risks of cardiovascular disease, diabetes, colon cancer, and obesity which potentially come from the *overconsumption* of meat (McAfee et al. 2010).

3   A note on terminology is in order. It is important to make a distinction between "lab-based" meat analogues which may in fact be "plant-based" but manufactured in a laboratory setting in an effort to recreate the taste and consistency of genuine meat; and those cultured-meat analogues that Newman is mostly concerned with in her chapter. The latter are not "plant-based" but rather seek to grow cellular cultures which are essentially identical to animal cells. We thus try to refer to "plant-based meat analogues" or "cultured meat analogues" to reflect this important difference.

References

Anderson, Kip. 2014. *Cowspiracy: The Sustainability Secret.* AUM Films and First Spark Media.

Animal Welfare Institute. 2016. "Consumer Perceptions of Farm Animal Welfare." Animal Welfare Institute. https://awionline.org/sites/default/files/uploads/documents/fa-consumer_perceptionsoffarmwelfare_-112511.pdf.

Arcari, Paula. 2017. "Normalised, Human-Centric Discourses of Meat and Animals in Climate Change, Sustainability and Food Security Literature." *Agriculture and Human Values* 34 (1): 69–86. https://doi.org/10.1007/s10460-016-9697-0.

Atkins, Eric. 2015. "Canadians Eating Less Meat, Taking a Bite out of Food Industry's Margins." *Globe and Mail*, 15 September 2015. http://www.theglobeandmail.com/report-on-business/canadians-eating-less-meat-taking-a-bite-out-of-food-industrys-margins/article26373758/.

Avery, Alex, and Dennis Avery. 2008. "Beef Production and Greenhouse Gas Emissions." *Environmental Health Perspectives* 116 (9): A374–5. https://doi.org/10.1289/ehp.11716.

Bakx, Kyle. 2016. "Earls Apologizes to Ranchers for Its 'Dumb Decision' to Take Canadian Beef Off the Menu." CBC News, 10 August 2016. http://www.cbc.ca/news/canada/calgary/earls-beef-timhortons-sustainable-1.3715275.

Bansback, Bob. 2014. "Future Directions for the Global Meat Industry?" *EuroChoices* 13 (2): 4–11. https://doi.org/10.1111/1746-692X.12056.

Beaulieu, Martin S. 2014. "Demographic Changes in Canadian Agriculture." 18 February 2014. http://www.statcan.gc.ca/pub/96-325-x/2014001/article/11905-eng.htm.

Bittman, Mark. 2008. "Rethinking the Meat-Guzzler." *New York Times*, 27 January 2008. http://www.nytimes.com/2008/01/27/weekinreview/27bittman.html.

Blair, Jennifer. 2015. "'Better Beef' Campaign Turns Out Just Fine for A&W."
    AGCanada.com. 9 October 2015. http://www.agcanada.com/2015/10/
    better-beef-campaign-turns-out-just-fine-for-aw.
Boer, Joop de, Hanna Schösler, and Jan J. Boersema. 2013. "Climate Change
    and Meat Eating: An Inconvenient Couple?" *Journal of Environmental
    Psychology* 33 (March): 1–8. https://doi.org/10.1016/j.jenvp.2012.09.001.
Bohne, Meagen, and Jean Halloran. 2012. "Meat on Drugs: The Overuse of
    Antibiotics in Food Animals and What Supermarkets and Consumers
    Can Do to Stop It." Yonkers, NY: Consumer Reports.
Capper, Judith L. 2011. "Replacing Rose-Tinted Spectacles with a High-
    Powered Microscope: The Historical versus Modern Carbon Footprint of
    Animal Agriculture." *Animal Frontiers* 1 (1): 26–32. https://doi.org/10.2527/
    af.2011-0009.
Carrington, Damian. 2018. "Avoiding Meat and Dairy Is 'Single Biggest Way'
    to Reduce Your Impact on Earth." *The Guardian*, 31 May 2018. http://www.
    theguardian.com/environment/2018/may/31/avoiding-meat-and-dairy-is-
    single-biggest-way-to-reduce-your-impact-on-earth.
Cerulli, Tovar. 2013. *Mindful Carnivore: A Vegetarian's Hunt for Sustenance.*
    New York: Pegasus Books.
Clapp, Jennifer. 2012. *Food.* Malden, MA: Polity Press.
Clapp, Jennifer, and Sarah J. Martin. 2013. "Food and Agriculture." In
    Routledge Handbook of Global Environmental Politics, edited by Paul G.
    Harris, 520–32. Abingdon, UK: Routledge.
Craig, Winston J., and Ann Reed Mangels. 2009. "Position of the American
    Dietetic Association: Vegetarian Diets." *Journal of the American Dietetic
    Association* 109 (7): 1266–82.
Dawkins, Marian Stamp, and Roland Bonney. 2008. *The Future of Animal
    Farming: Renewing the Ancient Contract.* Malden, MA: Blackwell.
Doane, Deborah. 2001. *Taking Flight: The Rapid Growth of Ethical
    Consumerism: Ethical Purchasing Index.* London, UK: New Economics
    Foundation.
Eisler, Mark C., Michael R.F. Lee, John F. Tarlton, Graeme B. Martin,
    John Beddington, Jennifer A. J. Dungait, Henry Greathead, et al. 2014.
    "Agriculture: Steps to Sustainable Livestock." *Nature News* 507 (7490): 32.
    https://doi.org/10.1038/507032a.
Fairlie, Simon. 2010. *Meat: A Benign Extravagance.* White River Junction, VT:
    Chelsea Green.
Foer, Jonathan Safran. 2010. *Eating Animals.* London: Penguin.
Friedmann, Harriet. 1992. "Distance and Durability: Shaky Foundations of
    the World Food Economy." *Third World Quarterly* 13 (2): 371–83.
– 1993. "The Political Economy of Food: A Global Crisis." *New Left Review* 1
    (197).

Frith, Sheldon. 2016. *Letter to a Vegetarian Nation: We Need Livestock for Sustainable Food Production and Environmental Restoration*. Self-published.

Froggatt, Antony, and Laura Wellesley. 2019. "Meat Analogues: Considerations for the EU." Research Paper. London: Chatham House, Royal Institute of International Affairs. https://www.chathamhouse.org/sites/default/files/2019-02-18MeatAnalogues3.pdf.

Gerber, P.J., H. Steinfeld, B. Henderson, A. Mottet, C. Opio, J. Dijkman, A. Falcucci, and G. Tempio. 2013. "Tackling Climate Change through Livestock: A Global Assessment of Emissions and Mitigation Opportunities." Rome: Food and Agriculture Organization of the United Nations.

Graham, David. 2012. "The New Vegetarians." Thestar.com. 7 December 2012. https://www.thestar.com/life/2012/12/07/the_new_vegetarians.html.

Grain. 2017. "Grabbing the Bull by Its Horns: It's Time to Cut Industrial Meat and Dairy to Save the Climate." Barcelona: GRAIN. https://www.grain.org/attachments/4150/download.

Gray, Louise. 2017. *The Ethical Carnivore: My Year Killing to Eat*. New York: Bloomsbury Natural History.

Haider, Lisa M., Lukas Schwingshackl, Georg Hoffmann, and Cem Ekmekcioglu. 2018. "The Effect of Vegetarian Diets on Iron Status in Adults: A Systematic Review and Meta-Analysis." *Critical Reviews in Food Science and Nutrition* 58 (8): 1359–74. https://doi.org/10.1080/10408398.2016.1259210.

Hall, Amy. 2012. "The Dark Side of Soya: How One Super Crop Lost Its Way." The Ecologist, 1 May 2012. http://www.theecologist.org/green_green_living/food_and_drink/1337453/the_dark_side_of_soya_how_one_super_crop_lost_its_way.html.

Haraway, Donna. 2008. "Chicken." In *Animal Subjects: An Ethical Reader in a Posthuman World*, edited by Jodey Castricano, 33–8. Waterloo, ON: Wilfrid Laurier University Press.

– 2015. "Anthropocene, Capitalocene, Plantationocene, Chthulucene: Making Kin." *Environmental Humanities* 6: 159–65.

Harvey, David. 1993. "The Nature of Environment: The Dialectics of Social and Environmental Change." In *The Socialist Register 1993: Real Problems False Solutions*, 29: 1–51. New York: Monthly Review Press.

Harvey, Fiona. 2016. "Eat Less Meat to Avoid Dangerous Global Warming, Scientists Say." *The Guardian*, 21 March 2016. http://www.theguardian.com/environment/2016/mar/21/eat-less-meat-vegetarianism-dangerous-global-warming.

Heinrich Böll Stiftung and Friends of the Earth Europe. 2014. "Meat Atlas: Facts and Figures about the Animals We Eat." Ahrensfelde, Germany: Heinrich Böll Stiftung and Friends of the Earth Europe. https://www.

foeeurope.org/sites/default/files/publications/foee_hbf_meatatlas_
jan2014.pdf.

Herrero, M., P.K. Thornton, A.M. Notenbaert, S. Wood, S. Msangi, H.A.
Freeman, D. Bossio, et al. 2010. "Smart Investments in Sustainable Food
Production: Revisiting Mixed Crop-Livestock Systems," *Science* 327 (5967):
822–5. https://doi.org/10.1126/science.1183725.

Herzog, Hal. 2014. "84% of Vegetarians and Vegans Return to Meat. Why?"
Psychology Today, 2 December 2014. http://www.psychologytoday.com/
blog/animals-and-us/201412/84-vegetarians-and-vegans-return-meat-why.

Jones, A.K., D.L. Jones, and P. Cross. 2014. "The Carbon Footprint of Lamb:
Sources of Variation and Opportunities for Mitigation." *Agricultural
Systems* 123 (January): 97–107. https://doi.org/10.1016/j.agsy.2013.09.006.

Joy, Melanie. 2011. *Why We Love Dogs, Eat Pigs and Wear Cows: An Introduction
to Carnism, the Belief System That Enables Us to Eat Some Animals and Not
Others*. San Francisco, CA: Conari Press.

Katz-Rosene, Ryan. 2016. "Don't Give Up Meat If You Want to Save the
Planet, Eat Less and Better." Rabble.ca. 11 July 2016. http://rabble.ca/blogs/
bloggers/views-expressed/2016/07/dont-give-meat-if-you-want-to-save-
planet-eat-less-and-better.

Kramberger, Albert. 2016. "Beaconsfield Council Promotes Meatless Monday
Initiative." *Montreal Gazette* (blog). 29 March 2016. http://montrealgazette.
com/news/local-news/west-island-gazette/beaconsfield-council-promotes-
meatless-monday-initiative.

Liusuwan, Nicholas. 2016. "Why Aren't All Buddhists Vegetarians?"
Huffington Post.com (blog). 3 May 2016. http://www.huffingtonpost.com/
nicholas-liusuwan/why-arent-all-buddhists-v_b_9812362.html.

Maple Leaf Foods. 2017. "Maple Leaf Foods Pursuing Ambition to Be
the Most Sustainable Protein Company on Earth." Maple Leaf Foods,
Inc. https://www.mapleleaffoods.com/news/maple-leaf-foods-pursuing-
ambition-to-be-the-most-sustainable-protein-company-on-earth/.

Mason, Pamela, and Tim Lang. 2017. *Sustainable Diets*. London: Taylor
and Francis.

McDonald, Kay. 2016. "What about This War on Meat?" Big Picture
Agriculture (blog). 8 June 2016. http://bigpictureagriculture.blogspot.
com/2016/06/what-about-this-war-on-meat.html.

Monbiot, George. 2018. "The Best Way to Save the Planet? Drop Meat
and Dairy." *The Guardian*, 8 June 2018. http://www.theguardian.com/
commentisfree/2018/jun/08/save-planet-meat-dairy-livestock-food-free-
range-steak.

Nijdam, Durk, Trudy Rood, and Henk Westhoek. 2012. "The Price of Protein:
Review of Land Use and Carbon Footprints from Life Cycle Assessments

of Animal Food Products and Their Substitutes." *Food Policy* 37 (6): 760–70. https://doi.org/10.1016/j.foodpol.2012.08.002.

Niman, Nicolette Hahn. 2014. *Defending Beef*. White River Junction, VT: Chelsea Green.

Osborne, Catherine. 1995. "Ancient Vegetarianism." In *Food in Antiquity*, edited by John Wilkins, David Harvey, and Michael J. Dobson, 214–24. Exeter: University of Exeter Press.

Piazza, Jared, Matthew B. Ruby, Steve Loughnan, Mischel Luong, Juliana Kulik, Hanne M. Watkins, and Mirra Seigerman. 2015. "Rationalizing Meat Consumption. The 4Ns." *Appetite* 91 (August): 114–28. https://doi.org/10.1016/j.appet.2015.04.011.

Pollan, Michael. 2010. "The Food Movement, Rising." *The New York Review of Books*, 10 June 2010. http://www.nybooks.com/articles/2010/06/10/food-movement-rising/.

Poore, J., and T. Nemecek. 2018. "Reducing Food's Environmental Impacts through Producers and Consumers." *Science* 360 (6392): 987–92. https://doi.org/10.1126/science.aaq0216.

Popkin, Barry M. 2009. "Reducing Meat Consumption Has Multiple Benefits for the World's Health." *Archives of Internal Medicine* 169 (6): 543–5. https://doi.org/10.1001/archinternmed.2009.2.

Potts, Annie, ed. 2016. *Meat Culture. Human-Animal Studies*, vol. 17. Leiden: Brill.

Premack, Rachel. 2016. "Meat Is Horrible." *Washington Post*, 30 June 2016. https://www.washingtonpost.com/news/wonk/wp/2016/06/30/how-meat-is-destroying-the-planet-in-seven-charts/.

Ritchie, Hannah, and Max Roser. 2017. "Meat and Seafood Production and Consumption." OurWorldinData.org (August). https://ourworldindata.org/meat-and-seafood-production-consumption.

Sagan, Aleksandra. 2018. "More Vegetarian and Vegan Options Offered at Fast Food Restaurants." CTV News. 31 October 2018. https://windsor.ctvnews.ca/more-vegetarian-and-vegan-options-offered-at-fast-food-restaurants-1.4157227.

Sans, P., and P. Combris. 2015. "World Meat Consumption Patterns: An Overview of the Last Fifty Years (1961–2011)." *Meat Science* 109 (November): 106–11. https://doi.org/10.1016/j.meatsci.2015.05.012.

Savory, Allan. 2013. *How to Fight Desertification and Reverse Climate Change*. Ted Talks. https://www.ted.com/talks/allan_savory_how_to_green_the_world_s_deserts_and_reverse_climate_change.

Schneider, Mindi. 2015. "Wasting the Rural: Meat, Manure, and the Politics of Agro-Industrialization in Contemporary China." *Geoforum*. https://doi.org/10.1016/j.geoforum.2015.12.001.

Schwartz, Judith D. 2013. *Cows Save the Planet: And Other Improbable Ways of Restoring Soil to Heal the Earth*. White River Junction, VT: Chelsea Green.

Shepard, Mark. 2013. "Livestock and Restoration Agriculture." In *Restoration Agriculture: Real-World Permaculture for Farmers*, 113–34. Austin, TX: Acres USA.

Singer, Peter. 1990. "The Significance of Animal Suffering." *Behavioral and Brain Sciences* 13 (1): 9–12.

Smil, Vaclav. 2013. *Should We Eat Meat? Evolution and Consequences of Modern Carnivory*. West Sussex: John Wiley and Sons.

Statistics Canada. 2007. "Farms, by Farm Type and Province (Census of Agriculture, 2001 and 2006)." Statcan.gc.ca. 16 May 2007. http://www.statcan.gc.ca/tables-tableaux/sum-som/l01/cst01/agrc35a-eng.htm.

Steinfeld, Henning, Pierre Gerber, T. Wassenaar, V. Castel, Mauricio Rosales, and C. de Haan. 2006. "Livestock's Long Shadow: Environmental Issues and Options." Rome: Food and Agriculture Organization of the United Nations. http://www.fao.org/docrep/010/a0701e/a0701e00.HTM.

Suzuki, David. 2016. "Eating Less Meat Will Reduce Earth's Heat." Rabble.ca. 17 May 2016. http://rabble.ca/blogs/bloggers/david-suzuki/2016/05/eating-less-meat-will-reduce-earths-heat.

Swyngedouw, Erik. 2007. "Impossible 'Sustainability' and the Postpolitical Condition." In *The Sustainable Development Paradox: Urban Political Economy in the United States and Europe*, edited by Rob Krueger and David Gibbs, 13–40. New York: Guilford Press.

Taylor, Peter Shawn. 2010. "Stop Eating Meat? Not Bloody Likely." Macleans.ca (blog). 30 March 2010. http://www.macleans.ca/society/life/stop-eating-meat-not-bloody-likely/.

Toensmeier, Eric. 2016. *The Carbon Farming Solution: A Global Toolkit of Perennial Crops and Regenerative Agriculture Practices for Climate Change Mitigation and Food Security*. White River Junction, VT: Chelsea Green.

Weersink, Alfons, Michael von Massow, and Molly Gallant. 2019. "Meat Consumption Is Changing but It's Not Because of Vegans." The Conversation.com. 11 March 2019. http://theconversation.com/meat-consumption-is-changing-but-its-not-because-of-vegans-112332.

Wellesley, Laura, Antony Froggatt, and Catherine Happer. 2015. "Changing Climate, Changing Diets: Pathways to Lower Meat Consumption." London: Chatham House, Royal Institute of International Affairs.

World Commission on Environment and Development. 1987. *Our Common Future*. Oxford: Oxford University Press.

Zaraska, Marta. 2016. *Meathooked: The History and Science of Our 2.5-Million-Year Obsession with Meat*. New York: Basic Books.

2

Confronting Meatification

Tony Weis

The Rise of the Doubling Narrative and the Contestable Trajectory of Dietary Change

Since around 2008, there has been an increasingly influential narrative that world crop production must double from current levels in order to feed over 9 billion people by 2050, often with the prefix "sustainably."[1] This emanated from a range of influential organizations like the Food and Agriculture Organization of the United Nations (FAO), as well as some academics (Ray et al. 2013; Tilman et al. 2011; Soil Association 2010; FAO 2009; UN 2009), and has been enthusiastically embraced and touted by large agro-input and agro-food corporations (Kowitt 2016; Philpott 2011; World Economic Forum 2011). Four prominent drivers feature in this doubling narrative: the magnitude of persistent hunger and malnourishment; continuing human population growth; expanded agro-fuel production; and expected dietary changes.

At first glance, this conveys the appearance of a sober, objective assessment about the fact that there are many people hungry today, there will be at least 2 billion more people on earth in the coming three decades, more land is being devoted to agro-fuels given the limits to conventional fossil energy supplies, and people with rising incomes will keep eating more animal products in line with past trends – what I have previously called the "meatification" of diets (Weis 2015). However, positioning prodigious growth in production as the central problem facing world agriculture amounts to a spin on the failed neoliberal promise that a "rising tide will lift all boats," as though increases in aggregate supply can surmount inequality. This serves to obscure deep structural problems, such as the long-term marginalization of peasantries and biodiverse farming systems; the growing rupture between cuisines and bioregions and breakdown of local agro-food networks; immense disparities in effective demand (i.e., if more is produced, there is no guarantee that the world's hungry and malnourished could afford it); and vulnerabilities associated with chronic food deficits in many of the world's poorest countries (Clapp 2016; Weis 2007).

One of the most crucial and misleading aspects of the doubling narrative is the assumption that the continuing meatification of diets is largely unstoppable. Rather than assuming that such increases are inevitable, this chapter makes a brief case for why challenging and reversing the current trajectory of meat production and consumption must be a pillar of struggles to build more sustainable, equitable, and humane food systems.

A Snapshot of Global Meatification: Consumption

The term meatification describes the movement of meat from the periphery of human consumption patterns – where it was for the great majority of agricultural history – to the centre. On a world scale, meatification has proceeded continuously since the middle of the twentieth century. The average person on earth today consumes nearly twice as much meat per year (over 44 kgs in 2016) as did the average person only two generations earlier (23 kgs in 1961), over a period when the human population leapt from roughly 3 billion people to 7.5 billion people.[2] By 2050, if the present course continues, there will be between 9 and 10 billion people consuming an average of more than 50 kgs of meat per year.

It is also important to recognize that meatification is extremely uneven and clearly reflects global inequalities. At the apex, the average US citizen consumes roughly 120 kgs of meat a year, whereas the average African consumes less than 20 kgs and the average South Asian less than 10 kgs. These consumption disparities also reflect how rising meat consumption is an underappreciated measure and aspiration of modernity, nourished by long-held views about the superiority of animal protein together with some potent cultural attitudes about meat. This can be clearly seen in the fact that increased per capita meat consumption in fast-growing countries – with important class differences – is projected to have the biggest role propelling meatification in the coming decades (Weis 2013).

Yet when discussing meatification we must be clear that there is no nutritional justification; on the contrary, the overwhelming weight of research on diet and epidemiological patterns strongly correlates this trajectory with an array of negative health outcomes. In particular, the increasing consumption of animal products is a major force in fast-rising levels of obesity and many non-communicable diseases (NCDs), or so-called diseases of affluence, such as cardiovascular disease, Type-2 diabetes, hypertension, fatty liver disease, and some cancers. According to the *Global Burden of Disease Study*, poor quality diets – marked by high levels of unhealthy fats, salt, sugar, and refined carbohydrates, and low levels of vegetables, fruits, and legumes – are the largest contributing factor to the magnitude of disease on a world scale, with diet-related NCDs responsible for 63 per cent of deaths. Notably, the incidence of NCDs is rising fastest among rapidly industrializing middle-income countries (Dinu et al. 2016; Springmann et al. 2016; Anand et al. 2015; Lim et al. 2012; Popkin et al. 2012; WHO 2010; Popkin 2009).

In short, in terms of consumption, meatification is first and foremost about palate pleasure and culture, not necessity or health. The demand for more meat in diets has been further fortified by a powerful economic motivation on the production side, as the cycling of feed through livestock has had a key function profitably absorbing grain and oilseed surpluses, in turn enabling their continuing growth when it would have otherwise devastated prices (Weis 2013; Winders and Nibert 2004; Berlan 1991). A range of agriculture and food corporations can be seen to have both responded to these tastes and culturally ingrained perceptions of meat and animal products and, at the same time, worked to enlarge this demand in order to increase their sources of profit. This promotion has taken various forms, from intensively lobbying state agencies that set nutritional guidelines to champion animal-derived protein (Nestle 2013), to a vast array of marketing tactics that frequently play on tropes of meat and masculinity (Adams 2015).

A Snapshot of Global Meatification: Production

The meatification of diets is entwined with soaring populations of animals and revolutionary changes in how they are raised. Until very recently, most livestock animals lived at relatively low densities, either herded extensively or reared in mixed farming systems, and had multifunctional roles as sources of labour, transport, and nutrient cycling in addition to producing milk, eggs, flesh, wool, and hides. This involved varying degrees of control, with most animals having some level of autonomy in securing their food by grazing on natural grasslands, rotated pasture, and crop stubble, and scavenging on the margins of croplands and households.

Extensive herding and ranching continue to be a major part of agro-food systems in some parts of the world, and pasture occupies by far the most total area of any human land use, between 22 and 25 per cent of all land (Foley et al. 2011; Steinfeld et al. 2006). Ruminant animals occupy almost all global pasture, much of this with very low stocking densities and in areas not suitable for crops. Over the past half-century, ruminant production (chiefly cattle, secondarily sheep and goats) has more or less kept pace with human population growth due to a combination of increased stocking densities in some areas, efforts to enhance some pastures, and ongoing conversions of forests and grasslands to pasture. Small livestock populations also persist in some mixed farming landscapes, especially in the Global South (Steinfeld et al. 2006).

But the story of global meatification – that is, increases in production and consumption over and above human population growth – has been driven largely by the industrial production of pigs and poultry birds (overwhelmingly chickens), which means that it centers on arable land rather than pasture. The lion's share of world food production comes from the 10–12 per cent of the earth's land area that is devoted to permanent crops, and industrial livestock production now effect-ively occupies close to one-third of this through its command of great volumes of feed crops, led by corn and soybeans (Monfreda et al. 2008; Foley et al. 2007; Steinfeld et al. 2006). This system of agriculture, the industrial grain-oilseed-livestock complex, can be likened to "islands" of concentrated animals within "oceans" of monocultures, which helps to highlight how animals are physically disarticulated from agricultural landscapes and rearticulated through flows of feed and other inputs (Weis 2013). A handful of transnational corporations exerts a tremendous amount of power over the trajectory of this system, from the nexus of seeds, agro-chemicals, and animal pharmaceuticals (e.g., Bayer-Monsanto, ChemChina-Syngenta, Dow-Dupont, BASF), to grain and oilseed processing (e.g., ADM, Bunge, Cargill, Louis Dreyfus), to livestock slaughter and packing (e.g., JBS, WH Group, Tyson, Perdue, Cargill), to fast-food restaurants (e.g., McDonald's, YUM Brands, Subway, Burger King, etc.) and other retailers (IPES 2017).

Pigs and poultry now account for over 70 per cent of the total volume of world meat production, and virtually all future growth on a world scale is expected to centre on pigs and chickens alone. Pig meat, poultry meat, and egg production are overwhelmingly industrialized in temper-ate countries, increasingly industrialized in fast-growing countries like China, Brazil, and Thailand, and beginning to industrialize across large areas of the Global South. Ruminant production is generally much less industrialized than pig and poultry production, although in temperate countries dairy cattle are increasingly being confined for much of their lives (Gillespie 2018) and connected to feed and most beef cattle are started on pasture and finished on feedlots.

Meatification and industrial livestock production, especially the explosion of poultry, are also central to the phenomenal rise in the population of individual animals raised and killed each year. Since 1960, there has been a near quadrupling in the population of livestock animals on earth at any one time, and a near ninefold increase in the annual population of animals killed for food, from around 8 billion to more than 70 billion today – a figure that is racing towards 120 billion should the trajectory of meatification continue.[3] This means that a large and growing share of the world's livestock population face conditions of life that defy those that have prevailed for most of agrarian history, in which animals do not touch the earth, breathe fresh air, experience natural seasonal and diurnal rhythms, or have anything resembling normal social interactions with fellow members of their own species (Weis 2016; Weis 2013). Harari (2015) stresses that these conditions are now inflicted on a large and growing share of the world's *total* population of mammals and birds, and calls this "one of the most pressing ethical issues of our time."

The Ecological Hoofprint

The ecological hoofprint is a conceptual framework for understanding why the trajectory of meatification and the industrial grain-oilseed-livestock complex are so important to struggles for a more sustainable, equitable, and humane world. At the basis of the ecological hoofprint framework is attention to how political-economic imperatives – most pivotally, the pursuit of economies of scale and the pressure to substitute capital and technology for labour – shape the ways that productive environments are organized in both the monoculture oceans and the islands of concentrated animals, driving biological simplification and standardization at every turn. The pressure to biologically simplify and standardize productive environments creates or exacerbates a series of intractable biological and physical problems. These barriers to industrial scale in industrial agriculture, or *biophysical contradictions*, are never resolved, but rather are perpetually met with short-term fixes, or *biophysical overrides*, which might temporarily mask problems even as they grow deeper or engender new risks. Understanding biophysical problems and overrides together opens up a way of comprehending resource budgets and pollution loads (Weis 2013).

Industrial monoculture production increases soil erosion, vulnerability to insects and weeds, and the demand for water. This is in contrast to traditional farming practices and modern agroecological methods, which involve a much greater range of crops (and genetic diversity within crops), more rotations and fallowing, less tillage and compaction, and more groundcover and complementary cropping patterns (i.e., crops grown in mutually beneficial associations). In monocultures, the problem of heightened soil erosion is repeatedly met through applications of nitrogen, phosphorous, and potassium fertilizers, the problem of heightened vulnerability to pests is met with a spectrum of pesticides, and the reduced soil moisture and water requirement of high yielding varieties necessitates heightened irrigation consumption. The biophysical contradiction-and-override dialectic helps to shed light on the resource intensity of feed crops. A key aspect of this is the fossil energy flowing through the system in the process of running farm machinery; manufacturing synthetic nitrogen fertilizer; mining and processing phosphorous and potassium fertilizers; manufacturing pesticides; producing specialized seeds on controlled plots; moving fertilizers, pesticides, and seeds, often over long distances; and pumping irrigation (which also hinges on great freshwater diversions from streams, rivers, and lakes, and the unsustainable drawdown of underground aquifers). These dynamics contribute to a series of pollution loads and public health risks, such as the CO_2 emissions from machinery, fertilizer and pesticide manufacturing, and moving materials over great distances; N_2O emissions from nitrogen fertilizers; the proliferation of persistent toxins into water, soils, and ecosystems; and the runoff of excess nitrates and phosphates from fertilizers that has damaging impacts on freshwater ecosystems (Sage 2012; Weis 2010; McIntyre et al. 2009; Kimbrell 2002).[4]

As with feed crop monocultures, the pursuit of scale and simplification in industrial livestock operations runs up against a range of biophysical barriers. Natural reproduction is too slow and unpredictable, unnatural densities of animals and enormous concentrations of feces and urine amplify the risks of contagious pathogens, and extreme crowding and immobility induces stress that adversely affects animal health. Here again, the problems associated with the pursuit of scale are never fundamentally resolved but rather are managed in a range of ways, including artificial insemination and the specialization of breeding sites; chronic antibiotic use; physical mutilations (e.g., beak tipping, tail docking, and teeth clipping, to prevent injuries from crowding-induced behavioural pathologies); and elaborate waste management systems (Weis 2013; Imhoff 2010; D'Silva and Webster 2010; Pew Commission 2008).

Again, the biophysical contradiction-and-override dialectic helps to illuminate resource budgets, pollution loads, and public health risks. The consumption of energy increases relative to non-industrial systems, because of the movement of newborn animals from sites of specialized breeding to sites of growing, the transport of feed and various inputs, and the powering of breeding sites and enclosures (e.g., regulating temperatures, monitoring ambient conditions, and running ventilation units). The energy intensity grows further when industrialized slaughterhouses and packing plants are taken into account, in powering the kill floor, the chilling or scalding of carcasses, the packing lines, and the subsequent refrigeration, and because many more animals are increasingly moved over longer distances to slaughter.[5] Water consumption is greatly enlarged because animals can no longer seek their own sources of moisture or gain it from roughage, unnatural concentrations of feces and urine must be repeatedly flushed out of enclosures, and there are heavy demands associated with processing flesh and cleaning corporal wastes from slaughter and packing lines (Weis 2013; Imhoff 2010; D'Silva and Webster 2010; Pew Commission 2008).

These dynamics reverberate in a series of burdens. Various fossil energy demands translate to CO_2 emissions. Wastewater lagoons produce methane emissions, localized airborne pollution (marked by a wretched stench that negatively impacts the health of surrounding communities), and excess nutrient loads that, like fertilizers, destabilize surrounding freshwater ecosystems.[6] Health risks include the management of chronic infectious disease (e.g., e-coli, salmonella, listeria), the long-term threat of more virulent pathogens (e.g., avian and swine flu) emerging, and the declining effectiveness of antibiotics in human populations due to overuse (Wallace 2016; Pew Commission 2008; Silbergeld et al. 2008). By focusing on how productive environments are organized, this framework also draws attention to the intensity with which animal lives are dominated as their "turnover time" is accelerated. Together, the intensity, speed, and scale of production – along with the increasing physical and cognitive distance between meat and animal lives – can be seen to constitute a revolution in interspecies relations from the sorts of relations that prevailed over the long history of domestication, herding, farming, and husbandry (Weis 2013).

The resource budgets and pollution loads of industrial monocultures and livestock operations get magnified by the basic nutritional wastage at their nexus. Cycling crops through animals to produce food is an extremely inefficient way of generating useable nutrition for human societies, as large portions of useable nutrition are burned in the metabolic processes of animals before being converted to flesh, milk, and eggs – what amounts to a net nutritional drain (Springmann et al. 2016; Foley et al. 2011; Pimentel and Pimentel 2003; Gerben-Leenes and Nonhebel 2002; Gilland 2002; Goodland 1997). This drain inevitably expands the overall land area, water, energy, and other resources that must be devoted to agriculture – more than would be needed if plant nutrition was consumed directly – thereby reducing space for ecosystems and other species, as well as contributing more pollutants and GHG emissions. The additional land required for crops is made worse by the fact that input-intensive monocultures do not support much biodiversity and reduce the capacity for carbon sequestration over a given landscape.[7]

Another basic characteristic of the biophysical contraction-and-override dialectic is that it is never stable. Because the pursuit of scale is incontestable, the mounting environmental problems associated with industrial livestock operations continue to be approached through science and engineering, with the faith that innovation can either fortify existing overrides or find new ones. A good example of this can be seen in attempts to capture methane emissions, from backpacks fitted to cows to biodigesters for fecal lagoons, which could simultaneously reduce the gases that end up in the atmosphere and offset some of the energy costs of operations (euphemized as methane gas "recovery"). Biodigesters are also geared to converting lagoon slurry into useable energy. The genetic engineering of animal bodies is another important realm of ostensible environmental innovation, now geared towards such ends as making wastes less polluting (as with the so-called Enviropig,[TM] designed to produce less phosphorous-laden manure) in addition to the long-established goal of reducing feed conversion losses.

Although the focus here has been on the industrial grain-oilseed-livestock complex, which entails significantly different socio-ecological and inter-species relations from pasture-raised livestock, this should not diminish the significance of debates over the future of pasture. As indicated, pasture occupies roughly twice as much land as crops on a world scale, and its expansion has been a major historic force in deforestation (Williams 2006) and the loss of natural grasslands, contributing to both biodiversity loss and climate change. The climate burden of pasture stems from the initial CO_2 emissions associated with the removal of natural vegetation (including from soil-based carbon), the diminished sequestration capacity of a given landscape over the long term, and the methane emissions from increasing populations of ruminants (Ripple et al. 2014). The need to stop the advance of the pasture frontier could not be clearer: the continuing expansion of pasture remains an especially destructive force in biodiversity loss and climate change in Amazonia (Hoelle 2015), and overgrazing is widely recognized as a major factor where desertification is occurring, most acutely in the semi-arid tropics, a problem that both contributes to and is worsened by climate change (Steinfeld et al. 2006; Geist and Lambin 2006).

Thornier debates surround the use of historically entrenched pasture, as it is far less resource intensive than industrial livestock production, involves better conditions of life for animals, and can, if well managed, maintain healthy soils. However, any attempt to justify pasture on environmental grounds must also recognize that historic deforestation is not immutable, and that in order to reduce the extent of biodiversity loss and climate change there is a pressing need to restore ecosystems and enhance carbon sequestration as widely as possible and reduce the GHG emissions from ruminants (Ripple et al. 2014). The ecological restoration imperative also needs to be seen in relation to the fact that wherever pasture occupies high quality arable land crop, cultivation can generate greater net nutritional product per land area. This implies that efforts to reduce the scale of pasture should start by targeting areas with the best soils and climate for cultivation, and the areas that are capable of supporting the most biodiversity or are most prone to degradation for re-naturalization.[8]

Conclusion

There is nothing inexorable about the continuing meatification of diets, and nothing neutral about calls to double world agricultural production in the coming decades. Rather, the doubling narrative mobilizes world hunger and food insecurity in a way that seeks to brace the dominant political-economic logic and constellation of power in agro-food systems, reifying corporate-led technological innovation as the key source of hope within the context of deepening market integration. Among other things, this helps obscure the multidimensional burden of meatification, including the profound consumption disparities it involves; the wastage of massive and growing volumes of useable nutrition (which serves to profitably absorb grain and oilseed surpluses); the dependence on unsustainable resource budgets; and the generation of pollution loads, public health risks, and an expanding world of animal suffering. The meatification of diets not only *reflects* global inequalities but is *exacerbating* them, especially given how it contributes to climate change and how climate change is making food insecurity much worse in some of the poorest parts of the world.

Instead of expecting meatification to continue and leaving biophysical contradictions beyond question, real prospects for enhancing food security sustainably into the future depend on reducing meat production and consumption, starting with efforts to dismantle the industrial grain-oilseed-livestock complex. In this light, it would be hard to overstate the urgent need to rethink the current role played by livestock in agro-food systems.

Notes

1 This is a significantly modified version of a paper that first appeared in *Canadian Food Studies* (Weis 2015). Permission to reuse segments and the title is gratefully acknowledged.
2 These statistics are derived from FAOSTAT (2018).
3 This is to say nothing of fish and aquaculture, which are undergoing an industrial revolution that has important parallels to livestock (Longo et al. 2015).
4 These nutrients stimulate the growth of algae which take up oxygen when they decompose, creating "dead zones" as fish and other aquatic creatures are killed.
5 This necessarily increases as landscapes specialize and livestock operations and slaughterhouses grow in scale but shrink in number.
6 This occurs both from unintended seepage and spills and deliberate field applications of slurry.
7 This reflects the fact that the nutritional and ecological inefficiency is not only a matter of what is lost to animal metabolic processes, but that the land currently given to industrial monocultures could simultaneously generate more useable nutrition with far less inputs through labour-intensive agroecological practices.
8 The potential environmental benefit from turning pasture to crops on quality arable land is only realizable if nutritional needs get met as efficiently as possible – that is, plants geared for human consumption rather than animal feed.

References

Adams, Carol J. 2015. *The Sexual Politics of Meat: A Feminist-Vegetarian Critical Theory*. 25th anniversary ed. New York: Bloomsbury.

Anand, Sonia S., Corinna Hawkes, Russell J. de Souza, Andrew Mente, Mahshid Dehghan, Rachel Nugent, Michael A. Zulyniak, et al. 2015. "Food Consumption and Its Impact on Cardiovascular Disease: Importance of Solutions Focused on the Globalized Food System: A Report From the Workshop Convened by the World Heart Federation." *Journal of the American College of Cardiology* 66 (14): 1590–614. https://doi.org/10.1016/j.jacc.2015.07.050.

Berlan, Jean-Pierre. 1991. "The Historical Roots of the Present Agricultural Crisis." In *Towards a New Political Economy of Agriculture*, edited by William H. Friedland, Lawrence M. Busch, Frederick H. Buttel, and Alan P. Rudy, 115–36. Boulder, CO: Westview Press.

Clapp, Jennifer. 2011. *Food*. Cambridge: Polity.

Clark, Jonathan L. 2012. "Ecological Biopower, Environmental Violence against Animals, and the 'Greening' of the Factory Farm." *Journal for Critical Animal Studies* 10 (4): 109–29.

Dinu, Monica, Rosanna Abbate, Gian Franco Gensini, Alessandro Casini, and Francesco Sofi. 2016. "Vegetarian, Vegan Diets with Multiple Health Outcomes: A Systematic Review with Meta-Analysis of Observational Studies." *Critical Reviews in Food Science and Nutrition* 57 (17): 3640–9. http://dx.doi.org/10.1080/10408398.2016.1138447

D'Silva, Joyce, and John Webster, eds. 2010. *The Meat Crisis: Developing More Sustainable Production and Consumption*. 1st ed. London: Earthscan.

Foley, Jonathan A., Chad Monfreda, Navin Ramankutty, and David Zaks. 2007. "Our Share of the Planetary Pie." *Proceedings of the National Academy of Sciences* 104 (31): 12585–6. https://doi.org/10.1073/pnas.0705190104.

Foley, Jonathan A., Navin Ramankutty, Kate A. Brauman, Emily S. Cassidy, James S. Gerber, Matt Johnston, Nathaniel D. Mueller, et al. 2011. "Solutions for a Cultivated Planet." *Nature* 478 (7369): 337–42. https://doi.org/10.1038/nature10452.

Food and Agriculture Organization Statistics Division. 2018. "FAOSTAT." http://www.fao.org/faostat/en/#home.

Food and Agriculture Organization of the United Nations (FAO). 2009. "How to Feed the World in 2050." Rome: FAO. http://www.fao.org/fileadmin/templates/wsfs/docs/expert_paper/How_to_Feed_the_World_in_2050.pdf.

Geist, Helmut J., and Eric F. Lambin. 2004. "Dynamic Causal Patterns of Desertification." *BioScience* 54 (9): 817–29. https://doi.org/10.1641/0006-3568(2004)054[0817:DCPOD]2.0.CO;2.

Gerbens-Leenes, P.W., and S. Nonhebel. 2002. "Consumption Patterns and Their Effects on Land Required for Food." *Ecological Economics* 42 (1): 185–99. https://doi.org/10.1016/S0921-8009(02)00049-6.

Gilland, Bernard. 2002. "World Population and Food Supply: Can Food Production Keep Pace with Population Growth in the Next Half-Century?" *Food Policy* 27 (1): 47–63. https://doi.org/10.1016/S0306-9192(02)00002-7.

Gillespie, Kathryn. 2018. *The Cow with Ear Tag #1389*. Chicago: University of Chicago Press.

Goodland, Robert. 1997. "Environmental Sustainability in Agriculture: Diet Matters." *Ecological Economics* 23 (3): 189–200. https://doi.org/10.1016/S0921-8009(97)00579-X.

Harari, Yuval Noah. 2015. "Industrial Farming Is One of the Worst Crimes in History." *The Guardian*, 25 September 2015. http://www.theguardian.com/books/2015/sep/25/industrial-farming-one-worst-crimes-history-ethical-question.

Hoelle, Jeffrey. 2015. *Rainforest Cowboys: The Rise of Ranching and Cattle Culture in Western Amazonia*. Austin: University of Texas Press.

IPES-Food. 2017. "Too Big to Feed: Exploring the Impacts of Mega-Mergers, Concentration, Concentration of Power in the Agri-Food Sector." International Panel of Experts on Sustainable Food Systems. http://www.ipes-food.org/images/Reports/Concentration_FullReport.pdf.

Kimbrell, Andrew, ed. 2002. *The Fatal Harvest Reader: The Tragedy of Industrial Agriculture*. Washington, DC: Island Press.

Kowitt, Beth. 2016. "How Monsanto's CEO Thinks We Can Feed the World." *Fortune*, 17 May 2016. http://fortune.com/2016/05/17/monsanto-ceo-feeding-planet/.

Lim, Stephen S., Theo Vos, Abraham D. Flaxman, Goodarz Danaei, Kenji Shibuya, Heather Adair-Rohani, Markus Amann, et al. 2012. "A Comparative Risk Assessment of Burden of Disease and Injury Attributable to 67 Risk Factors and Risk Factor Clusters in 21 Regions, 1990–2010: A Systematic Analysis for the Global Burden of Disease Study 2010." *The Lancet* 380 (9859): 2224–60. https://doi.org/10.1016/S0140-6736(12)61766-8.

Longo, Stefano B., Rebecca Clausen, and Brett Clark. 2015. *The Tragedy of the Commodity: Oceans, Fisheries, and Aquaculture*. New Brunswick, NJ: Rutgers University Press.

McIntyre, Beverly D., Hans R. Herren, Judi Wakhungu, and Robert T. Watson, eds. 2009. *Agriculture at the Crossroads*. International Assessment of Agricultural Knowledge, Science, and Technology for Development. Washington, DC: Island Press.

McMichael, Anthony J., John W. Powles, Colin D. Butler, and Ricardo Uauy. 2007. "Food, Livestock Production, Energy, Climate Change, and Health." *The Lancet* 370 (9594): 1253–63. https://doi.org/10.1016/S0140-6736(07)61256-2.

Monfreda, Chad, Navin Ramankutty, and Jonathan A. Foley. 2008. "Farming the Planet: 2. Geographic Distribution of Crop Areas, Yields, Physiological Types, and Net Primary Production in the Year 2000." *Global Biogeochemical Cycles* 22 (1). https://doi.org/10.1029/2007GB002947.

Nestle, Marion. 2013. *Food Politics: How the Food Industry Influences Nutrition, and Health*. 3rd ed. Berkeley: University of California Press.

Pew Commission. 2008. *Putting Meat on the Table: Industrial Farm Animal Production in America*. Washington, DC: The Pew Charitable Trusts and the Johns Hopkins Bloomburg School of Public Health.

Philpott, Tom. 2011. "Big Ag Won't Feed the World." *Mother Jones*, 15 June 2011. https://www.motherjones.com/food/2011/06/vilsack-usda-big-ag/.

Pimentel, David, and Marcia H. Pimentel. 2003. "Sustainability of Meat-Based and Plant-Based Diets and the Environment." *The American Journal of Clinical Nutrition* 78 (3): 660S–3S. https://doi.org/10.1093/ajcn/78.3.660S.

Popkin, Barry M. 2009. "Reducing Meat Consumption Has Multiple Benefits for the World's Health." *Archives of Internal Medicine* 169 (6): 543–5. https://doi.org/10.1001/archinternmed.2009.2.

Popkin, Barry M., Linda S. Adair, and Shu Wen Ng. 2012. "NOW AND THEN: The Global Nutrition Transition; The Pandemic of Obesity in Developing Countries." *Nutrition Reviews* 70 (1): 3–21. https://doi.org/10.1111/j.1753-4887.2011.00456.x.

Ray, Deepak K., Nathaniel D. Mueller, Paul C. West, and Jonathan A. Foley. 2013. "Yield Trends Are Insufficient to Double Global Crop Production by 2050." *PLoS One* 8 (6): e66428. https://doi.org/10.1371/journal.pone.0066428.

Ripple, William J., Pete Smith, Helmut Haberl, Stephen A. Montzka, Clive McAlpine, and Douglas H. Boucher. 2013. "Ruminants, Climate Change and Climate Policy." *Nature Climate Change* 4 (1): 2–5. https://doi.org/10.1038/nclimate2081.

Sage, Colin. 2011. *Environment and Food*. London: Routledge.

Silbergeld, Ellen K., Jay Graham, and Lance B. Price. 2008. "Industrial Food Animal Production, Antimicrobial Resistance, and Human Health." *Annual Review of Public Health* 29: 151–69. https://doi.org/10.1146/annurev.publhealth.29.020907.090904.

Soil Association. 2010. "Telling Porkies: The Big Fat Lie about Doubling Food Production." UK: The Soil Association. https://www.soilassociation.org/media/4906/policy_telling_porkies.pdf.

Springmann, Marco, H. Charles J. Godfray, Mike Rayner, and Peter Scarborough. 2016. "Analysis and Valuation of the Health and Climate Cobenefits of Dietary Change." *PNAS* 113 (15): 4146–51. https://doi.org/10.1073/pnas.1523119113.

Steinfeld, Henning, Pierre Gerber, T. Wassenaar, V. Castel, Mauricio Rosales, and C. de Haan. 2006. "Livestock's Long Shadow." Rome: Food and Agriculture Organization. http://www.fao.org/docrep/010/a0701e/a0701e00.HTM.

Tilman, David, Christian Balzer, Jason Hill, and Belinda L. Befort. 2011. "Global Food Demand and the Sustainable Intensification of Agriculture." *Proceedings of the National Academy of Sciences* 108 (50): 20,260–4. https://doi.org/10.1073/pnas.1116437108.

United Nations (UN). 2009. "Food Production Must Double by 2050 to Meet Demand from World's Growing Population." GA/EF/3242. Sixty-Fourth

General Assembly, Second Committee, Panel Discussion. United Nations. https://www.un.org/press/en/2009/gaef3242.doc.htm.

Wallace, Rob. 2016. *Big Farms Make Big Flu: Dispatches on Infectious Disease, Agribusiness, and the Nature of Science*. New York: Monthly Review Press.

Weis, Tony. 2007. *The Global Food Economy: The Battle for the Future of Farming*. London: Zed Books.

– 2010. "The Accelerating Biophysical Contradictions of Industrial Capitalist Agriculture." *Journal of Agrarian Change* 10 (3): 315–41. https://doi.org/10.1111/j.1471-0366.2010.00273.x.

– 2013. *The Ecological Hoofprint: The Global Burden of Industrial Livestock*. London: Zed Books.

– 2015. "Meatification and the Madness of the Doubling Narrative." *Canadian Food Studies / La Revue Canadienne Des Études Sur l'alimentation* 2 (2): 296–303. https://doi.org/10.15353/cfs-rcea.v2i2.105.

– 2016. "Towards 120 Billion: Dietary Change and Animal Lives." *Radical Philosophy* 199 (5): 8–13.

Williams, Michael. 2006. *Deforesting the Earth: From Prehistory to Global Crisis*. Chicago: University of Chicago Press.

Winders, Bill, and David Nibert. 2004. "Consuming the Surplus: Expanding 'Meat' Consumption and Animal Oppression." *International Journal of Sociology and Social Policy* 24 (September): 76–96. https://doi.org/10.1108/01443330410790786.

World Economic Forum. 2011. "Realizing a New Vision for Agriculture: A Roadmap for Stakeholders." Geneva: World Economic Forum. http://wef.ch/1mvrblU.

World Health Organization (WHO). 2010. "Global Status Report on Non-Communicable Diseases 2010." Geneva: World Health Organization.

3

How Do Livestock
Impact the Climate?

Ryan M. Katz-Rosene

In 2006, Al Gore produced *An Inconvenient Truth*, a film that has since been credited with playing a significant role in bringing the challenge of climate change into popular consciousness.[1] It is worth noting that the film does not mention the livestock sector in any significant sense, nor does it identify "animal agriculture" as a leading cause in anthropogenic warming. Despite this, it would seem that now – about a decade and a half later – it is increasingly becoming "common sense" that the production and consumption of meat is "*bad* for the climate." In this chapter I will argue that this emergent common-sense wisdom offers an oversimplified view of livestock production. Such oversimplifications could yield equally simplistic policy responses, which may be counterproductive and unjust. In short, this chapter outlines how this narrative, which seemingly paints all livestock in the world with the same brush, (1) has led to inflated assessments of the climatic footprint of livestock animals themselves; (2) fails to make a crucial distinction between "agro-ecological" and "industrial" models of livestock production; and (3) is unduly discriminating in its focus on emissions *generated* by the sector globally, which in turn works to sideline the rather important role played by livestock within various forms of sustainable agri-food systems.[2] Let me be clear: my aim is certainly not to say that "the consumption of meat is *good* for the climate"! This would be just as simplistic and misleading as its opposing claim. Rather, the objective of this chapter, by problematizing the dominant meat-climate narrative today, is to cause readers to think critically about the significant qualitative differences between, say, the climatic footprint of meat from an organic mixed farming operation supplying local consumers, and from an industrial feedlot producing meat for export on the global market. In short, if climate mitigation is the underlying goal, then rather than identify "animal agriculture" as a climate culprit, it makes far more sense to target fossil fuel-intensive practices *within* agri-food systems while supporting livestock production methods in which animals provide positive ecosystem services, at a scale that can be sustained by the planet.

From "A Higher Share than Transport" to "The Best Thing You Can Do to Save the Planet"

How is it that in such a short period of time the production and consumption of meat has become internalized as being bad for the climate? Certainly, the publishing of the Food and Agriculture Organization of the United Nations' (FAO) report *Livestock's Long Shadow* (Steinfeld et al. 2006) in the same year as Gore's film – when climate change was catapulted into the public psyche – appears to have played an important part. As the FAO trumpeted in its report, "the livestock sector is a major player [in climate change], responsible for 18 per cent of greenhouse gas (GHG) emissions measured in [carbon dioxide (CO_2)] equivalent. *This is a higher share than transport*" (Steinfeld et al. 2006, xxi; emphasis added). Since that time, the figure of 18 per cent has been widely publicized, as has the comparison with transport. It was, however, eclipsed by Kip Anderson's 2014 documentary *Cowspiracy*. Anderson refers to a report by the Worldwatch Institute, whose authors claim that livestock are responsible for 51 per cent of global GHG emissions (Goodland and Anhang 2009, 11) – a figure that, thanks to *Cowspiracy*'s popularity, is now widely disseminated in the digital media as well (see Bekhechi 2016 or McMahon 2016 for recent examples). In the lead-up to the 2015 Paris Climate Conference, the Royal Institute of International Affairs published research seeking in part to address what it saw as an "awareness gap regarding the links between livestock, diet and climate change," asserting that the livestock sector's emissions were "equivalent to tailpipe emissions from all the world's vehicles" (Wellesley, Froggatt, and Happer 2015, vii; see also Bailey, Froggatt, and Wellesley 2014).

More recently there was the publication of Poore and Nemecek's meta-data study in *Science* on the wide-ranging ecological footprints of different types of agricultural production, wherein the authors conclude that there is "transformative potential" in having the world shift "to a diet that *excludes* animal products" (Poore and Nemecek 2018, 991; emphasis added). Much of the press coverage of the study is unequivocal in reaffirming the notion that by *not consuming* animal-based foods such as meat and dairy, humans could take a significant step towards mitigating serious global environmental challenges such as global warming and the sixth mass extinction. Two headlines from *The Guardian* are telling in this regard: upon interviewing one of the study's lead authors, the newspaper's environment editor Damian Carrington wrote a piece entitled "Avoiding Meat and Dairy Is 'Single Biggest Way' to Reduce Your Impact on Earth" (Carrington 2018), while acclaimed environmental columnist George Monbiot's op-ed covering the study is similarly entitled "The Best Way to Save the Planet? Drop Meat and Dairy" (Monbiot 2018).

In the wake of these wide-ranging environmental criticisms of the livestock sector, a number of popular campaigns and programs calling for a reduction in meat consumption have been implemented or proposed as a means of tackling climate change. For instance, there has been the implementation of "Meatless Mondays" at different institutions (Kramberger 2016), proposed taxes on meat (see Premack 2016), and it is now more common to see popular treatises calling for an *end to all animal agriculture* on environmental grounds (such as *Cowspiracy*). With only a few rebuttals to such claims in the sphere of popular culture (some literary examples include Fairlie 2010; Schwartz 2013; and Niman 2014), the correlation between meat and climate change appears to be more and more subsumed within an emergent "common-sense"[3] narrative. This is not to suggest that everybody thinks this way, but rather that there is a critical mass of the population that accepts this logic, particularly in "Western" societies. Of course, as with all pieces of common sense, there is indeed a kernel of truth involved. In this sense, the growing attention toward the environmental impacts of livestock production is indeed a welcome development. Certainly, as argued in other parts of this book, there is a good case to be made for *reducing* meat consumption in order to maintain a more sustainable diet. Yet as Gramsci pointed out, "common sense" is not necessarily "good sense." One key problem, as I explore below, is that there are many different forms and expressions of livestock production and meat consumption throughout the world, some of which are likelier to have an amplified and detrimental impact on the climate system, while others take great pains to integrate livestock into ecologically restorative practices (Shepard 2013; Rodale Institute 2014; Toensmeier 2016). It is therefore not only unfair, but also inaccurate, to place the blame universally on "livestock" or "meat" – as the common-sense wisdom appears to do – when it is *certain types of agricultural practices* (like intensive grain- and fossil fuel-reliant industrialized systems, or deforestation) that are the primary culprits when it comes to the sector's contributions to anthropogenic global warming.

Inflated Numbers

A detailed analysis of the assessments by FAO and Worldwatch suggests that common-sense claims about animal agriculture's contribution to global GHG emissions are susceptible to inflation and mischaracterization. To be fair, it should be noted that calculating the global GHG emissions from livestock production is a highly subjective process. It requires multiple decisions on what to include in the calculations, and importantly how to weigh carbon found in methane (CH_4) and nitrous oxide (N_2O) as compared to CO_2 (see below). The Intergovernmental Panel on Climate Change (IPCC) and the FAO are considered the leading authorities on how this is calculated, and even the latter has admitted, "data on GHG emissions from agriculture, forestry and other land use (AFOLU) activities are poorly known, including for recent years" (Tubiello et al. 2014, 2). The assumptions that go into these calculations are such that the results could be different by orders of magnitude *in either direction*.[4] Hence the figure for the global percentage of GHGs resulting from livestock varies significantly, depending on who is doing the math, and the nature of their underlying motivations.

At the lower end of the spectrum we find a 2005 study by World Resources Institute, which claims that livestock *directly* are responsible for 5.1 per cent of global emissions (Baumert, Herzog, and Pershing 2005). In the middle we find the FAO, who after revising its earlier calculations in *Livestock's Long Shadow* says the livestock sector now produces 14.5 per cent of global GHG emissions (Gerber et al. 2013, xii), putting it on par with transport *tailpipe* emissions.[5] At the extreme high end, with 51 per cent, we have the aforementioned Worldwatch report quoted in *Cowspiracy* (Goodland and Anhang 2009, 11).

In what sense are the latter figures inflated? First, consider the 51 per cent figure: as many have pointed out (for a vegan's critique of the report, see Chivers 2016), the Worldwatch study is methodologically unsound because – among other errors – it incorrectly incorporates animal *respiration* in its calculations, which in turn is based on a rather spurious figure (for a thorough critique of the Worldwatch Institute's assessment, see chapter 13 of Fairlie 2010, "Global Warming: Cows or Cars?"). The Worldwatch report, in other words, does not accurately depict the carbon cycle. Yet arguably the FAO's figures are inflated as well: its claim that livestock are responsible for 14.5 per cent of global emissions (equivalent to 7.1 gigatons CO_2-eq) is a measure of the entire livestock production chain. That is, the figure incorporates a significant amount of GHG emissions from categories that are only *indirectly* related to livestock. For instance, nearly half of these emissions come from the

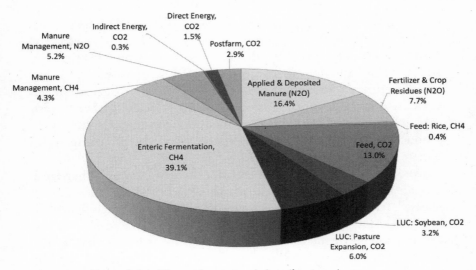

Figure 3.1   Share of global livestock sector emissions (by source)

Sources: Gerber et al. 2013, with data on global emissions from IPCC Fifth Assessment 2014.

production, fertilization, and processing of animal feeds, as well as post-farm transport (Gerber et al. 2013, 17; see figure 3.1). This is an important distinction because, presumably, many of the latter emissions would continue to occur if the decision was made to switch the recipients of such crop production toward humans instead of animals. CO_2 would be produced whether those crops are intended for animal or human consumption, and of course the same can be said of the processing and transport of those crop products to the consumers – be they human or otherwise. This raises the question of whether it is really fair to label these emissions as "livestock sector" emissions specifically.[6] Industrial crop production also requires fossil fuels to manufacture fertilizers through the Haber-Bosch process (Smil 2004), regardless of whether the crops are fed to animals or humans. Similarly, industrial production of feed[7] is unique to industrial livestock systems, which rely upon such feed as an external input, as opposed to restorative systems which seek as much as possible to feed animals through natural forages grown on site (see Shepard 2013). As such, many of these emissions sources could be significantly reduced – if not eliminated – if *different* livestock production methods and consumptive relations were brought into force.

It is therefore important to note that the FAO's figure for live-stock emissions is made up of both *direct* and *indirect* emissions. As Fairlie points out, if we follow this logic then emissions falling under the transport sector also ought to include indirect emissions from the manufacture of vehicles, road construction, transport hubs (like airports, train stations), and even the production of fuels and electricity used to power cars, planes, and trains. These are emissions that are typically slotted under other sectors like "industry" or "buildings" or "manufacturing" (Fairlie 2010, 159–60). There is a case to be made to *not* attribute feed production emissions to the "livestock sector," or at least to do a better job of clarifying direct and indirect emissions from feed production, and to clarify that the livestock-transport GHG comparison is of an apples-oranges character.[8]

Another site of indirect GHG emissions is deforestation. When land is cleared for the express purpose of raising or feeding animals, CO_2 is released. Yet burning forest for the purpose of industrial agriculture, such as sugar cane for ethanol or soy for export, is just as devastating, and it is unfair to categorize such emissions under the *livestock* sector. It does not make ecological sense in this era to clear forest for *any reason*, but the point here is that animals are not the problem per se; the problem is the human practice of burning or clearing forestland for agro-industrial purposes. To be clear, clearing forestland is not a requirement for animal agriculture. When *Livestock's Long Shadow* came out, it noted that more than a third of livestock sector emissions (34 per cent) were a direct result of deforestation, the idea being that massive tracts of land were being cleared strictly for the purpose of raising livestock. However, the FAO has since revised its calculations, no longer assuming that *all* agricultural deforestation is necessarily tied to livestock production. It notes, for instance, that there is ongoing "debate surrounding the key drivers of deforestation," and further that "grazing does not appear to be a significant driver of deforestation in Africa" (Gerber et al. 2013, 8, 9), as opposed to Latin America, where it *does* continue to be a problem. It also estimates what percentage of soy – the main crop planted in Latin America's recently deforested areas – typically goes into the global livestock feed trade, and what percentage of land cleared goes towards pasture for animals, noting that these two categories combined are cumulatively responsible for only 9.2 per cent of livestock sector emissions: in other words, less than a third of the value previously attributed to the sector within *Livestock's Long Shadow*.[9] This change in our understanding of the drivers of deforestation is one of the main reasons for the FAO's downward revision of the sector's estimated GHG emissions between 2006 and 2013. The point to emphasize here is that "rainforest meat" is very different in its GHG footprint from a grass-based cow-calf operation in the Canadian Prairies, for example.[10]

Further, it is apparent when drawing from the FAO's recent reports and the latest climate assessment by the IPCC that only about *half* of

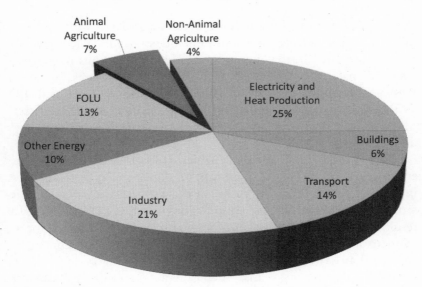

Figure 3.2   Share of global GHG emissions (by economic subsector)
Sources: IPCC Fifth Assessment 2014,,with data on AFOLU from FAO 2014.

the sector's emissions are *directly* related to livestock. The categories of emissions that the FAO's most recent assessment attributes to "livestock production"[11] amount to 3.5 gigatons, equivalent to 7.1 per cent of the global total GHG emissions in 2010 (see figure 3.2). It is worth underscoring here that these direct livestock emissions are *half* the value of global transport emissions. It is also worth emphasizing that not all of those livestock are intended for meat.[12] To put it differently, if we were to completely phase out meat production, the maximum GHG emissions savings are a fraction of those we could gain from completely phasing out fossil fuel-based transport. As I explain below, there are further reasons why targeting fossil fuel-based sectors and subsectors would be more effective in tackling climate change.

Differentiating between Animal and Human-Driven Emissions

So far this discussion has centred on CO_2, mostly because global GHG emissions are calculated in terms of CO_2 *equivalents* despite there being a handful of other significant GHGs. Here it is worth considering that the emissions coming directly from animals are qualitatively different from the emissions indirectly associated with animal agriculture, that is, emissions from human-driven processes associated with livestock production (for instance, emissions from industrial animal feed production). If it is not already apparent, the *indirect* emissions mentioned above are made up of CO_2 and N_2O in about equal measures. Emissions *directly* related to livestock are made up almost entirely of CH_4 and N_2O (with CH_4 taking the lion's share). This is our first clue that "direct" GHG emissions and "indirect" GHG emissions in the livestock sector are different beasts.

There are only a few ways in which animals directly cause new emissions of GHGs. First, a significant amount of CH_4 gas is released in the digestive process of ruminants, a process known as enteric fermentation.[13] Second, there are emissions of both N_2O and CH_4 that result from the decomposition of animal manure. The latter process happens in many different ways, but whether manure is applied to croplands as fertilizers, left on pastures, or concentrated in so-called manure management systems,[14] such gases are unavoidably released as a by-product.[15]

This qualitative difference between direct and indirect emissions in the livestock sector complicates matters because, as Suzuki (2016) points out, both CH_4 and N_2O are much "stronger" GHGs than CO_2 (on a weight-by-weight basis). At the same time, they are more fleeting because they do not stay in the atmosphere for nearly as long.[16] This poses a unique challenge: direct animal agriculture emissions are playing an emphasized role in pushing the climate to planetary tipping points in the present moment, yet compared to emissions from the transport and manufacturing sectors (mostly CO_2) such emissions are relatively short lived. This paradox has led some to argue that eliminating livestock poses the quickest "fix" for the climate (for instance, Russell, Singer, and Brook 2008). Others argue the very opposite, that any genuine lasting solution to climate change will be completely futile unless it confronts CO_2 from fossil fuels (for instance, see Fairlie 2010, 184). Allen et al. (2018) have argued that the typical way that CH_4 has been weighted[17] does not accurately reflect the "flow" nature of CH_4 as compared to the "stock" nature of CO_2. As a result, over a 100-year period, the contribution of CH_4 to global temperature change is less than implied by the current weighting of methane (Allen et al. 2018).[18]

This relates to another qualitative difference between direct and indirect emissions in the livestock sector. GHG emissions coming directly from animals in the form of CH_4 from enteric fermentation, and in the form of N_2O from manure left on pasture, are what we might call "surface-level" or biospheric emissions. These mostly release carbon (in the case of CH_4) or nitrogen (in the case of N_2O), as part of natural biogeochemical cycles that take place regardless of human intervention on a relatively short timescale. That is, the carbon released in the form of CH_4 from enteric fermentation had to come from the plant matter eaten by the animals. Such plant matter would have, in turn, obtained that carbon from the atmosphere through photosynthesis (Ballerstedt 2012). This is not a "direct exchange" of gases, as occurs in respiration, so it is still worth noting in the carbon accounting. However, it takes place at a much different timescale than emissions of CO_2 from fossil fuel combustion.[19]

Enteric fermentation is a natural part of the digestive process for both domesticated and wild ruminants such as cows, deer, elk, moose, goats, sheep, and bison.[20] CH_4 is produced by anaerobic bacteria in the animals' guts called "methanogens" as they help decompose the feed. There are some ways to reduce the amount of CH_4 produced by a ruminant, namely fine-tuning its diet. For agro-ecological livestock producers this means improving the quality of animal forages, such as increasing the amount of legumes in the pastures. The Union of Concerned Scientists notes that "the use of pasture management practices that improve the nutritional quality of forage crops could reduce CH_4 emissions from pasture beef by about 15 to 30 percent" (Gurian-Sherman 2011, 2).

N_2O from animals is also qualitatively different from N_2O released by human-driven processes. Animal urine and dung contains ammonia (NH_3), which plays an essential role as a natural plant fertilizer thanks to its nitrogen content. However, some of the nitrogen therein eventually oxidizes, releasing N_2O into the atmosphere. Similarly, when synthetic fertilizers are applied to agricultural crops, a small portion of the nitrogen will also oxidize and release N_2O *at the same rate* as natural fertilizers (Fairlie 2010, 168). Nitrogen is a requirement for all agricultural production, so fertilizer-related releases of N_2O are an inevitable result of food production everywhere, whether for meat, grains, or vegetables. However, an energy-intensive process known as Haber-Bosch is used to produce a *synthetic* nitrogen fertilizer. The process converts atmospheric nitrogen into NH_3 by reacting it with hydrogen, which is typically derived from hydrocarbons. The hydrocarbons are derived from fossil CH_4, which is extracted from the earth after being sequestered there for hundreds of millions of years.[21] In contrast, animals obtain nitrogen and hydrogen from their food, water, and air[22] in very short-term cycles – a matter of hours or days.

Agro-ecological and industrial livestock systems also diverge in how they deal with manure, releasing both CH_4 and N_2O in different ways.

The main deciding factors for how much CH_4 is emitted from manure are the method of manure storage and the ambient climate, since CH_4 production requires an anaerobic environment for bacterial reproduction – thus higher temperatures will result in more emissions (Jun, Gibbs, and Gaffney 2000, 322). Here large feedlots or other industrial models where animals are highly concentrated are problematic, since the manure is often contained in large lagoons or holding tanks. In this condition they cannot undergo "natural" degradation.[23] In contrast, on pastures countless species of dung-breeding insects help to reduce CH_4 from cow pats. These insects quickly degrade the pats, scatter the manure, and even bury parts of it underground, thereby aerating and draining the pats (Floate 2012).[24]

N_2O emissions can also be reduced by improving the quality of what the livestock eat, in part because more nutritious feeds allow animals to grow more quickly, thereby spending less time producing manure overall. Furthermore, higher-quality feeds shift some of the nitrogen from the animals' urine to dung (Gurian-Sherman 2011, 11, 26).[25] In agro-ecological systems, manure is spread out on pasture rather than collected in large heaps (as is typically required in industrial settings). This can also reduce N_2O emissions, since it increases the chance that the underlying soil can "use" the nitrogen and thereby sequester it, thereby building soil fertility rather than releasing it into the atmosphere.

None of the above discussion is intended to claim that CH_4 and N_2O emissions from livestock are *inconsequential*. We *do* need to think carefully about how to minimize these emissions – most notably by tackling the *scale* of the problem generated by growing global demand. The point, however, is that animals (in particular ruminants) will continue to release CH_4 through enteric fermentation regardless of whether they are wild or domesticated for the purposes of livestock production. Similarly, some of the nitrogen found in animal urine and manure will find its way back into the atmosphere regardless of whether the offending animals are domesticated or not. In contrast, the human-related emissions of fossil fuel-based CH_4, CO_2, and N_2O all stem from industrial-era and industrial-scale technologies that mark a break with the natural cycling of such gases and their elemental components.[26]

There is a notable puzzle in global CH_4 stocks, which the FAO itself has acknowledged, that speaks to qualitative differences in agricultural practices. In 2008 a joint report by the FAO and International Atomic Energy Agency (IAEA) found that the strong correlation between the rising global livestock numbers and the growth in global CH_4 emissions before 1999 could no longer be detected. The organizations concluded that "this change in relationship between the atmosphere and ruminant numbers suggests that the role of ruminants in greenhouse gasses may be less significant than originally thought, with other sources and sinks playing a larger role in global methane accounting" (FAO and IAEA 2008). Indeed, recent studies have found that fugitive emissions of CH_4 from fossil fuel production are responsible for a much greater portion of global CH_4 stocks than previously thought (Schwietzke et al. 2016; Rice et al. 2016).[27]

This all makes the problem of animal-related GHG emissions largely one of form and scale. Let us not forget that there were "tens of millions" of CH_4-belching and NH_3-excreting ruminant bison in the North American plains before industrialization (Shaw 1995).[28] There were also 100 million small antelope,[29] all while global atmospheric concentrations of CH_4 and N_2O remained within "natural" historical ranges. This suggests that the significant emissions sources of CH_4 and N_2O started with the Industrial Revolution and are associated with industrial activities.[30] It also suggests that there is a certain bandwidth for "allowable" CH_4 and N_2O emissions within a sustainable climate system (albeit a much smaller range than what is presently generated).

Partly Negating Emissions through Sequestration

The close attention paid to livestock-produced GHG emissions diverts attention away from the role that certain livestock management systems can play in sequestering atmospheric carbon in agricultural soils. Since the dawn of agriculture, notes Toensmeier, the clearing of land has resulted in the "loss" of 320 billion tons of carbon from soil (Toensmeier 2016, 23). This is because common agricultural practices like tilling, producing annual crops, and leaving soil bare for periods of time result in releases of carbon from soil to the atmosphere. In contrast, agricultural practices that do not use tillage and encourage growth of perennial plants tend to sequester carbon. In a pasture setting this generally happens in four main ways. First, when the aboveground biomass (i.e., leaf or other residues) dies and falls to the ground, it decomposes and some gets subsumed into soil organic matter. Second, perennial plants are consumed by grazing animals and then deposited on the ground in the form of manure. Part of this carbon-rich manure becomes soil organic matter. Third, the underground plant biomass (roots) dies when animals clip off the top foliage.[31] The dead roots decompose into soil organic matter. Finally, the plants directly exude carbon-rich compounds deep into the soil through their roots in a process called the "liquid carbon pathway" (Toensmeier 2016, 21–2; Jones 2008). All of this is to say that, in general, agricultural methods that encourage no-till and perennial crops[32] will see carbon sequestered into the soil.

The big question, of course, is how much carbon can be sequestered, and what are the limitations of this process? More specifically, does this sequestered carbon merely offset part of the aboveground emissions (CH_4 and N_2O in particular), or does it entirely negate them? The scientific evidence suggests that there is simply no singular answer to this because there are so many contextual factors affecting the rate of carbon sequestration, and different agricultural practices shaped by different geographical contexts.[33] In fact, the best science shows that, in some cases, livestock can help in sequestration and in others it can actually hinder the process (McSherry and Ritchie 2013). However, at the global scale, organizations like the FAO focus on livestock-based sequestration because grasslands make up a significant portion of agricultural lands,[34] and therefore offer significant climate change mitigation potential since even a small amount of sequestration could yield major gains (Toensmeier 2016, 85).

Just as there exists a range of assessments on what percentage of global GHGs are emitted by livestock, there is also a range of estimates regarding the sequestration potential of various livestock grazing practices. The Rodale Institute claims that if pasture management and improved grass forages are practised on a global level then animal agriculture could sequester 37 Gt CO_2 *per year*. This would be equivalent to about 70 per cent of the world's entire GHG emissions in 2012 (Rodale Institute 2014, 9).[35] The Savory Institute has a similar take, suggesting that if holistically planned grazing was practised on the world's 5 billion hectares of degraded grasslands then it "could return 10 or more gigatons of excess atmospheric carbon to the terrestrial sink annually.[36] This would have the impact of lowering GHGs concentrations to pre-industrial levels in a matter of decades" (Savory Institute 2015, 3). These are the enthusiasts.

In the middle, the Union of Concerned Scientists has suggested that better management of pasture and rangeland soils could sequester 13–70 million metric tons (MMT) of carbon per year in the United States. When this is combined with better crop management, such practices could reduce the US's annual GHG emissions by about 15 per cent (Gurian-Sherman 2011, 26). The FAO is much more conservative in its assessment of the overall potential for carbon sequestration from livestock grazing. Nevertheless, it is enthusiastic about this potential due to the sheer scale of net carbon sequestered if practised on a global level. For instance, the FAO claims that grassland carbon sequestration within the livestock sector could "significantly offset emissions, with global estimates of about 0.6 gigatons CO_2-eq per year" (Gerber et al. 2013, xiii). This is equivalent to only around 1.2 per cent of all anthropogenic emissions using the same base year as the FAO in its report. However, even this minimal figure is substantial, given that livestock themselves directly generate around 7.1 per cent of global GHG emissions. This all leads one to wonder about the significant potential offered by certain livestock systems in offering meat, fiber, and muscle power – among other "services" – while mitigating the sector's very own emissions.

Conclusion

To summarize, it seems to this author that the common-sense wisdom about meat being necessarily bad for the climate is overly simplistic and, in some instances, wrongheaded. A better job needs to be done to differentiate between "agro-ecological" models of livestock production and "industrial" models of livestock production. The former strives to produce meat and other services in ways that usually emit negligible amounts of GHGs – if not yielding a net sequestration of GHGs. The latter, among so many other environmental problems, tends to rely upon energy-intensive processes, at the primary and secondary levels, which until now have been dependent on fossil fuels. A better job also needs to be done to provide context and nuance to the "livestock sector" – particularly when discussing the sector's carbon footprint. Failing to do so leads passive observers to assume that eliminating all *livestock* would result in the elimination of all those emissions, which clearly is incorrect. Finally, when it comes to discussions around meat and climate change, a better job needs to be done to explain to the public that livestock animals are not just "GHG-emitting machines." These animals – given the right agricultural contexts – can be key partners in humanity's effort to address climate change while supporting global food security and nutrition targets. The risk of *not* getting this discussion right and *not* delving into the nuances and complexities is that simplistic representations yield simplistic solutions. These simplistic solutions could be counterproductive and/or unjust, which could mean both small-scale livestock producers and the climate become the victims of well-intentioned but misinformed policies.

Notes

1   Indeed, Gore was later awarded the Nobel Peace Prize for this important –
    and, one might add, long overdue – endeavour.

2   Including the potential – to a limited though not insignificant degree –
    to support carbon dioxide (CO_2) sequestration in some circumstances.

3   I use the term "common sense" here in the Gramscian sense of the word –
    meaning that it represents a general uncritical popular understanding of a
    given concept (Gramsci 1971).

4   The IPCC claims its agriculture sector GHG calculations have an estimation
    uncertainty of between 10 per cent and 150 per cent (Tubiello et al. 2014, 1).
    In part, this is because there are a great deal of assumptions that go into
    "bottom-up" modelling, which in the case of livestock estimates usually
    involves multiplying the number of animals by average emissions figures
    based on what is known about various production methods – the problem
    being that these calculations may or may not match real agricultural
    practices, and may not account for variations in natural "checks" and
    "balances" in the system (natural carbon sinks, for instance) from one place
    to another.

5   Though as I note below, transport still serves as a poor comparison.

6   Of course, critics will note that because of different energy conversion rates
    for meat and protein crops, *less land* would be required if we just used those
    croplands to make food for humans, rather than feed animals first and then
    feed the animal proteins to humans. This, in turn, would presumably free
    up land for restoration, which would in theory help sequester more carbon.
    This is a valid counterargument, but it is not without its own problems. First,
    due to the nutritional density of meat-based proteins vis-à-vis plant-based
    proteins, one typically requires *more* of the latter in terms of net weight to
    achieve the same quality of human-useable protein overall (Layman 2018;
    Baber, Sawyer, and Wickersham 2018). Thus, if the decision was made to
    switch out all livestock feed crop production over to human-grade protein
    crop production, then there would be a significant protein shortfall which
    would need to be met, presumably by planting additional protein crops.
    Second, a considerable amount of animal feed is from "crop residues" or low-
    quality crops deemed unfit for human consumption (in fact, about 86 per
    cent of livestock feed globally is *not* human-edible; Mottet et al. 2017). This
    is to say that a considerable amount of crop products fed to livestock are
    essentially "wasted" human food crops. As such, in the absence of livestock
    to make use of that "waste," humans would need additional croplands to
    account for a certain percentage of the annual harvest which turns out to be
    unsuitable to humans.

7 Typically corn, soy, and other cereal grains.

8 Interestingly, Henning Steinfeld, the lead author of that original FAO report
   which compared livestock emissions to the transport sector, has recently
   clarified that this comparison is inaccurate (MacMillan 2018).

9 This 9.2 per cent comes from CO_2 from pasture expansion, which is 6 per
   cent of sector emissions, and from the clearing of land for the express
   production of soybean-based animal feeds, which is 3.2 per cent of sector
   emissions (Gerber et al. 2013, 17).

10 Vast differences would also be observed in the broader ecological
   implications of these different types of meat production (for instance,
   see Pittman 2018 for an explanation of the role cattle play in preserving
   biodiversity on the Canadian Prairies).

11 As opposed to "feed production" or "post-farm" emissions.

12 It also includes, for instance, laying hens and dairy cows and sheep and
   alpacas raised for wool, etc.

13 The so-called – and largely mislabelled – cow farts problem. Ruminant
   flatulence does exist, but the more significant issue, as far as methane release
   is concerned, is from ruminant belching or "eructation."

14 So-called slurry lagoons, for instance.

15 As mentioned above, it is true that animal respiration (in other words, the
   CO_2 exhaled by animals) is in theory a form of GHG emissions directly
   related to livestock, but climate scientists have been clear to note the folly
   of incorporating respiration in the calculation of animal agriculture's
   "contribution" to climate change (as Anhang and Goodland do), since there
   is a direct exchange of carbon to the atmosphere from the photosynthesizing
   plants that removed said carbon in the first place before being eaten by
   animals (for similar reasons, we do not consider human respiration as a cause
   of climate change either; see Steinfeld et al. 2006, 95).

16 CH_4 is up to twenty-eight times as powerful as CO_2 in terms of warming
   the planet, but it only stays in the atmosphere for about a decade; N_2O is
   265 times more powerful than CO_2, and it stays in the atmosphere for about
   a century. Meanwhile, CO_2 stays in the atmosphere for *thousands of years*.

17 Using a Global Warming Potential over 100 years.

18 As one of the study's co-authors recently explained on Twitter, CH_4 is given
   a Global Warming Potential of 28, but "if you want to know how important
   different emissions are for warming in 2100, this metric is no good. Methane
   does not give 28× more warming in 2100 than CO_2, as CH_4 has a half-life of
   ~10 years so it's mostly gone by then!"

19 This type carbon accounting returns carbon to the atmosphere after it
   has effectively been sequestered in the lithosphere for *300 million years*
   (US Department of Energy 2013).

20   Termites, while not ruminants, also happen to produce lots of CH_4, with one
     estimate claiming that the insect species alone is responsible for 4 per cent of
     global CH_4 emissions (Sanderson 1996).

21   While the GHG emissions associated with the energy used to produce
     synthetic fertilizers (in the Haber Bosch process) are supposedly included
     within the FAO's livestock sector estimates (Gerber et al. 2013, 17, 20), it
     would seem that the fugitive GHG emissions resulting from the industrial
     production of hydrogen (an essential feedstock used in the Haber Bosch
     process) are attributed to *other* sectors. In fact, the FAO's recent report on GHG
     emissions in the entire AFOLU sector (Tubiello et al. 2014, 35) only include
     N_2O emissions from synthetic fertilizers, not any CO_2 emissions associated
     with synthetic fertilizer *production*. It is no wonder then that "livestock"-
     related emissions would seem to take up such a prominent role in the
     agriculture sector.

22   It then cycles them through to their next elemental stage.

23   Though as industrial advocates note, there is great potential here to "capture"
     the methane and then use it as fuel for either heat or an electrical generator.

24   There are some 450 known species of insects that depend on cattle dung in
     North America. Industrial sewage lagoons therefore pose a threat to these
     species.

25   Urine has a higher concentration of NH_3. As Gurian-Sherman (2011) points
     out, one study found that this technique could reduce the nitrogen content
     in the urine of dairy cows by up to 28 per cent.

26   I have not discussed N_2O emissions from the transport sector, as this is a
     whole other can of worms. The key takeaway is that *industrial* processes –
     including synthetic fertilizer – have caused N_2O levels in the atmosphere
     to increase by 16 per cent since the industrial revolution: "Burning fossil
     fuels and wood is one source of the increase in atmospheric nitrous oxide,
     however the main contributor is believed to be the widespread use of
     nitrogen-based fertilisers," for crop production, notes the BBC Weather
     Centre (2014).

27   At the same time, "biological sources" of CH_4 from (rice cultivation, swamp
     gas, and enteric fermentation) also appear to be a growing contributing
     source to global stocks in recent years, *particularly in tropical regions*, in what
     is very likely a positive feedback loop related to global warming (Nisbet et al.
     2016). This is undoubtedly troubling, but clearly the solution is not to single
     out just *one* of these biological CH_4 sources.

28   Shaw points out that most estimates (usually in the 30–60 million range)
     face a high margin of error.

29   These numbers are comparable to the 12 million cattle in Canada (Kay 2015)
     plus 92 million in the US (National Cattlemen's Beef Association 2016).

30   This would admittedly include *industrial* livestock production.

31 This can happen either as a result of natural root death, or it can be encouraged by grazing, since plants that have just been grazed will then shed the equivalent amount of removed aboveground biomass from their root structure in order to compensate for the imbalance.

32 This certainly *includes* a variety of agro-ecological livestock production methods, but *excludes* most industrial livestock production methods.

33 For instance, one study of different livestock management practices in Colombia found that regular pasture-based grazing strategies typically saw carbon sequestration only partially offsetting the aboveground methane and nitrous oxide emissions, while silvopastoral practices (which integrate pastures with trees) actually allowed for net gains in GHG accounting (Cardona et al. 2014).

34 About 3.5 billion of 5 billion hectares.

35 When combined with the switch to regenerative organic agriculture methods in crops around the world, the Rodale Institute claims that "we could sequester more than 100% of current annual CO_2 emissions" (2).

36 The FAO claims that there are in fact only 3.5 billion hectares of arable grasslands, which it describes as land suitable for "pasture" or "fodder crops."

References

Allen, Myles R., Keith P. Shine, Jan S. Fuglestvedt, Richard J. Millar, Michelle Cain, David J. Frame, and Adrian H. Macey. 2018. "A Solution to the Misrepresentations of CO_2 –Equivalent Emissions of Short-Lived Climate Pollutants under Ambitious Mitigation." *Npj Climate and Atmospheric Science* 1 (1): 16. https://doi.org/10.1038/s41612-018-0026-8.

Baber, Jessica R., Jason E. Sawyer, and Tryon A. Wickersham. 2018. "Estimation of Human-Edible Protein Conversion Efficiency, Net Protein Contribution, and Enteric Methane Production from Beef Production in the United States." *Translational Animal Science* 2 (4): 439–50. https://doi.org/10.1093/tas/txy086.

Bailey, Rob, Antony Froggatt, and Laura Wellesley. 2014. "Livestock – Climate Change's Forgotten Sector: Global Public Opinion on Meat and Dairy Consumption." December 2014. https://www.chathamhouse.org/sites/files/chathamhouse/field/field_document/20141203LivestockClimateChangeBaileyFroggattWellesley.pdf?dm_i=1TY5,30JLo,BHZILT,AUGSP,1.

Ballerstedt, Peter. 2012. "The Reality of Ruminants and Liebig's Barrel: Examining the New 'Conventional Wisdom.'" Presented at the Ancestral Health Symposium, Boston, MA, 9 August.

Baumert, Kevin A., Timothy Herzog, and Jonathan Pershing. 2005. "Navigating the Numbers: Greenhouse Gas Data and International

Climate Policy." Washington, DC: World Resources Institute. http://pdf.wri.
org/navigating_numbers.pdf.

BBC Weather Centre. 2014. "Nitrous Oxide." Climate Change from the BBC
Weather Centre. 24 September 2014. http://www.bbc.co.uk/climate/
evidence/nitrous_oxide.shtml.

Bekhechi, Mimi. 2016. "No Meat? No Problem!" Huffington Post.com.
3 October 2016. http://www.huffingtonpost.co.uk/mimi-bekhechi/
no-meat-no-problem_b_12266088.html.

Cardona, Cuartas, César A., Naranjo Ramírez, Juan F., Tarazona Morales,
Ariel M., Enrique Murgueitio Restrepo, et al. 2014. "Contribution of
Intensive Silvopastoral Systems to Animal Performance and to Adaptation
and Mitigation of Climate Change." *Revista Colombiana de Ciencias
Pecuarias* 27 (2): 76–94.

Carrington, Damian. 2018. "Avoiding Meat and Dairy Is 'Single Biggest Way'
to Reduce Your Impact on Earth." *The Guardian*, 31 May 2018. http://www.
theguardian.com/environment/2018/may/31/avoiding-meat-and-dairy-is-
single-biggest-way-to-reduce-your-impact-on-earth.

Chivers, Danny. 2016. "Cowspiracy: Stampeding in the Wrong
Direction?" *New Internationalist*, 10 February 2016. https://newint.org/
blog/2016/02/10/cowspiracy-stampeding-in-the-wrong-direction/.

Fairlie, Simon. 2010. *Meat: A Benign Extravagance*. White River Junction, VT:
Chelsea Green.

FAO and IAEA. 2008. "Belching Ruminants, a Minor Player in Atmospheric
Methane." Joint FAO/IAEA Programme: Nuclear Techniques in Food
and Agriculture. Rome: FAO/IAEA. http://www.naweb.iaea.org/nafa/aph/
stories/2008-atmospheric-methane.html.

Floate, Kevin. 2012. "Calling on More Troops – New Beetles Help Degrade
Dung on Canadian Pastures." Agriculture and Agri-Food Canada. 2012.
http://www.agr.gc.ca/resources/prod/doc/sci/pdf/fs_degrade_dung_eng.pdf.

Gerber, P.J, H. Steinfeld, B. Henderson, A. Mottet, C. Opio, J. Dinkman,
A. Falcucci, and G. Tempio. 2013. "Tackling Climate Change through
Livestock – A Global Assessment of Emissions and Mitigation
Opportunities." Rome: Food and Agriculture Organization of the
United Nations.

Goodland, Robert, and Jeff Anhang. 2009. "Livestock and Climate Change."
World Watch Magazine, December: 10–19.

Gramsci, Antonio. 1971. *Selections from the Prison Notebooks of Antonio
Gramsci*. Edited by Geoffrey Nowell-Smith and Quintin Hoare. London:
Lawrence and Wishart.

Gurian-Sherman, Doug. 2011. "Raising the Steaks: Global Warming and
Pasture-Raised Beef Production in the United States." Cambridge, MA:
Union of Concerned Scientists.

Niman, Nicolette Hahn. 2014. *Defending Beef*. White River Junction, VT: Chelsea Green.

Jones, Christine. 2008. "Liquid Carbon Pathway Unrecognized." Australian Farm Journal. http://amazingcarbon.com/PDF/JONES-LiquidCarbonPathway(AFJ-July08).pdf.

Jun, Paul, Michael Gibbs, and Kathryn Gaffney. 2000. "CH_4 and N_2O Emissions from Livestock Manure." In *Good Practice Guidance and Uncertainty Management in National Greenhouse Gas Inventories*, 321–38. Montreal: Intergovernmental Panel on Climate Change.

Kay, Steve. 2015. "Is Canada's Cattle Herd at Its Lowest Level in 20 Years?" Canadian Cattlemen.ca (blog). 9 February 2015. http://www.canadiancattlemen.ca/2015/02/09/its-all-about-the-cattle-numbers/.

Kramberger, Albert. 2016. "Beaconsfield Council Promotes Meatless Monday Initiative." *Montreal Gazette* (blog), 29 March 2016. http://montrealgazette.com/news/local-news/west-island-gazette/beaconsfield-council-promotes-meatless-monday-initiative.

Layman, Donald K. 2018. "Assessing the Role of Cattle in Sustainable Food Systems." *Nutrition Today* 53 (4): 160. https://doi.org/10.1097/NT.0000000000000286.

MacMillan, Susan. 2018. "FAO on the Common but Flawed Comparisons of Greenhouse Gas Emissions from Livestock and Transport." ILRI Clippings (blog). 19 September 2018. https://clippings.ilri.org/2018/09/19/fao-on-the-common-but-flawed-comparisons-of-greenhouse-gas-emissions-from-livestock-and-transport/.

McMahon, Jeff. 2016. "Paris Agreement Portends a Reckoning for Meat and Dairy." *Forbes*, 1 January 2016. http://www.forbes.com/sites/jeffmcmahon/2016/01/01/paris-agreement-will-impact-meat-and-dairy/.

McSherry, Megan E., and Mark E. Ritchie. 2013. "Effects of Grazing on Grassland Soil Carbon: A Global Review." *Global Change Biology* 19 (5): 1347–57. https://doi.org/10.1111/gcb.12144.

Monbiot, George. 2018. "The Best Way to Save the Planet? Drop Meat and Dairy." *The Guardian*, 8 June 2018. http://www.theguardian.com/commentisfree/2018/jun/08/save-planet-meat-dairy-livestock-food-free-range-steak.

Mottet, Anne, Cees de Haan, Alessandra Falcucci, Giuseppe Tempio, Carolyn Opio, and Pierre Gerber. 2017. "Livestock: On Our Plates or Eating at Our Table? A New Analysis of the Feed/Food Debate." *Global Food Security* (issue on Food Security Governance in Latin America) 14 (September): 1–8. https://doi.org/10.1016/j.gfs.2017.01.001.

National Cattlemen's Beef Association. 2016. "Beef Industry Statistics." Denver, CO: National Cattlemen's Beef Association. 2016. http://www.beefusa.org/beefindustrystatistics.aspx.

Nisbet, E.G., E.J. Dlugokencky, M.R. Manning, D. Lowry, R.E. Fisher, J.L. France, S.E. Michel, et al. 2016. "Rising Atmospheric Methane: 2007–2014 Growth and Isotopic Shift." *Global Biogeochemical Cycles* 30 (9): 1356–70. https://doi.org/10.1002/2016GB005406.

Pittman, Jeremy. 2018. "How Cattle Ranching Can Help Preserve Species at Risk in Canada's Grasslands." *Canadian Geographic*, 24 July 2018. https://www.canadiangeographic.ca/article/how-cattle-ranching-can-help-preserve-species-risk-canadas-grasslands.

Poore, J., and T. Nemecek. 2018. "Reducing Food's Environmental Impacts through Producers and Consumers." *Science* 360 (6392): 987–92. https://doi.org/10.1126/science.aaq0216.

Premack, Rachel. 2016. "Meat Is Horrible." *Washington Post*, 30 June 2016. https://www.washingtonpost.com/news/wonk/wp/2016/06/30/how-meat-is-destroying-the-planet-in-seven-charts/.

Rice, Andrew L., Christopher L. Butenhoff, Doaa G. Teama, Florian H. Röger, M. Aslam K. Khalil, and Reinhold A. Rasmussen. 2016. "Atmospheric Methane Isotopic Record Favors Fossil Sources Flat in 1980s and 1990s with Recent Increase." *Proceedings of the National Academy of Sciences* 113 (39): 10791–6. https://doi.org/10.1073/pnas.1522923113.

Rodale Institute. 2014. "Regenerative Organic Agriculture and Climate Change: A Down-to-Earth Solution to Global Warming." Kutztown, PA: Rodale Institute. http://rodaleinstitute.org/assets/WhitePaper.pdf.

Röös, Elin, Mikaela Patel, Johanna Spångberg, Georg Carlsson, and Lotta Rydhmer. 2016. "Limiting Livestock Production to Pasture and By-Products in a Search for Sustainable Diets." *Food Policy* 58 (Supplement C): 1–13. https://doi.org/10.1016/j.foodpol.2015.10.008.

Russell, Geoff, Peter Singer, and Barry Brook. 2008. "The Missing Link in the Garnaut Report." *Sydney Morning Herald*, 10 July 2008. http://www.smh.com.au/federal-politics/the-missing-link-in-the-garnaut-report-20080709-3cjh.html.

Sanderson, M.G. 1996. "Biomass of Termites and Their Emissions of Methane and Carbon Dioxide: A Global Database." *Global Biogeochemical Cycles* 10 (4): 543–57.

Savory Institute. 2015. "Restoring the Climate through Capture and Storage of Soil Carbon through Holistic Planned Grazing." 2015. http://savory.global/assets/docs/evidence-papers/RestoringClimateWhitePaper2015.pdf.

Schwartz, Judith D. 2013. *Cows Save the Planet: And Other Improbable Ways of Restoring Soil to Heal the Earth.* White River Junction, VT: Chelsea Green.

Schwietzke, Stefan, Owen A. Sherwood, Lori M. Bruhwiler, John B. Miller, Giuseppe Etiope, Edward J. Dlugokencky, Sylvia Englund Michel, et al. 2016. "Upward Revision of Global Fossil Fuel Methane Emissions

Based on Isotope Database." *Nature* 538 (October): 88–91. https://doi.org/10.1038/nature19797.

Shaw, James H. 1995. "How Many Bison Originally Populated Western Rangelands?" *Rangelands* 17 (5): 148–50.

Shepard, Mark. 2013. *Restoration Agriculture: Real World Permaculture for Farmers*. Austin, TX: Acres USA.

Smil, Vaclav. 2004. *Enriching the Earth: Fritz Haber, Carl Bosch, and the Transformation of World Food Production*. Cambridge, MA: MIT Press.

Steinfeld, Henning, Pierre Gerber, T. Wassenaar, V. Castel, Mauricio Rosales, and C. de Haan. 2006. "Livestock's Long Shadow: Environmental Issues and Options." Rome: Food and Agriculture Organization of the United Nations. http://www.fao.org/docrep/010/a0701e/a0701e00.htm.

Suzuki, David. 2016. "Eating Less Meat Will Reduce Earth's Heat." Rabble.ca. 17 May 2016. http://rabble.ca/blogs/bloggers/david-suzuki/2016/05/eating-less-meat-will-reduce-earths-heat.

Toensmeier, Eric. 2016. *The Carbon Farming Solution: A Global Toolkit of Perennial Crops and Regenerative Agriculture Practices for Climate Change Mitigation and Food Security*. White River Junction, VT: Chelsea Green.

Tubiello, F.N, M. Salvatore, R.D. Cóndor Golec, A. Ferrara, S. Rossi, R. Biancalani, S Federici, H. Jacobs, and A. Flammini. 2014. "Agriculture, Forestry and Other Land Use Emissions by Sources and Revomals by Sinks." Working Paper Series ESS/14-02. Rome: Food and Agriculture Organization of the United Nations. http://www.fao.org/docrep/019/i3671e/i3671e.pdf.

US Department of Energy. 2013. "How Fossil Fuels Were Formed." US Department of Energy. 12 February 12 2013. http://www.fe.doe.gov/education/energylessons/coal/gen_howformed.html.

Wellesley, Laura, Antony Froggatt, and Catherine Happer. 2015. "Changing Climate, Changing Diets: Pathways to Lower Meat Consumption." London: Chatham House, Royal Institute of International Affairs.

4

Does Meat Belong in a Sustainable Diet?

Caitlin M. Scott

Introduction

Despite increasing awareness of the heavy carbon footprint and water and land use associated with global industrial meat production (Weis 2013), the competing interests and scientific uncertainty in debates over meat consumption create questions around what constitutes a "sustainable diet." The call for sustainable diets puts the reduction of meat consumption centre stage and incorporates a variety of voices. Academics and members of civil society have been active in the ensuing debates, bringing the environmental impacts of meat production to light with life cycle assessments and information campaigns. However, they may sometimes lose sight of the nuance in broader sustainability debates, as well as the social and cultural challenges to changing diets. Despite its success in bringing sustainable diets to the forefront, civil society's collaboration with business to build momentum around common ground serves to legitimize change-making in the form of apolitical nudges, rather than shifting consumption patterns. Governments have done relatively little to take on the challenge of sustainable diets, with only a few changes in food guidelines and even fewer far-reaching reforms of policy, like taxes and subsidies. Finally, sustainable diets pose a challenge to industry's business model. Agri-food industries have adopted discourses of efficiency and productivity, and point to the larger environmental impacts of other industries. This chapter argues that efforts to define what counts as a sustainable diet give rise to various, contrasting sustainability discourses surrounding meat consumption, where powerful actors compete to influence the universal definition to align with their own interests. This effort is problematic because it does not take into consideration the complexity of global food systems that may arise from different contexts and entail various types of sustainable diets.

The following chapter will explore how recent debates on sustainable diets have unfolded, highlighting the discourses from a variety of actors and problematizing their positions. It is not meant to capture every voice on the matter, but to shed light on some of the key issues and stakeholders, including academics, government, civil society, and business. In the drive for a universal definition of "sustainable diet," not only are important voices being left out of the conversation entirely, some narratives are louder than others. In efforts to make the argument for reduced meat consumption, the complexity of dietary choices and social change are being simplified in ways that may be problematic for animal life, equity, and the ecological health of the planet. This chapter will give a brief overview of the early work on sustainable diets and some of the academic literature that has emerged on this topic. It will then survey how different civil society organizations are pushing for action on sustainable diets, and the response from governments thus far. Finally, it will show how different business interests are using the sustainable diets debate to their advantage or are disputing the need for a change to meat consumption patterns altogether.

Sustainable Diets in Review: From Defining Moments to the Academic Literature

The term "sustainable diet" was first coined by Gussow and Clancy (1986) in a paper arguing for better integration of environmental factors in nutritional guidelines, but the concept has been around much longer. At the time, sustainable diets failed to gain popular attention, but in the last decade there has been a proliferation of work that has aimed to explore and quantify the environmental impacts of food production, and in turn, to define "sustainable diets" (see Mason and Lang 2017; Jones et al. 2016).

The commonly accepted definition of "sustainable diets" comes from a report on an FAO-funded scientific symposium held in 2010. The community of scientists, academics, and policy professionals at the event agreed on the following definition: sustainable diets are those "with low environmental impacts which contribute to food and nutrition security and to a healthy life for present and future generations. Sustainable diets are protective and respectful of biodiversity and ecosystems, culturally acceptable, accessible, economically fair and affordable; nutritionally adequate, safe and healthy; while optimizing natural and human resources" (FAO in Burlingame and Dernini 2012, 264–5).

This broad definition does not provide prescriptive means of achieving these attributes. Instead the debate remains open, and academic, civil society, and policy communities continue to qualify and quantify sustainable diets in contrasting ways. But these efforts have led to further studies and conflicting priorities. The vast majority of research on sustainable diets has focused on the environmental impacts of meat consumption. However, as the following sections will show, the act of defining sustainable diets, and the focus on meat consumption specifically, has limitations, including simplifying the complex measures necessary to achieve a sustainable food future.

This chapter takes the view, similar to Mason and Lang (2017), that sustainability in the context of diets and food systems requires a more nuanced and complex approach than the traditional three pillars of environment, society, and economy. Mason and Lang go on to argue that there should instead be six headings under which to view sustainable diets: quality, health, environment, social values, economy, and governance. These groupings build on the six broad categories of criteria outlined by the FAO-Bioversity International model of sustainable diets: well-being and health; biodiversity, environment, and climate; equity and fair trade; eco-friendly, local, and seasonal foods; cultural heritage and skills; and food and nutrient needs, food security, and accessibility (ibid., 15). Likewise, Johnston, Fanzo, and Cogill (2014) established five determinants of sustainable diets: agriculture, health, sociocultural, environmental, and socio-economic factors. However, all of these approaches are quite anthropocentric, failing to fully consider the rights and suffering of animals that often results from food production. Additionally, as will be shown, while various authors provide a number of criteria by which sustainable diets can be measured, it is evident that some aspects are better understood than others. Thus, in considering what a sustainable diet is, this chapter understands sustainability as contextual and nuanced, requiring critical readings of discourse.

Mason and Lang (2017, 8) note that there can be "soft" and "hard" sustainable diets using the notion of a meal that is healthy and has one environmentally sound element vs. one that is entirely low impact, low sugar, low fat, and seasonal. While this concept of a soft or hard understanding of sustainable diet is reminiscent of "strong" vs. "weak" sustainability, the authors admit that both could be considered sustainable and do not take into consideration the even broader criteria of sustainable diets. What is evident is the lack of clarity around the concept, and many of the concepts within the official definition of sustainable diets. This makes the discussion of discourses, and critical understandings of how different actors are assessing sustainability, that much more important.

The majority of studies that use the term "sustainable diets" focus narrowly on quantifying the environmental impacts of food production. More narrowly they tend to focus on greenhouse gas emissions (GHGs), land use, or water availability (Jones et al. 2016). For example, the academic literature on sustainable diets has grown due to the increased use of life cycle assessment or analysis (LCA) in the agri-food sector (Freidberg 2014). LCA is the process by which the environmental impact of a product is calculated throughout its life cycle, from "cradle to grave," and it forms the basis for many of the arguments for sustainable diets. The International Standards Organisation (ISO) has published guidelines on this process, and the growth in LCA has spurred numerous conferences and journals that publish life cycle studies (e.g., *The International Journal for Lifecycle Assessment*). Many of the papers exploring the potential for sustainable diets attempt to quantify reductions in carbon emissions by modelling changes to diets, which is reliant on data from LCA studies (Eshel and Martin 2006; Zhu, van Wesenbeeck, and van Ierland 2006; Carlsson-Kanyama and González 2009; Tilman and Clark 2014; Tom, Fischbeck, and Hendrickson 2016).

Nevertheless, research focused on LCA and dietary patterns fails to recognize many dimensions of sustainability (as described by Johnston, Fanzo, and Cogill 2014 or Mason and Lang 2017). The LCA studies and sustainable diets literature, to date, have largely focused on conventional livestock operations, ignoring insights from different methods of farming and their respective ecosystem services. Freidberg (2014, 572) points out that LCA studies cannot resolve complex debates such as sustainability as a normative goal, or the possible trade-offs between eco-efficiency, healthfulness, and the well-being of workers and animals (Freidberg 2014). LCA may provide an effective big picture view of the environmental impacts of diets, but it cannot provide the diversity and nuanced experiences of the food sector that could lead to a sustainable future. In turn, using LCA as a basis for arguments for sustainable diets provides opportunities for sustainability narratives to be shaped by different actors, and in turn allows power dynamics to dictate how these narratives become the foundation for governance.

Numerous studies on sustainable diets attempt to quantify nutritional needs in relation to varied amounts of animal products included in diets (Aston, Smith, and Powles 2012; de Carvalho et al. 2013; Perignon et al. 2016; Temme et al. 2015; Soret et al. 2014; Scarborough et al. 2012). Authors have looked at these modelled scenarios to assess potential acceptability among different populations, and the impact that only small reductions in meat consumption might have (Vieux et al. 2012; Macdiarmid et al. 2011). Others have attempted to explore the ability of vegetarian and vegan diets to reduce the occurrence of health issues and prevent diet-related mortality, both of which have profound economic impacts (Springmann et al. 2017). There is some debate in the public health and nutrition field over what nutritionally adequate diets look like at a population level, and whether the goal is "optimum nutrition for the individual or good enough nutrition for society as a whole" (Garnett 2014, 6). Saturated fats and sugar have become key areas of contention in these debates, with some authors arguing that sugar and diets high in processed carbohydrates are the sources of ill health, while advocating for diets that are considerably lower in carbohydrates and higher in animal products. Alternatively, critical nutrition studies scholars have pushed back against the reductive focus on nutrients, with authors calling for new understandings of food that take into account quality, tradition, culture, and sensual and practical experiences around food (Scrinis 2013; Biltekoff 2013).

Studies demonstrating the ability to meet current dietary criteria while considerably reducing meat consumption provide the impetus for policy change and overarching recommendations to reduce consumption. Several studies consider consumer choice related to narrowly defined aspects of sustainable food consumption, including organic, fair trade, or vegetarian diets specifically (Jones et al. 2016). Much of the work is quantitative in nature and gives overall indications about consumer perceptions and motivations related to food consumption choices by defining the percentages of people willing to spend more to purchase "sustainable" food or potentially give up meat in their diets. However, there is a recognition that reductions would entail dramatic changes to the status quo.

A gap in the literature remains when it comes to the cultural and social drivers of dietary change in relation to sustainability. More work is needed to understand why people may change their diet, and how to create large shifts in the cultural acceptance of meat consumption and production. Macdiarmid, Douglas, and Campbell (2016) found focus group participants ill-informed or skeptical about the links between environmental degradation and meat consumption, which inhibited their willingness to reduce or give up meat. A Chatham House report with similar findings linked awareness of the diet and climate issue with acceptance of reduced consumption and policy reforms with this goal (Wellesley 2015, viii).

The academic literature on sustainable diets has grown exponentially in a short time but has failed to significantly affect public consciousness and political decision-making. Fuchs et al. (2016) argue that power is often a critical element left out of discussions on sustainable consumption and policy efforts, citing the politics of meat as a prime example. Academic literature on sustainable diets can be similarly critiqued because few researchers delve into the political struggles and powerful interests involved in what defines a sustainable diet. The tendency to ignore power and politics and to focus on quantitative measurements of environmental impact has affected how civil society and business interests engage in their work on sustainable diets.

Civil Society and Government Efforts on Sustainable Diets

Civil society has been actively pursuing the issue of dietary sustainability for many years, with a wide variety of organizations urging its inclusion in policies related to food and diets. The primary strategies to encourage sustainable diets include changing dietary guidelines, advocating for taxes on high-carbon products, public education on meat and its environmental impacts, and collaborations with industry. These strategies have served to legitimize certain forms of policy and action, while reducing the debate on alternatives.

Civil society's strength lies in turning the academic information on sustainable diets into efforts to build public awareness, critical for a reduction in meat consumption. The Barilla Center for Food and Nutrition Foundation (BCFN) is a private non-profit think tank that has been particularly prominent in the movement for sustainable diets. The BCFN developed the Double Pyramid, a combination of a traditional food pyramid and environmental pyramid, which shows the relationship between health and nutrition, and its environmental impact (Barilla Center for Food and Nutrition 2015). Barilla's Double Pyramid is frequently mentioned to demonstrate the win-wins from reducing dietary environmental impacts, pointing to the health benefits accompanying this change. In 2015, BCFN used mostly academic studies to compile 1,222 data points on the environmental impacts of various food products from 385 sources, a significant increase from their 2010 report, which used 140 data points from thirty-five sources. Like the academic literature that the Double Pyramid work is based on, the majority (71 per cent) of the data used for the Double Pyramid report focuses on carbon footprints, with only 15 per cent looking at water footprints and 14 per cent looking at ecological footprints (Barilla Center for Food and Nutrition 2015). The dependence on academic studies means that civil society suffers from many of the same pitfalls, neglecting qualitative approaches that provide more diverse interpretations and outcomes.

Civil society campaigns in Europe like the "Livewell" plate,[1] a partnership of wwf uk and Friends of Europe, aim to raise public awareness of the environmental impacts of meat consumption by engaging media attention. The Livewell project developed a number of reports and case study dietary scenarios to show the potential for sustainable diets throughout Europe. Simple messaging was developed to guide consumers on improving the sustainability of their diet. Eating Better, another uk organization, has also worked across sectors to develop consistent messaging for policy and cultural change towards eating less meat (EatingBetter.org 2016). Simple messaging and effective media campaigns have brought sustainable diets to the public consciousness in Europe; however, it is unclear whether significant progress is being made towards eating sustainably.

The approach of civil society organizations to sustainable diets is similar to other environmental campaigns that insist that it will not take significant sacrifice or change to individuals' consumption. The trend of individualized responsibility, with little institutional or policy change, has been a growing tactic of the environmental movement, but as Maniates points out, these approaches "constrain our imagination about what is possible and what is worth working towards" (Maniates 2001, 50). For example, the bcfn's 2015 Double Pyramid report claims, "Food is one of the areas of life where personal well-being can be reconciled with that of the Planet. Without giving anything up" (Barilla Center for Food and Nutrition 2015, 57). Although this strategy aims to push citizens slowly and non-confrontationally towards sustainable diets, interventionist measures have proven more effective in achieving the scale of behavioural shift required to meaningfully contribute to reductions in environmental impacts from the meat industry (Wellesley, Happer, and Froggat 2015, 15). Campaigns that promote Meatless Mondays and other slow nudges in the direction towards reduced meat consumption from civil society constrain our collective ability to question and shift the culture of meat consumption.

Advocacy for more sustainable diets has led civil society organizations to collaborate with consulting firms and industry on policy advocacy and programs that focus on consumer choice. A number of wwf publications[2] demonstrate the choices that citizens could make to reduce their dietary impact. Some of these publications use Agri-Footprint® Life Cycle Inventory and the Optimeal® modelling program for dietary environmental impact developed by the Blonk Consultants, a Dutch firm specializing in sustainability. Other organizations have made headlines in the past year with multiple reports coming out of Chatham House on meat and sustainability. Shortly after, the Carbon Trust, a corporate consultation service, published the *Case for Protein Diversity*, sponsored by a leading UK meat alternatives producer, Quorn.

Collaborative projects between business and civil society have emerged to change consumption and to develop sustainable diets that will be supported by consumers. The Forum for the Future is a collaborative project between civil society organizations including the WWF, the Global Alliance for Improved Nutrition (GAIN), and a number of business actors, including Quorn, the Hershey Company, and Target. A recent report aimed to "raise the profile of protein as an integral part of a sustainable food system," and "change the conversation … from 'good' and 'bad' sources towards a better balance of sustainable protein" (Forum for the Future 2016). In 2016, The World Resources Institute (WRI) put out a working paper on dietary change, *Shifting Diets for a Sustainable Future*, that garnered significant media attention. This report explores different dietary scenarios and strategies for shifting consumption and includes a visual shift wheel that highlights cultural barriers and solutions for moving towards more sustainable food consumption patterns (Ranganathan et al. 2011). As part of their effort, the WRI partnered with Google, Sainsbury's, and research and marketing specialists to launch the Better Buying Lab in 2016 to encourage consumers to choose more sustainable diets. These collaborative efforts show how civil society, business, and government can find common ground on sustainable diets.

But, as Dauvergne (2016) argues, these collaborations often legitimize a version of *corporate sustainability* rather than environmental sustainability. Civil society organizations working towards sustainable diets can be caught between these two aims. The WWF promotes the Livewell plate on one hand, and on the other hand is actively engaged in the Global Roundtable on Sustainable Beef. The increasing business-civil society collaborations may be problematic, while promoting a version of sustainability that does "little to challenge … the increasing dominance of a market liberal worldview," and in turn, does not challenge the expansion of meat production and diets heavy in animal products globally (Dauvergne 2016, 393). One area that requires more research is the role that governments must play in sustainable diets, a role that has thus far been relatively unexplored.

Guidelines over Taxes: Government Complacency in Sustainable Diets

Government involvement in the sustainable diets debate has been limited, with relatively little concrete or coordinated action. One way a few governments in higher-income countries engage with the sustainable diets issue is through their dietary guidelines (Lang 2017). Civil society and academia were the primary groups that pushed for the inclusion of sustainability in dietary guidelines (Fischer et al. 2016). An analysis of dietary guidelines found that four countries include environmental sustainability in their official dietary guidelines – Germany, Brazil, Sweden, and Qatar (Fischer et al. 2016). There are also a number of countries that currently have quasi-official guidelines that include sustainability criteria, including the Netherlands, the Nordic countries, Estonia, the United Kingdom, and France (Fischer et al. 2016). Fischer et al. (2016) found great variation in the focus and incorporation of environmental and sustainability information in the guidelines. Both the United States and Australia saw political battles over their guidelines end in government decisions to exclude discussions of the sustainability of food (Aubrey 2015; Fischer et al. 2016). Strong counter-narratives in these countries, and power relations amongst governments and industry, created conditions where sustainability was ultimately left out (Freidberg 2016).

A more direct government policy that is being explored is taxes on meat. Taxes and price increases for beef have been advocated as an effective way to change consumption behaviour (Vaughan 2016; Wellesley 2015; Springmann et al. 2016 or Springmann et al. 2017). The Danish Ethics Council (2016) released a recommendation to tax all foods based on their carbon intensity starting with beef and moving to all other red meat (Withnall 2015). However, beyond the Danish context, taxes to change consumptive behaviour have been unpopular – despite showing success in reducing consumption. In the US, a variety of state- or city-level proposals to tax or ban sugary beverages have been met with backlash, depicted as "nanny state" efforts (Nestle 2015, 399). Similarly, the UK effort to tax sugar has faced criticism, along with attempts to discredit it as an implausible and ineffective mechanism, even while the Mexican government has shown reductions in the purchase of sugary beverages from their tax (Campbell, Smithers, and Butler 2016). Taxes have also been criticized because of their potentially disproportionate effect on the poorest demographic groups (Wellesley, Froggat, and Happer 2015). But research has shown that negative impacts can be reduced through social safety nets, education, and by providing access to alternatives (Wellesley, Happer, and Froggat 2015; World Health Organization 2016b).

Debate on sustainable diets policy has been mostly limited to dietary guidelines though alternative governance mechanisms that are available to change consumption. This restriction could be reflective of the lack of coordination in food governance (Clapp 2015). However, limited government action on sustainable consumption is also due to complex power relations (Lorek and Fuchs 2013). Fuchs et al. (2016) show that consumption debates have ignored power, and show the ways that structural, instrumental, and discursive power work across supply chains to make consumption changes more difficult to govern and achieve. They demonstrate the many ways that the meat industry holds power to sustain a market for their products, such as keeping the prices of their products low (Fuchs et al. 2016). In the US, the livestock and meat industries are supported through subsidies and a strong lobby that hinder access to more sustainable and healthy food options (Wellesley, Happer, and Froggat 2015).

The current lack of policy integration and coordination of sustainable diets and food consumption is mixed with discourses that downplay sustainable diets and use anthropocentric visions of sustainability changes. Paula Arcari (2017) analyzed global and Australian policy documents on environmental change, sustainability, and food security. Her analysis shows that livestock farming is justified throughout this literature as a human need (Arcari 2017, 1). At the same time, Arcari (2017, 83) found that the literature regularly downplays or ignores the viability of alternatives like plant-based diets. Arcari concludes that human-centric notions of the value of animals for food need to be destabilized, as "only then will their use, in any way, become a topic worthy of serious ethical consideration creating a valid counter-discourse to current efforts to 'solve' the problems of meat by producing it more 'sustainably,' making it 'healthier' and treating the animals more 'humanely.'" In these debates, the harmful environmental, climate, and animal and human health outcomes are set aside.

The fragmented efforts of a few governments, with dominant discourses that normalize animals for use by humans, are entrenched in the political battles over food consumption policy. Governments have made little progress towards concrete policy on sustainable diets (and thus meat consumption), but continued efforts by academics and civil society are promising avenues towards change. However, as noted previously, making changes that take a wide variety of factors into account may depend on ensuring that visions of sustainability and equity for the planet and its citizens are put ahead of business interests. In order for this to occur, there must be progressive government policy that takes a broader scope in considering meat consumption in human diets.

The Business of Sustainable Diets:
Winners and Losers Emerge

The business world is divided on the issue of sustainable diets. Here, winners and losers emerge, with businesses using a variety of narratives to sell new products or stave off attacks to their bottom line. A variety of companies in the food industry have begun to take sustainable diets seriously, realizing that a growing recognition of the problems associated with animal agriculture can mean large profits for business. Big food companies that manufacture processed foods are buying up smaller companies marketed as sustainable, as well as introducing new product lines with sustainability-focused marketing to diversify their portfolios. This growing market was solidified by an investor initiative in 2016 called Farm Animal Investment Risk Reduction, which highlighted the growing risk to businesses from industrial animal agriculture (FAIRR 2016). FAIRR has continued to work on this project, doubling their investors from 2016 to 2018. The initiative shows that plant-based meat alternatives have grown 8 per cent a year on average since 2010, and projected growth potential of the meat alternatives market will "expand at a compound annual growth rate (CAGR) of 8.29% between 2017 and 2021" (FAIRR 2018, 10).

At the same time, a variety of smaller-scale producers of meat, egg, and dairy alternatives have begun to emerge, leveraging sustainability debates to convince both investors from Silicon Valley and potential consumers of their products. In March 2016, the Plant Based Foods Association was launched, and has gained sixty-three members in less than a year (Plant Based Foods Association 2016). Between egg replacers (e.g., Just Inc., formerly Hampton Creek, and Clara), traditional meat alternatives (Sweet Earth, Beyond Meat, Impossible Foods), cultured meats (Mosa Meat, Memphis Meat), and edible insects (Bitty Foods, Big Cricket Farms, Entomo Farms), entrepreneurs of the food industry are taking sustainable diets seriously and capitalizing with alternatives to the industrial meat supply. Companies in the alternatives industry are using the same narratives of sustainability being put forth by academics and civil society about the environmental impacts of conventional animal agriculture. Additionally, they are using the "doubling narrative," calling for 50 to 70 per cent increases in food production by 2050 to meet future food needs, assuming that meat consumption will continue to grow (Weis 2013). Using this logic, these companies are making a compelling case for the future of their products and profits. Big business is taking note, with companies like Tyson, Kellogg's, and General Mills starting venture capital funds to invest in food start-ups. Tyson has been particularly active in pursuing protein alternatives, after slowing profits in 2016 (Kell 2017). In Canada, Maple Leaf Foods has made their goal "to be the most sustainable protein company on Earth," investing in protein alternatives and pledging to reduce their environmental footprint by 50 per cent by 2025 (Maple Leaf Foods 2018).

The restaurant industry has also begun to pursue what they see as more sustainable and ethical products for their outlets, with notable examples like McDonald's setting goals for sourcing cage-free eggs and working on the issue of sustainable beef, or A&W introducing the Beyond Meat plant-based burger (Canadian Press 2018; McDonald's Corporation 2015). The Global Roundtable on Sustainable Beef (GRSB) is playing an important role in providing legitimacy to companies that are not about to give up meat in their business but still want to show they are taking sustainability seriously. Michele Banik-Rake of McDonald's stated on the first Conference on Sustainable Beef that "one of the things that this whole group had in common was that their livelihoods were under attack" (Makower 2014). The recognition that sustainable diets pose a threat to their bottom line has spurred these companies to join the GRSB to show the benefits of sustainable beef.

The GRSB (2016) sets out five broad principles and criteria for adoption and adaption to the regional and national contexts of its members. Despite being embraced by industry, questions have been raised about how the principles were decided on, the vagueness of the principles and criteria, and the GRSB's call for increased production of beef. Environmental organizations have criticized the GRSB because, they contend, it represents an attempt by industry to "greenwash" beef (Friends of the Earth 2014). Academics have also criticized the initiative, with Gidon Eshel, a professor of environmental science at Bard College, arguing that "the only sustainable beef is beef that was never produced or consumed" (Rothman 2014). The GRSB is reflective of the variety of counter-narratives being put forward as the pressure to reduce meat consumption grows. No actor has a larger stake in this debate than the meat industry itself, and it has worked to advance a narrative of its own, discussed below.

"Sausage: The Original Sustainable Food" and Other Narratives of Sustainable Meat

Not all are winners in the growing awareness of the environmental impacts of meat production and the need for sustainable diets. The meat industry is under threat and is actively pursuing alternative narratives that present themselves as though they are taking sustainability seriously while working to reduce the threat to their business model. The meat industry has tried a number of narratives to demonstrate their sustainability, even claiming that processed meat would fall under this category. Janet Riley, senior vice president of the North American Meat Institute, claims, "Processed meats like bacon and lunch meats are sustainable because they take cuts of meat that might otherwise not be used, and that cuts down on waste … sausage was the original sustainable food" (Foran 2015). In addition to claims of reducing waste, the industry has used a variety of arguments to downplay the environmental impacts of meat, while declaring it an essential part of healthy and balanced diets. The following section will provide an overview of some of the most common assertions coming from the meat industry with respect to the environmental impacts of these products.

Industry's primary tactic has been to highlight the efficiency improvements made over time (Capper 2011). Studies funded by the industry conclude that productivity improvements have been made through the use of technology and operational changes that have drastically increased the weight of animals slaughtered, while reducing the time to slaughter (Stackhouse et al. 2012; Capper and Bauman 2013). These studies demonstrate the reductions in water and emissions per kilogram of meat produced, and are used to justify intensive production systems. Here, there is an interesting juxtaposition in the use of similar data by academic and civil society with drastically different conclusions. By focusing on only a few environmental factors, the LCA data that academic and civil society advocates use has produced the ability for industry to demonstrate their efficiency gains. This narrative has of course been questioned, with the use of efficiency in this way being problematized by others (Garnett, Röös, and Little 2015).

Industry has also compared the productivity of conventional systems against grass-fed production systems, using similar measures to show that conventional systems are more "efficient" (Capper 2011). This research has been used to vilify farmers who are not using "modern technologies," accusing them of causing increased environmental pressures while not being as economically competitive (Sustainable Beef Resource Center 2012). The Sustainable Beef Resource Center, formerly the Growth Enhancement Technology Team (or GET IT) is composed of representatives from global animal-health companies (Sustainable Beef Resource Center 2012). It has promoted the use of technology to increase the sustainability, efficiency, and productivity of the beef supply chain. While these major industry players focus on the efficiency of large-scale livestock operations, they demonize grass-fed or small-scale beef production – which others claim are environmentally preferable to industrial food production (see chapters 3 and 5 of this volume).

Debate between small-scale, grass-fed beef producers and industrial livestock producers resurfaced during updates to the 2015 United States Dietary Guidelines. The Dietary Guidelines Advisory Committee (DGAC), a committee of fifteen experts on nutrition, medicine, and public health, published their report with the inclusion of sustainability, which caused considerable contention throughout the process. Public comment on the report included a vocal outcry from those in the grass-fed beef industry who felt they were being unfairly lumped in with industrial practices, with one farmer declaring that the emissions from grass-fed beef were offset by "the lessened air and water pollution from feedlots, [eschewing] the soil destruction from monocropped grain production used for animal feed, and the reduced need for petrochemical inputs" (Freidberg 2016, 76). Livestock producers from the Great Plains prairies also decried the recommendations, stating that livestock grazing was critical for this ecosystem (ibid., 75). In other words, debates over meat consumption are often heavily focused on conventional industrial livestock systems. That the livestock industry is not homogenous is a given; however, these industry debates may leave out the reality that the vast majority of meat consumed, in the US in particular, does come from conventional livestock systems where environmental impacts are compounded by the sheer size of these systems (FAIRR 2016; Food and Water Watch 2015).

The livestock industry maintains that meat is a necessary and healthy part of a diet, even with growing understanding and warnings of the link between red and processed meat and cancer (World Health Organization 2016a or World Health Organization 2016b). The meat industry has fought back on this point, arguing that lean red meat is part of a healthy lifestyle in addition to exercise and not smoking (Shalene McNeill of the National Cattleman's Beef Association, as quoted in Petroff 2015). Betsy Booren of the North American Meat Institute (NAMI) has argued that the World Health Organization "tortured the data to ensure a specific outcome" (Petroff 2015). NAMI has been the most vocal source of this narrative, using health as a justification in its arguments against the inclusion of sustainability in the US dietary guidelines. Janet Riley, the NAMI senior vice president of public affairs, was quoted as saying: "This needs to be about nutrition. The purpose here is to give Americans the information they need to make healthy choices. This is not the time or the place to get into sustainability" (Foran 2015).

The uncomfortable relationship between industry funding and scientific research has been highlighted in the case of tobacco and nutrition science (Brownell and Warner 2009), and more recently in the case of sugar science (Holpuch 2016; Chartres, Fabbri, and Bero 2016). Similarly, a number of industry-funded academics have written articles that aim to dispute the arguments for sustainable diets. Many of these studies exploit the uncertainty left in the science to discredit the concept of sustainable diets. The limitations of the LCA data are used in calling for additional interdisciplinary study before policy changes can be made (Auestad and Fulgoni 2015). These tactics align with attempts to point to other sectors that contribute to GHG emissions, claiming that they should be prioritized over dietary change (ibid.), or to discredit the figures that compare transport sector and livestock sector emissions (Mitloehner 2015).

Frank Mitloehner is a professor of Animal Sciences at University of California, Davis who has actively argued against the livestock sector's contribution to climate change, most famously challenging the FAO's *Livestock's Long Shadow* Report. He published a short critique through the American Feed Industry Association claiming that politics was in play in the assessment of beef's effect on the climate (Mitloehner 2015). The piece criticized the use of Meatless Monday as a way of reducing emissions by comparing it to changing light bulbs (ibid., 2) and argued that Mexican and Indian beef production was less efficient than US beef (ibid., 3). Mitloehner's article was refuted by a group of researchers at Johns Hopkins University who countered that his calculations made unfair assumptions about global GHG emissions vs. US emissions, as well as left out important parts of the beef supply chain to claim that it only contributes 4.2 per cent to US GHG emissions (Fry et al. 2016). These researchers argue that while all sectors need to play a part to keep climate change below 2 degrees Celsius, drastic reductions in meat and dairy consumption will be a critical part of that effort (ibid.).

Finally, interpretation of data based on different metrics can skew perceptions of the sustainability of different foods. A popular narrative in this vein claims that vegan and vegetarian diets may be just as bad or worse if they depend on certain high-emission fruits and vegetables, or products like soy that may exacerbate Brazilian deforestation (Union of

Concerned Scientists 2017). In 2015, the media reported heavily on a new study with headlines claiming that lettuce is worse for the environment than bacon (Rea 2015; Withnall 2015). It turned out that the provocative headline was provided by the university public relations team and later acknowledged as misleading by the author of the study (Nosowitz 2015). The figures were derived by using calorie counts that would unfairly make low-calorie foods (like lettuce) look high in emissions when compared with higher-calorie foods (ibid.).

Conclusions

The notion that a universal conception of sustainable diets can be agreed upon is called into question when the complexities and variety of considerations in play are made apparent. While academics and civil society rely on LCA to show the high impacts of meat, they may lose the nuance of broader sustainability debates, equity issues, and cultural change required to move populations to more sustainable diets. At the same time, civil society's collaboration with business bumps up against uncomfortable questions about how we make change, and what strategies are actually worth pursuing in this vein. Finally, sustainable diets, which – most evidence suggests – requires reduced meat consumption, challenge the meat industry's entire business model. The industry, in turn, defends its efficiency and productivity, but this will not be sufficient to reduce environmental impacts at levels required. Although the issue of sustainable diets has gained considerable attention, it is important to question the assumptions and trade-offs being made in the quest for a "universal sustainable diet." Rather than strive for the latter, we must learn to live with complexity while accounting for nuance and differences across place and space, and we must endeavour for effective research and policy that accounts for the influences of power relations in governance processes and discourse.

Notes

1 The Livewell Plate is a visual representation of what foods should be included in a more sustainable diet and what foods should be eaten more sparingly (Livewell for Life 2017).
2 Including: *A Balance of Healthy and Sustainable Food Choices for France, Spain and Sweden*; *Eating for 2 Degrees: New and Updated Livewell Plate* (revised edition); *and Eating Our Way to a Healthy Planet.*

References

Arcari, Paula. 2017. "Normalised, Human-Centric Discourses of Meat and Animals in Climate Change, Sustainability and Food Security Literature." *Agriculture and Human Values* 34 (1): 69–86. https://doi.org/10.1007/s10460-016-9697-0.

Aston, Louise M., James N. Smith, and John W. Powles. 2012. "Impact of a Reduced Red and Processed Meat Dietary Pattern on Disease Risks and Greenhouse Gas Emissions in the UK: A Modelling Study." *BMJ Open* 2 (5): e001072. https://doi.org/10.1136/bmjopen-2012-001072.

Aubrey, Allison. 2015. "Will the Dietary Guidelines Consider the Planet? The Fight Is On." *The Salt* (blog). 26 February 2015. https://www.npr.org/sections/thesalt/2015/02/26/389276051/will-the-dietary-guidelines-consider-the-planet-the-fight-is-on.

Auestad, Nancy, and Victor L. Fulgoni. 2015. "What Current Literature Tells Us about Sustainable Diets: Emerging Research Linking Dietary Patterns, Environmental Sustainability, and Economics." *Advances in Nutrition* 6 (1): 19–36. https://doi.org/10.3945/an.114.005694.

Barilla Center for Food and Nutrition (BCFN). 2015. "Double Pyramid 2015: Recommendations for a Sustainable Diet." Italy: Barilla Center for Food and Nutrition. https://www.barillacfn.com/m/publications/dp-2015-en.pdf.

Biltekoff, Charlotte. 2013. *Eating Right in America: The Cultural Politics of Food and Health*. Durham, NC: Duke University Press.

Brownell, Kelly D., and Kenneth E. Warner. 2009. "The Perils of Ignoring History: Big Tobacco Played Dirty and Millions Died. How Similar Is Big Food?" *The Milbank Quarterly* 87 (1): 259–94. https://doi.org/10.1111/j.1468-0009.2009.00555.x.

Burlingame, Barbara, and Sandro Dernini. 2012. "Sustainable Diets and Biodiversity: Directions and Solutions for Policy, Research and Action." Proceedings of the International Scientific Symposium Biodiversity and Sustainable Diets United against Hunger, 3–5 November 2010. Rome: Nutrition and Consumer Protection Division, FAO.

Campbell, Denis, Rebecca Smithers, and Sarah Butler. 2016. "Sugar Tax: Osborne's Two-Tier Levy Brings Mixed Response." *The Guardian*, 17 March 2016. https://www.theguardian.com/uk-news/2016/mar/16/budget-2016-george-osborne-sugar-tax-mixed-response.

Canadian Press. 2018. "'Beyond Meat' Burgers Arrive at A&W in Canada." Huffington Post.ca. 10 July 2018. https://www.huffingtonpost.ca/2018/07/10/beyond-meat-burger-aw-canada_a_23478741/.

Capper, Judith L. 2011. "The Environmental Impact of Beef Production in the United States: 1977 Compared with 2007." *Journal of Animal Science* 89 (12): 4249–61. https://doi.org/10.2527/jas.2010-3784.

Capper, Judith L., and Dale E. Bauman. 2013. "The Role of Productivity in Improving the Environmental Sustainability of Ruminant Production Systems." *Annual Review of Animal Biosciences* 1 (January): 469–89. https://doi.org/10.1146/annurev-animal-031412-103727.

Carlsson-Kanyama, Annika, and Alejandro D. González. 2009. "Potential Contributions of Food Consumption Patterns to Climate Change." *The American Journal of Clinical Nutrition* 89 (5): 1704S–9S. https://doi.org/10.3945/ajcn.2009.26736AA.

Carvalho, Aline Martins de, Chester Luiz Galvão César, Regina Mara Fisberg, and Dirce Maria Lobo Marchioni. 2013. "Excessive Meat Consumption in Brazil: Diet Quality and Environmental Impacts." *Public Health Nutrition* 16 (10): 1893–9. https://doi.org/10.1017/S1368980012003916.

Chartres, Nicholas, Alice Fabbri, and Lisa A. Bero. 2016. "Association of Industry Sponsorship with Outcomes of Nutrition Studies: A Systematic Review and Meta-Analysis." *JAMA Internal Medicine* 176 (12): 1769–77. https://doi.org/10.1001/jamainternmed.2016.6721.

Clapp, Jennifer. 2015. "Food Security and Contested Agricultural Trade Norms." https://uwspace.uwaterloo.ca/handle/10012/11536.

Danish Ethics Council. 2016. "Stort Flertal i Det Etiske Råd Anbefaler En Klimaafgift På Oksekød." 25 April 2016. http://www.etiskraad.dk/etiske-temaer/natur-klima-og-foedevarer/publikationer/etisk-forbrug-af-klimabelastende-foedevarer-2016/pressemeddelelse.

Dauvergne, Peter. 2016. "The Sustainability Story: Exposing Truths, Half-Truths, and Illusions." In *New Earth Politics: Essays from the Anthropocene*, edited by Simon Nicholson and Sikina Jinnah, 387–404. Cambridge, MA: MIT Press.

EatingBetter.org. 2016. "Eating Better – What Is Eating Better?" https://www.eating-better.org/about.html.

Eshel, Gidon, and Pamela A. Martin. 2006. "Diet, Energy, and Global Warming." *Earth Interactions* 10 (9): 1–17. https://doi.org/10.1175/EI167.1.

FAIRR. 2016. "The Future of Food: The Investment Case for a Protein Shake Up." http://www.fairr.org/wp-content/uploads/FAIRR-and-ShareAction-Protein-Briefing-September-2016.pdf.

– 2018. "Plant-Based Profits: Investment Risks and Opportunities in Sustainable Food Systems." http://www.fairr.org/resource/plant-based-profits-investment-risks-opportunities-sustainable-food-systems/.

Fischer, Carlos Gonzalez, Tara Garnett, University of Oxford, Food Climate Research Network, and Food and Agriculture Organization of the United Nations. 2016. *Plates, Pyramids, and Planets: Developments in National Healthy and Sustainable Dietary Guidelines: A State of Play Assessment.* http://www.fao.org/3/a-i5640e.pdf.

Food and Water Watch. 2015. "Factory Farm Nation: 2015 Edition." https://www.foodandwaterwatch.org/insight/factory-farm-nation-2015-edition.

Foran, Clare. 2015. "The Political Battle over Red Meat." *The Atlantic* (blog), 3 February 2015. https://www.theatlantic.com/politics/archive/2015/02/the-political-battle-over-red-meat/443790/.

Forum for the Future. 2016. "The Protein Challenge 2040." Forum for the Future. https://www.forumforthefuture.org/protein-challenge.

Freidberg, Susanne. 2014. "Footprint Technopolitics." *Geoforum* 55 (August): 178–89. https://doi.org/10.1016/j.geoforum.2014.06.009.

– 2016. "Wicked Nutrition: The Controversial Greening of Official Dietary Guidance." *Gastronomica: The Journal of Critical Food Studies* 16 (2): 69–80. https://doi.org/10.1525/gfc.2016.16.2.69.

Friends of the Earth. 2014. "Leading NGOs Slam Greenwashing by Meat Industry, Demand Beefier Sustainability Standards. Friends of the Earth." Friends of the Earth. https://foe.org/news/2014-11-leading-ngos-slam-greenwashing-by-meat-industry-demand-beefier-sustainability-standards/.

Fry, Jillian, Roni Neff, Bob Martin, Rebecca Ramsing, Claire Fitch, Brent Kim, Erin Biehl, and Raychel Santo. 2016. "A Response to Dr. Frank Mitloehner's White Paper, 'Livestock's Contributions to Climate Change: Facts and Fiction.'" 2016. https://www.jhsph.edu/research/centers-and-institutes/johns-hopkins-center-for-a-livable-future/_pdf/about_us/FSPP/letter-policymakers/20160512_Mitloehner_Response12.pdf.

Fuchs, Doris, Antonietta Di Giulio, Katharina Glaab, Sylvia Lorek, Michael Maniates, Thomas Princen, and Inge Røpke. 2016. "Power: The Missing Element in Sustainable Consumption and Absolute Reductions Research and Action." *Journal of Cleaner Production* 132 (September): 298–307. https://doi.org/10.1016/j.jclepro.2015.02.006.

Garnett, Tara. 2014. "What Is a Sustainable Healthy Diet? A Discussion Paper." Oxford: Food Climate Research Network. https://fcrn.org.uk/sites/default/files/fcrn_what_is_a_sustainable_healthy_diet_final.pdf.

Gussow, Joan Dye, and Katherine L. Clancy. 1986. "Dietary Guidelines for Sustainability." *Journal of Nutrition Education* 18 (1): 1–5. https://doi.org/10.1016/S0022-3182(86)80255-2.

Holpuch, Amanda. 2016. "Sugar Lobby Paid Scientists to Blur Sugar's Role in Heart Disease – Report." *The Guardian*, 12 September 2016. https://www.theguardian.com/society/2016/sep/12/sugar-industry-paid-research-heart-disease-jama-report.

Johnston, Jessica L., Jessica C. Fanzo, and Bruce Cogill. 2014. "Understanding Sustainable Diets: A Descriptive Analysis of the Determinants and Processes That Influence Diets and Their Impact on Health, Food Security, and Environmental Sustainability123." *Advances in Nutrition* 5 (4): 418–29. https://doi.org/10.3945/an.113.005553.

Jones, Andrew D., Lesli Hoey, Jennifer Blesh, Laura Miller, Ashley Green, and Lilly Fink Shapiro. 2016. "A Systematic Review of the Measurement

of Sustainable Diets." *Advances in Nutrition* 7 (4): 641–64. https://doi.
org/10.3945/an.115.011015.

Kell, John. 2017. "Why Tyson Foods Is Investing in Alternative Proteins."
Fortune, March 2017. http://fortune.com/2017/03/03/tyson-foods-new-ceo-
acquisitions/.

Lang, Tim. 2017. "Re-Fashioning Food Systems with Sustainable Diet
Guidelines – Food Policy Briefings – Food Research Collaboration." 2017.
http://foodresearch.org.uk/publications/re-fashioning-food-systems-with-
sustainable-diet-guidelines/.

Livewell for Life. 2017. "LiveWell Plate." http://livewellforlife.eu/livewell-plate.

Lorek, Sylvia, and Doris Fuchs. 2013. "Strong Sustainable Consumption
Governance – Precondition for a Degrowth Path?" *Journal of Cleaner
Production* (issue on Degrowth: From Theory to Practice) 38 (January):
36–43. https://doi.org/10.1016/j.jclepro.2011.08.008.

Macdiarmid, Jennie I., Flora Douglas, and Jonina Campbell. 2016. "Eating Like
There's No Tomorrow: Public Awareness of the Environmental Impact
of Food and Reluctance to Eat Less Meat as Part of a Sustainable Diet."
Appetite 96 (January): 487–93. https://doi.org/10.1016/j.appet.2015.10.011.

Macdiarmid, Jennie, Janet Kyle, Graham Horgan, Jennifer Loe, Claire Fyfe,
Alex Johnstone, and Geraldine McNeill. 2011. "Livewell: A Balance of
Healthy and Sustainable Food Choices." Godalming, UK: WWF-UK. https://
www.fcrn.org.uk/research-library/new-wwf-report-livewell-uk-balance-
healthy-and-sustainable-food-choices.

Makower, Joel. 2014. "Can the Beef Industry Collaborate Its Way to
Sustainability?" *GreenBiz* (blog). 9 January 2014. https://www.greenbiz.
com/blog/2014/01/09/can-beef-industry-collaborate-its-way-sustainability.

Maniates, Michael F. 2001. "Individualization: Plant a Tree, Buy a Bike, Save
the World?" *Global Environmental Politics* 1 (3): 22.

Maple Leaf Foods. 2018. "To Be the Most Sustainable Protein Company
on Earth." https://www.mapleleaffoods.com/stories/to-be-the-most-
sustainable-protein-company-on-earth/.

Mason, Pamela, and Tim Lang. 2017. *Sustainable Diets: How Ecological
Nutrition Can Transform Consumption and the Food System.* 1st ed.
London and New York: Routledge.

McDonald's Corporation. 2015. "McDonald's to Fully Transition to Cage-
Free Eggs for All Restaurants in the U.S. and Canada." 9 September 2015.
https://news.mcdonalds.com/node/7816.

Mitloehner, Frank. 2015. "Livestock's Contributions to Climate Change:
Facts and Fiction." White Paper. Arlington, VA: American Feed Industry
Association. http://cekern.ucanr.edu/files/256942.pdf.

Nestle, Marion. 2015. *Soda Politics: Taking on Big Soda.* Oxford: Oxford
University Press.

Nosowitz, Dan. 2015. "Is Eating Lettuce Really Worse for the Environment than Eating Bacon?" *Modern Farmer* (blog), 18 December 2015. https://modernfarmer.com/2015/12/is-eating-lettuce-really-worse-for-the-environment-than-eating-bacon/.

Perignon, Marlène, Gabriel Masset, Gaël Ferrari, Tangui Barré, Florent Vieux, Matthieu Maillot, Marie-Josèphe Amiot, and Nicole Darmon. 2016. "How Low Can Dietary Greenhouse Gas Emissions Be Reduced without Impairing Nutritional Adequacy, Affordability and Acceptability of the Diet? A Modelling Study to Guide Sustainable Food Choices." *Public Health Nutrition* 19 (14): 2662–74. https://doi.org/10.1017/S1368980016000653.

Petroff, Alanna. 2015. "Processed Meat Causes Cancer, Says WHO." CNNMoney (blog). 26 October 2015. https://money.cnn.com/2015/10/26/news/red-meat-processed-cancer-world-health-organization/index.html.

Plant Based Foods Association. 2016. "About Us." *Plant Based Foods Association* (blog). https://plantbasedfoods.org/about/.

Ranganathan, Janet, Daniel Vennard, Richard Waite, Patrice Dumas, Brian Lipinski, and GLOBAGRI-WRR Model Authors. 2016. "Shifting Diets for a Sustainable Food Future." Working Paper 11. Creating a Sustainable Food Future. Washington, DC: World Resources Institute. http://www.wri.org/publication/shifting-diets.

Rea, Shilo. 2015. "Vegetarian and 'Healthy' Diets Could Be More Harmful to the Environment." Carnegie Mellon University newsfeed, 14 December 2015. http://www.cmu.edu/news/stories/archives/2015/december/diet-and-environment.html.

Rothman, Lauren. 2014. "Large-Scale Sustainable Beef Is Still an Empty Promise." Munchies (blog). 1 December 2014. https://munchies.vice.com/en_us/article/qkxqb5/large-scale-sustainable-beef-is-still-an-empty-promise.

Scarborough, Peter, Steven Allender, David Clarke, Kremlin Wickramasinghe, and Mike Rayner. 2012. "Modelling the Health Impact of Environmentally Sustainable Dietary Scenarios in the UK." *European Journal of Clinical Nutrition* 66 (6): 710–15. https://doi.org/10.1038/ejcn.2012.34.

Scrinis, Gyorgy. 2013. *Nutritionism: The Science and Politics of Dietary Advice*. New York: Columbia University Press.

Soret, Samuel, Alfredo Mejia, Michael Batech, Karen Jaceldo-Siegl, Helen Harwatt, and Joan Sabaté. 2014. "Climate Change Mitigation and Health Effects of Varied Dietary Patterns in Real-Life Settings throughout North America." *The American Journal of Clinical Nutrition* 100, Supplement 1 (July): 490S–5S. https://doi.org/10.3945/ajcn.113.071589.

Springmann, Marco, H. Charles J. Godfray, Mike Rayner, and Peter Scarborough. 2016. "Analysis and Valuation of the Health and Climate Change Cobenefits of Dietary Change." *Proceedings of the National*

Academy of Sciences 113 (15): 4146–51. https://doi.org/10.1073/pnas.1523119113.

Springmann, Marco, Daniel Mason-D'Croz, Sherman Robinson, Keith Wiebe, H. Charles J. Godfray, Mike Rayner, and Peter Scarborough. 2017. "Mitigation Potential and Global Health Impacts from Emissions Pricing of Food Commodities." *Nature Climate Change* 7 (1): 69–74. https://doi.org/10.1038/nclimate3155.

Stackhouse, Kim R., C. Alan Rotz, James W. Oltjen, and Frank M. Mitloehner. 2012. "Growth-Promoting Technologies Decrease the Carbon Footprint, Ammonia Emissions, and Costs of California Beef Production Systems." *Journal of Animal Science* 90 (12): 4656–65. https://doi.org/10.2527/jas.2011-4654.

Sustainable Beef Resource Center. 2012. "New Research Reveals Consequences of Not Using Technologies to Raise Beef Cattle." 2012.

Temme, Elisabeth H.M., Helena M.E. Bakker, S. Marije Seves, Janneke Verkaik-Kloosterman, Arnold L. Dekkers, Joop M.A. van Raaij, and Marga C. Ocké. 2015. "How May a Shift towards a More Sustainable Food Consumption Pattern Affect Nutrient Intakes of Dutch Children?" *Public Health Nutrition* 18 (13): 2468–78. https://doi.org/10.1017/S1368980015002426.

Tilman, David, and Michael Clark. 2014. "Global Diets Link Environmental Sustainability and Human Health." *Nature* 515 (7528): 518–22. https://doi.org/10.1038/nature13959.

Tom, Michelle S., Paul S. Fischbeck, and Chris T. Hendrickson. 2016. "Energy Use, Blue Water Footprint, and Greenhouse Gas Emissions for Current Food Consumption Patterns and Dietary Recommendations in the US." *Environment Systems and Decisions* 36 (1): 92–103. https://doi.org/10.1007/s10669-015-9577-y.

Union of Concerned Scientists. 2017. "What's Driving Deforestation: Soybeans." Union of Concerned Scientists. https://www.ucsusa.org/global-warming/stop-deforestation/drivers-of-deforestation-2016-soybeans.

Vaughan, Adam. 2016. "UN Expert Calls for Tax on Meat Production." *The Guardian*, 25 May 2016. https://www.theguardian.com/environment/2016/may/25/un-expert-calls-for-tax-on-meat-production.

Vieux, Florent, Nicole Darmon, Djilali Touazi, and Louis Georges Soler. 2012. "Greenhouse Gas Emissions of Self-Selected Individual Diets in France: Changing the Diet Structure or Consuming Less?" *Ecological Economics* 75 (Supplement C): 91–101. https://doi.org/10.1016/j.ecolecon.2012.01.003.

Weis, Tony. 2013. *The Ecological Hoofprint: The Global Burden of Industrial Livestock*. London: Zed Books.

Wellesley, Laura. 2015. "Changing Climate, Changing Diets: Pathways to Lower Meat Consumption." Chatham House. 24 November 2015. https://www.chathamhouse.org//node/19095.

Wellesley, Laura A., Catherine Happer, and Antony Froggat. 2015. "Changing
    Climate, Changing Diets: Pathways to Lower Meat Consumption."
    London: Chatham House, Royal Institute of International Affairs.
    https://www.chathamhouse.org/publication/changing-climate-changing-
    diets%20.
Withnall, Adam. 2015. "Lettuce Is 'Three Times Worse than Bacon' for
    Emissions." *The Independent*, 15 December 2015. http://www.independent.
    co.uk/news/science/vegetarian-diet-bad-for-environment-meat-study-
    lettuce-three-times-worse-emissions-bacon-a6773671.html.
World Health Organization. 2016a. "Fiscal Policies for Diet and the
    Prevention of Noncommunicable Diseases." WHO. 2016. http://www.who.
    int/dietphysicalactivity/publications/fiscal-policies-diet-prevention/en/.
– 2016b. "Q&A on the Carcinogenicity of the Consumption of Red Meat
    and Processed Meat." WHO. 2016. http://www.who.int/features/qa/cancer-
    red-meat/en/.
Zhu, Xueqin, Lia van Wesenbeeck, and Ekko C. van Ierland. 2006.
    "Impacts of Novel Protein Foods on Sustainable Food Production and
    Consumption: Lifestyle Change and Environmental Policy." *Environmental
    and Resource Economics* 35 (1): 59–87. https://doi.org/10.1007/s10640-006-
    9006-2.

PART TWO

Getting It Right: Case Studies and Specific Practices

5

The Evidence for
Holistic Planned Grazing

Sheldon Frith

Introduction

Controversy seems to follow Allan Savory. The octogenarian ecologist and co-founder of the Savory Institute was cast into the limelight in 2013 after giving a widely watched Ted Talk in which he claimed – in contravention to conventional wisdom – that "only livestock can reverse desertification," further noting that by grazing livestock on the earth's grasslands, the world could potentially sequester enough carbon dioxide (CO_2) to reverse anthropogenic climate change (Savory 2013). These admittedly grandiose claims, and Savory's heavy reliance on visual and anecdotal evidence rather than scientific peer-reviewed studies, have led to a considerable amount of criticism and even personal attacks (Savory 2013; Monbiot 2014; Ketcham 2017). It is true that some of Savory's ideas lack peer-reviewed scientific proof, as he himself acknowledges (Savory 2013); yet part of the reason is that it is difficult, if not impossible, to replicate the specific grazing management strategy he advocates (known as "holistic management," hereafter HM) in a controlled trial setting. And yet, as I argue below, there is a strong case to be made that the underlying theories about which Savory speaks, regarding goal-oriented approaches to ecological livestock management, do have scientific and socio-economic merit. Further, HM has served as a powerful theory of business management for environmentally conscious farmers, providing tools to raise livestock using more sustainable production methods – and, contrary to what some critics have argued, farmers who have adopted HM swear by this methodology. This chapter examines the anecdotal and scholarly evidence for the claims of HM related to farming with animals; in particular, it argues that "holistic planned grazing" (HPG) can result in higher levels of soil organic carbon (SOC), improved forage productivity, improved water retention, and increases in biodiversity above and below the ground. While claims about the specific merits of HPG will continue to result in scientific debate, this chapter shows that there is a growing body of supporting evidence from farmers like me who practise a variant of HPG. In addition, there are indications of recent scientific studies also supporting its founding premises.

What Is the Theory behind Holistic Planned Grazing?

Holistic planned grazing is just one component of a broader systems-oriented agricultural strategy called holistic management. Savory coined the term in the 1960s after theorizing that pastoralists could earn their livelihood, feed their communities, and restore their lands by practising holistic livestock management. However, today Savory is just one among myriad HM advocates. A number of other individuals and associations – most notably Holistic Management International – have championed HM as a "value-based decision-making framework that integrates all aspects of planning for social, economic, and environmental consider-ations" (Holistic Management International 2017).[1] Savory and other HM advocates apply an ethos where *grazing* is just one dimension of the much broader framework.

The terminology related to HPG can be confusing, as there are many different terms – including "regenerative grazing," "rotational grazing," "management intensive grazing" (MIG), "Adaptive Multi-Paddock Grazing" (AMP), and "mob grazing" – which are often used interchange-ably to refer to HPG, or sometimes grazing systems *very different* than HPG. For the sake of clarity, when I refer to HPG I only mean grazing where the animals are managed according to *the specific method* detailed in Allan Savory's handbook on holistic management (Savory and Butterfield 1999). The key to HPG is to focus on the role of *livestock*, and in particular the management of ruminants (like sheep, cattle, goats, etc.), in an agricultural ecosystem – although similar types of foundational assumptions relate to the management of grazing monogastrics (pigs, poultry, etc.). Most of the evidence (both anecdotal and peer-reviewed) supporting HPG's effectiveness in restoring ecosystem health is situated in non-humid climates; yet in more humid climates there are a wide variety of similar grazing management methods that have also proven effective. The specific strategies and practices of HPG are important because much of the scientific research claiming to have studied HPG has in fact studied something else entirely, which can be misleading.

At its core, HPG strategies mimic (to as great a degree as possible) the movement of wild animal herds, while also taking into account the economic and social needs of the producers. Wild animal herds fulfill a number of important ecological functions as they move across a landscape, including fertilizing the land and providing sustenance for predators up the food chain. HM practitioners in non-humid climates report that grazing animals break the hard cap on the soil surface, which allows water infiltration and seed germination, and knocks down dormant plant material so that new growth can form. In humid climates, ranchers point to observed improvements in ecosystem health and productivity because of the way that herds compact standing plant material into close contact with the soil surface, which protects the soil and increases decomposition.

From an ecological point of view, there are layers upon layers of biological services provided by various animals thanks to their specific behavioural and physiological characteristics. For instance, not only do ruminants deposit high-quality fertilizer on the ground, but their cloven hooves help work in the manure and aerate the soil by puncturing the very top layer of the ground. When chickens and pigs follow ruminants in a pasture rotation, they can scratch (and spread and aerate) the manure, help manage the population of insects, and so on. Similarly, the cropping of perennial plants by grazers enables sunlight to reach growth points at the ground level (fulfilling a plant's evolutionary function in a grassland) (Smith and Smith 2017). Additionally, HPG advocates will suggest that humans may not be fully aware of all the synergies and functions of animals in sustaining a range of bio-geochemical cycles.[2] For instance, it has been observed that ruminant saliva contains enzymes that help to kickstart regrowth in grass species, and it has also been shown that the presence of ruminants increases the number of methanotrophic bacteria (which help degrade methane; see Abell et al. 2009). Functions like these are mediated by scale, time, and a host of other natural and human-influenced conditions. For instance, allowing a lower density of grazing animals to have prolonged "continuous" access to a large grazing plot can very easily lead to *overgrazing* (often resulting in the compaction of soils and, relatedly, a reduction in soil biota), and certainly does not mimic the natural movement of a tightly bunched group of animals across a landscape as they are continually moving in search of greener pastures, access to available water, and a safe haven away from predators.[3] This is why practitioners of HPG move a higher-density group of livestock from one paddock to another (sometimes called "rotating") – as a means of mediating the amount of time and level of impact upon a piece of land based on a range of factors, like how quickly the forage crops are (re)growing, how quickly and how much the animals are eating, how hard or soft the ground is, how much precipitation there has been, and so on.

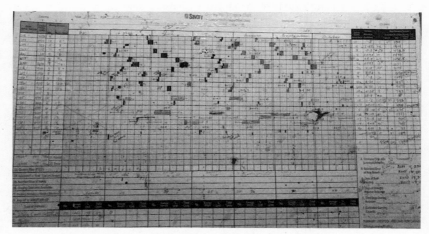

Figure 5.1 Example of a well-used holistic planned grazing chart.
Reproduced with the permission of Phyllis Van Amburgh

To the extent that farms and ranches are human-managed ecosystems, farmers and ranchers thinking ecologically about their land will try to use human management strategies to attempt to mimic nature as much as possible. Usually animals are kept at a fairly high stocking density in HPG systems but are moved quickly from paddock to paddock while accounting for a range of changing circumstances (hence the "adaptive" part), including, above all, ensuring that grazed plants are given adequate time to recover before being grazed again. The "planned" part of "holistic planned grazing" refers to a grazing plan that is created for each grazing season to inform the movements of the animals through each paddock. This grazing plan is created on a specific type of chart, using a very specific step-by-step process developed by Allan Savory over decades of on-the-ground experimentation on ranches around the world (see figure 5.1). The chart and process together allow the manager to account for the huge number of variables that must be considered when figuring out where and when to move the animals.

There are countless vocal supporters and practitioners of HPG who have seen healthier soils, rich biodiverse farmscapes, and carbon-sequestering plant growth. Often ranchers have come to HPG after having troubles with soil fertility on lands that were previously managed conventionally. As an example, Beatrice Krehl, head gardener of Waltham Place Farm in Berkshire, UK, helped shift the farm to an HPG system after having difficulties with water retention and plant growth in their fields. After only a few years of holistic management with cattle, sheep, pigs, and poultry, Waltham Place has found improvements in grass availability, soil build-up, and improvements in biodiversity, as noted by Natasha

Giddings in *Permaculture* magazine: "Beatrice was particularly happy to discover how cattle can be used to improve the health of ecosystems and create biodiversity rather than just being perceived as the cause of many environmental problems. In a matter of just a couple of years she has observed a significant increase in floral diversity as a result of the change in management and that is good for the butterflies and other insects too" (Alfaro-Arguello et al. 2010).

These types of responses are typical of ranchers who have "switched" from conventional methods to a form of HPG. This is unsurprising, given that a clear benefit (for the farmer) in recreating systems that cycle nutrients and essential elements naturally is that no additional inputs are required (such as chemical fertilizers, weed/pest controls, etc.). This not only helps the farmer by creating a more robust (and healthy) farm ecosystem, it also minimizes the requirement of expensive supplements from off the farm.

How Does HPG Produce Ecological Benefits Specifically?

An important starting point for considering the ecological benefits from HPG is to note the rather synergistic relationship between fully functioning nutrient cycles, healthy soils, and healthy plants and animals. When plant productivity is high it means that more photosynthesis is occurring and there is more carbon available to be sequestered in the soils, in addition to more food for the grazers above ground. More carbon stored in the soils means more "food" for soil organisms below ground, and more food for the grazers above ground means more natural fertilizers (including plant litter and manure) deposited at ground level. These processes lead to the build-up of dark black carbon-rich soil, which in addition to holding water more effectively (helping with soil stability) improves future plant productivity. As Abbey and Spencer Smith put it, "this soil is fertilizer for next year's grasses, which allows more grass plants to grow" (Smith and Smith 2017). It is one virtuous self-sustaining circle, which can easily turn to a "vicious cycle" if one part of the chain is thrown out of sync.

The key point here is that HPG practitioners do not view soil simply as a medium for chemically growing substances by applying whatever nutrient the soil analysis reveals is lacking. Rather, the soil is actively growing in its own right, teeming with microorganisms, fungi, nematodes, insects, and all kinds of bacteria that – when they are not killed by sprays or by tillage – actually work to break down the mineral substrate and whatever is deposited onto the soil (like manure and plant litter), and make all of these nutrients, sugars, and water available to the growing plants and grazing animals. Clearly the biological diversity in such soils is rich, yet good grazing practices, compared to other systems of farming, can also go a long way to preserving wildlife habitat above ground too. For instance, by avoiding the requirement for chemical sprays, HPG is good for local pollinator species and other non-farm wildlife. This is because HPG system boundaries are typically more permeable due to the use of temporary short-duration fencing (or even herding by humans) which often allows larger wildlife to transit through for much of the year. The regenerated soils in HPG systems yield healthy, nutrient-dense, and diverse forage. In contrast to conventional and industrial farming, which frames wild animals and insects as pests, HPG is a symbiosis with songbirds, insects, rodents, amphibians, and other predator species (foxes, martens, birds of prey, etc.), since habitats are only temporarily disturbed in a given plot of land.

As mentioned above, healthy carbon-rich soil helps with water retention as well (Department of Agriculture and Food 2016). The soil mycelium acts as a sponge, holding water that otherwise would run off as erosion, carrying with it dissolved nutrients and depositing them in groundwater runoff deposits like creeks and lakes. Tillage physically disrupts the mycelium, and when erosion is present, nutrients are literally carried away from the grazing lands, making them unavailable for plant life or animal life to consume. This water can be used by the plants later into the season, and in instances of temporary drought, it can keep plants alive and growing longer than in agricultural systems with poor water retention.

Active soil life is one of the key differences between depleted and healthy soils – in conventional agriculture, nutrients are applied topic-ally, and the annual plants take up some of those nutrients, with the remainder being washed away through erosion or surface runoff. The soil in a regenerative grazing system is alive, with the microorganisms therein actively cycling minerals and water (Smith and Smith 2017; Alfaro-Arguello et al. 2010; Savory and Butterfield 1999). The manure deposited by grazing animals and the grasses trampled into the ground provide ample feedstuffs for this microscopic cornucopia. Hoof action begins to incorporate some of this material into the soil, and hoof impressions (along with worm tunneling below ground) allow many small collection points for water to permeate the soil. The conventional approach considers soil *chemistry*, but not the soil *biology*. A biologically active soil has nutrients that are more available to the growing plants, and hence, to the grazing animals – whether it is livestock or wild animals. Livestock farmers see these benefits through rapid regrowth of the forages, and greater bodyweight gains in their livestock.

This explains why HPG practitioners place a premium on the concept of soil organic carbon (SOC) in particular, a key component of the organic matter in soils that serves as an indicator of the soil's overall health.[4] While it typically only makes up a small percentage of soil, organic matter is absolutely vital in a range of biochemical functions, including "nutrient turnover and cation exchange capacity, soil structure, moisture retention and availability, degradation of pollutants, greenhouse gas emissions and soil buffering" (Department of Agriculture and Food 2016). In short, soils with higher SOC content are healthier and more productive, thereby helping to pull carbon out of the atmosphere by supporting healthy rapidly growing plant life above ground, and further improving water retention, as well as soil fertility and structure! By taking steps to achieve these ecological functions, holistic land managers can simultaneously build up the biological diversity in the broader farmscape by mitigating the amount of damage to wildlife habitat and migration corridors.

Where Is the Evidence?

Decades of on-the-ground experimentation by ranchers has indicated that grazing management methods can be an extremely effective way of building up SOC, as well as providing a host of other benefits. There are many producers who have had third parties conduct soil carbon tests to verify their results. The Soil Carbon Coalition is perhaps the best example of this: they have compiled and conducted soil carbon tests on dozens of sites across North America, recording impressive carbon sequestration rates. Their regular soil tests of three holistically managed ranches in Saskatchewan, Canada, for example, have returned rates varying between 22 and 48 tonnes of carbon sequestered per year per hectare, on land upon which no other tool was being used except livestock (Soil Carbon Coalition 2017). Gabe Brown, a North Dakota farmer renowned for his sustainable methods, is another example; he conducted many soil tests on his property over a period of twenty years and recorded a 9 per cent increase of soil organic matter (SOM) thanks to high rates of carbon sequestration, using a combination of HPG and no-till crop production. West Wind Farm in West Virginia, US, has also had their pasture soils tested for carbon content and found over ten years that they were sequestering 2 tonnes of carbon per year per hectare using management-intensive grazing practices. These are just a few of the many reports from the farming community that support the efficacy of regenerative grazing using a citizen science approach to compiling evidence. One can go to the Soil Carbon Coalition map page to examine dozens of test plots throughout North America which have seen measurable net gains in the soil carbon, recorded using a scientific procedure called CN analysis throughout a ten-year measurement period (Soil Carbon Coalition 2017).

While the peer-reviewed literature on HPG has lagged behind the decades of anecdotal evidence, there are nevertheless several recent studies that support the claims being made by ranchers and other proponents of HPG. Machmuller et al. (2015) suggests an average *net* rate (meaning that above-ground *emissions* were also accounted for against the carbon sequestered) of 1.58 tonnes of carbon sequestered in soil per year per hectare using "management intensive grazing" with fast movements between paddocks and a very high stock density. This was a study conducted over seven years on land that was previously used for row-crop agriculture. The recovery period (time that each paddock was allowed to rest between grazing) was quite low, however, and anecdotal accounts from ranchers who use this style of grazing suggest that if the study had used a longer recovery period, the soil carbon sequestration rate may have been even higher. The study was conducted in the warm-temperate, humid environment of the southeast United States.

Another 2015 study published in the journal *Sustainability* compared the net carbon sequestration of three different grazing systems over a ten-year period in the arid Southern Great Plains (SGP) of the United States (light continuous grazing, heavy continuous grazing, and rotational multi-paddock grazing). Despite the poor forage quality in the area (which typically leads to an increase in methane emissions from the livestock), *all three* grazing systems were sequestering more carbon in the soil than they emitted above ground. The best grazing system was the adaptive multi-paddock system (with long recovery periods, and low stock density), with an average net rate of 2 tonnes of carbon sequestered per year per hectare, leading the authors to conclude the following: "Our analysis indicated cow-calf farms converting from continuous to MP [multi-paddock] grazing in SGP region are likely net carbon sinks for decades" (Wang et al. 2015).

Another study, reported by Doornbos and Ampt (2011) at the University of Sydney, examined the results of ten years of Holistic Planned Grazing combined with "pasture cropping" on a ranch in Australia. The study was not published in a peer-reviewed journal but was conducted to a high academic standard with sound scientific methodology. It found an average carbon sequestration rate of 1 tonne per year per hectare. Unfortunately, above-ground GHG emissions were not accounted for in the study. However, a more robust study published in the *Journal of*

Soil and Water Conservation, which examined the biophysical impacts and magnitude of *all* GHG emissions from key agricultural production activities, concluded that the long-term sustainability and ecological resilience of agricultural systems ought to include ruminant grazing: "Incorporating forages and ruminants into regeneratively managed agroecosystems can elevate soil organic C, improve soil ecological function by minimizing the damage of tillage and inorganic fertilizers and biocides, and enhance biodiversity and wildlife habitat" (Teague et al. 2016). This study also notes how, by growing forages for grazing (as opposed to growing industrial grains for livestock), farmers do not need to use inputs such as inorganic fertilizers and biocides – directly translating into agrological ecosystems that are more biologically diverse and robust (Teague et al. 2016).

It is unsurprising that the systems that yield higher levels of SOC will also likely achieve greater success with water retention and biodiversity rates, since (as noted above) soils with higher SOC will typically be healthier, more fertile soils with better structure, thus facilitating plant growth. This too is shown in the scientific literature: one study in Idaho comparing HPG, "rest rotation," and "total rest" found that the HPG pastures showed both "significantly higher" rates of water retention and higher amounts of ground litter (and found the two factors related), concluding that "holistic planned grazing appears to offer a management alternative with beneficial results measured on this landscape" (Weber and Gokhale 2010). While the relationship between SOC and water retention capacity in a soil is mediated by a range of complex factors (most notably the specific textural properties of the soil), the science suggests that in most instances an increase in SOC will lead to improvements in water retention.[5]

Higher water retention not only helps with plant productivity, but also the overall use of water resources on given farm. A 2010 study in Mexico comparing holistic and conventional ranches found that the former had double the "energy sustainability index" – a measure of both the farm's productivity and its resource usage. That study concluded that productivity and ecological management go hand in hand in HPG systems: "Productivity can be maintained as the sustainability of rural dairy ranches is increased. These results also show that local knowledge and understanding of the surrounding ecosystem can drive positive environmental change in production systems" (Alfaro-Arguello et al. 2010).

To be clear, none of these studies affirms that HPG will *inevitably and always* lead to improvements in the areas of SOC build-up, improved water retention, and improved biodiversity. What they do show, however, is first and foremost the immutable complexity of agricultural systems, and second, the real measured potential of various grazing strategies when carefully planned and deployed using an adaptive framework. This is because even minute changes to the underlying conditions can yield drastically different outcomes. For instance, a study published in the *Journal of Environmental Quality* (Liebig et al. 2010) highlights how even a slight variation in the forage content (that is, what species of plants are being grazed) can have a significant impact on the net emissions of GHGs. The study looked at three different grassland systems over a three-year period. It was found that native pasture with moderate stock density continuous grazing sequestered 0.78 tonnes of carbon per year per hectare (accounting for emissions), native pasture with high stock density continuous grazing sequestered 0.6 tonnes of carbon per year per hectare (accounting for emissions), and yet crested wheatgrass pasture with high stock density continuous grazing was a net source of carbon (released into the atmosphere). HPG grazing management systems were not studied in this case, but the point to belabour is how even a slight change in the underlying conditions can yield substantially different results (and further, that some grazing systems were able to achieve net reductions in GHG emissions).

HPG does not always provide a solution to every problem – nor does it claim to. In one study examining whether HPG could restore riparian areas and water quality in Northwest Zimbabwe (as compared with nearby continuously grazed communal lands) during a severe drought, the authors found no general improvement to the streambank structure and water quality in the tested area. Yet it is important to note that the authors do not *repudiate* HPG. In fact, they describe how adaptive management was particularly useful in allowing the community to reduce pressures on forage and water sources in settled areas. The authors conclude that even though both holistically managed and low-intensity continuous grazing systems degraded the little-available water resources during the drought, "this snapshot does not provide the entire picture, and long-term analysis of the sustainability of such management on a larger scale is still needed to understand the intra- and inter-annual fluctuations" (Strauch, Kapust, and Jost 2009). Once again, the scientific evidence paints a complex picture – highlighting above all the importance of adaptive responses to the changing underlying conditions on a given piece of land. This is ultimately the value of HPG.

So Why Is There Criticism of HPG?

It seems fairly straightforward that trying to manage animals in a way that mimics natural processes as much as possible would be largely welcomed by environmental thinkers, particularly when the industrial model of livestock production strays from this type of "natural systems" thinking so dramatically (see chapter 1 of this volume). Yet as noted above, HPG has nevertheless faced different types of criticism. There are a few main reasons why this is so.

First, Savory's claims about using livestock to "reverse" global-scale problems like climate change and desertification admittedly over-generalize the potential benefits of HPG in *specific* settings, which likely fuels skeptics, given that the theories run counter to the prevailing "common-sense" notions of livestock as having a detrimental impact (see chapter 3). One of Savory's arguments is to use livestock in this way to "regenerate" grasslands. The idea, in its simplest iteration, suggests that one of the main problems facing degenerated grasslands (many of which are becoming desertified) is their historic *loss* of animals – thus the solution is to put animals *back* on the land, not to remove them from the system! The trick, however, is to do so in a carefully managed way such that the human-managed system mimics natural processes rather than throws them out of balance. According to this theory, letting a herd of cows graze freely and continuously on an open grassland while limiting predators could easily lead to a state of overgrazing (and thus land degeneration). In contrast, carefully timing the movement (and return) of the animals to a given segment of the land while managing density and the rate of forage regeneration (along with monitoring environmental conditions) could ensure that the land is regenerated (Regeneration International 2018).[6]

This relates to a second main reason why HPG is sometimes criticized: much of the support for HPG comes in the way of anecdotal evidence from farmers and ranchers, which, despite often being carried out with rigour, does not find its way into peer-reviewed scientific journals. Further, as I note below, a number of peer-reviewed assessments claim to have found that HPG is not any more effective than other grazing methods in producing the types of ecological benefits claimed by its proponents, and thus this has led some opponents to claim that HPG is "unscientific" (Hawkins 2017). Nevertheless, I explain below why this is a misreading of the scientific literature. First, it is important to note why peer-reviewed studies may not be finding the types of benefits that HPG practitioners seem to find in their own experiences with this grazing method. Although Briske et al. (2008) and Briske et al. (2014) hypothesize that the main reason for this discrepancy is that HPG practitioners are more likely to *believe* that their methods work, in my view a more likely explanation for the discrepancy is that all existing reviews of HPG in the peer-reviewed literature have not been reviews of HPG at all, but actually are reviews of grazing systems with only the most superficial similarities to HPG. When I conducted an in-depth review of the twenty-nine studies included in Hawkins's (2017) meta-analysis of HPG, I found that only one study qualified as having accurately used HPG, and only four others used methods somewhat resembling HPG (see Frith 2017). More interestingly, when I cross-referenced my analysis with the findings in the meta-studies, the obvious emerging trend was that the more a study examined grazing management practices resembling HPG, the more likely it was to have had positive effects on plant biomass and cover.

HPG is exceptionally difficult to measure or replicate in a scientific setting. This is because the whole concept of adaptive management – the notion that the farmer must closely monitor the evolving conditions, which change from year to year and place to place – does not lend itself to certain forms of scientific assessment; the latter typically requires controlled variables. That is, what qualifies as holistic management on one piece of land at one given time of year may not qualify as holistic management on an adjacent piece of land (e.g., perhaps one piece of land is on a steeper slope, increasing the rate of water runoff and thus influencing the rate of plant growth and the speed at which the animals must be moved; or perhaps the local livestock market is different and only allows for one type of animal to be raised profitably, etc.). This makes genuine comparisons of HPG with other grazing systems very difficult to carry out methodologically.

This relates to the third main reason why HPG is sometimes criticized: a misrepresentation of the scientific assessment of HPG. As noted above, a number of scientific studies have supposedly not found any particular benefit of HPG *over* "conventional grazing systems" in terms of ecological outcomes (see Allen et al. 2014; Badgery et al. 2013; Carter et al. 2014). This is to say that a common conclusion in scientific studies is that the proposed benefits of HPG (including greater carbon sequestration, improved plant productivity and species composition, and improved soil quality) can be found in a variety of different grazing methods (including continuous grazing). In short, *other* factors, particularly regional precipitation levels and plant productivity, are said to be better predictors of the extent to which grazing will accrue such benefits (Briske et al. 2014). Yet while these findings are sometimes misrepresented as wholesale *repudiations* of HPG's claimed benefits, in fact they offer evidence that grazing practices *can* indeed help to keep agricultural ecosystems functioning healthily, and that there are clear benefits to thinking holistically about an agricultural landscape. For instance, even in one of the leading assessments of HPG from a policy perspective, the authors admit that "adaptive management would appear to benefit all grazing management strategies and more broadly all activities associated with ecosystem management" – their point being that it is possible to use adaptive management in a variety of grazing systems, not just HPG. Nevertheless, as practitioners of HPG will attest, the ecological benefits of HPG are indeed real, and contrary to what some critics argue, there is scientific evidence to support HPG.

Moving Forward with HPG

So what types of studies do we need to see in order to move forward on the issue of HM and HPG? There are a few key things that need to happen, which address the main shortcomings in the current scientific literature on the subject. First and foremost, the researchers and those designing the study need to be well versed in Holistic Management, both as it is formally laid out in the Holistic Management textbook and handbook *and* as it is actually practised on real-world farms and ranches around the world. Next, and related to the first point, researchers need to actually test HM or HPG itself, *not* management or grazing systems that may be similar to HPG (such as management intensive grazing, cell grazing, rotational grazing, etc.). This may seem trite or obvious, but it is overlooked surprisingly often in the current scientific literature (Firth 2017). Third, the variables being measured in the study (for example, profitability, soil organic matter, forage production, livestock weight gain, etc.) *must* be things that are included in the "Holistic Contexts"[7] of the ranchers being studied. This is because HM claims only one thing fundamentally: that it will help people to achieve or move closer to whatever is included in their Holistic Contexts. These three suggestions for researchers would solve the most glaring issues with the current scientific literature discussing HM and HPG, and would finally allow for an evidence-based debate to take place on whether HM and HPG are worthwhile or not.

What Would Be the Impact of Widespread Adoption of HM?

Some believe that the widespread adoption of HM would require huge changes to the food system and consumer diets (primarily in the context of North American and European food systems, where factory livestock farming is the norm). This is based on the false idea that HM means the adoption of specific farm production models (such as grass-finished beef, pastured poultry and pigs, no annual cropping, etc.). The reality is that HM does not *prescribe* any production model; instead it provides an efficient way for producers to evaluate which production model is right for them, and it provides tools to make their operation more sustainable, no matter what production model they are using (Savory and Butterfield 1999). This means that HM farmers, for example, only switch to grass-finishing their beef if the market allows them to do so. Most HM ranchers in North America are part of the industrial beef production system; many are "cow-calf" producers (they raise calves on grass, and then sell them to feedlots where they are grain-finished). Switching these types of producers over to HM practices does not require any prior changes to the industrial food system or in consumption, and yet it can still have major environmental benefits, given the amount of land currently under "cow-calf" style production. In the end, farmers cannot *sustainably* produce grass-finished beef (or pasture raised monogastrics) if consumers are not willing to pay for them. On the other hand, if consumers *do* start demanding more environmentally friendly agricultural production styles, HM offers valuable tools (such as planned grazing) to make them more efficient and profitable.

Conclusion: Evidence Supporting HPG

If the above combination of anecdotal and scientific evidence is anywhere near correct, then regenerative forms of HPG are among the best-known solutions for building up SOC in agricultural soils (and thus removing greenhouse gasses from the atmosphere in agricultural settings). In fact, it is hard to think of any other human-managed practices already in operation (aside from maintaining wilderness conservation areas) that do the work of combatting climate change *and* regenerating ecosystems at the same time. On top of that, HPG has the added benefits of providing high quality proteins to people and livelihoods to farmers, ranchers and pastoralists. Despite the lack of proof or disproof from the scientific world, land managers are taking up various regenerative grazing strategies *en masse*, because the anecdotal evidence supporting it is very compelling. The main routes by which managers are convinced of the benefits of Holistic Planned Grazing is through word of mouth and through their own experiences. There are thousands of producers using systems like holistic management, or adaptive multi-paddock grazing, and they overwhelmingly report great benefits from these management methods, including improved soil quality and depth, which are good indications of increased soil carbon stores and water retention. I invite you to go and see for yourself – there are countless practitioners out there, including an online directory of holistic managers (Holistic Management International 2018). You can also easily "see" the benefits online, by looking at photographs of land before and after holistic planned grazing was practised on the land. Such comparative photos exist for plots of land all over the world, and clearly show the restorative power of holistic management, benefitting the soil and biodiversity. The next time someone says that science shows that livestock destroy the environment, tell them about the regenerative potential of holistic grazing, and that this is backed by both experiential and experimental evidence.

Notes

1   The term "holistic management" is now officially a registered trademark of Holistic Management International.
2   Consider a recent finding by Canadian scientists in the Arctic who discovered that bird populations were playing an important role in regional temperature regulation. The birds produce exceptional amounts of nitrogen-rich guano, which releases large amounts of ammonia in the atmosphere, which in turn seeds "brighter" clouds that help reflect solar radiation away from the earth. In the grand scheme of things, it is just one of nature's myriad symbiotic processes working to keep biogeochemical cycles functioning properly (Simpkins 2017).
3   Some studies claim that farmers *can* use continuous grazing productively if stocking densities are appropriate, without leading to overgrazing (Briske et al. 2008), but practitioners of HPG would be skeptical of this approach.
4   Usually carbon makes up about 58 per cent of the organic matter in soils, but thanks to its easy measurability, SOC often serves as a stand-in measurement for the relative amount of organic matter in soils.
5   The main exception is fine textured soils at low existing carbon content (Rawls et al. 2003).
6   Admittedly, this is a simplistic example, and there may be specific circumstances that warrant no-grazing or low-grazing scenarios in a given piece of land. Yet this type of ecologically based assessment of a given piece of land qualifies as HM – sometimes the best grazing practice is to hold for another season!
7   A "Holistic Context" is a unique concept from HM which is used like a complex vision statement to guide all management decisions being made.

104   Sheldon Frith

References

Abell, Guy C.J., Nancy Stralis-Pavese, Angela Sessitsch, and Levente Bodrossy. 2009. "Grazing Affects Methanotroph Activity and Diversity in an Alpine Meadow Soil." *Environmental Microbiology Reports* 1 (5): 457–65. https://doi.org/10.1111/j.1758-2229.2009.00078.x.

Alfaro-Arguello, Rigoberto, Stewart A.W. Diemont, Bruce G. Ferguson, Jay F. Martin, José Nahed-Toral, J. David Álvarez-Solís, and René Pinto Ruíz. 2010. "Steps toward Sustainable Ranching: An Emergy Evaluation of Conventional and Holistic Management in Chiapas, Mexico." *Agricultural Systems* 103 (9): 639–46.

Allen, D.E., M.J. Pringle, S. Bray, T.J. Hall, P.O. O'Reagain, D. Phelps, D.H. Cobon, P.M. Bloesch, and R.C. Dalal. 2014. "What Determines Soil Organic Carbon Stocks in the Grazing Lands of North-Eastern Australia?" *Soil Research* 51 (8): 695–706. https://doi.org/10.1071/SR13041.

Badgery, W., H. King, A. Simmons, B. Murphy, A. Rawson, and E. Warden. 2013. "The Effects of Management and Vegetation on Soil Carbon Stocks in Temperate Australian Grazing Systems." *Revitalising Grasslands to Sustain Our Communities: Proceedings, 22nd International Grassland Congress, 15–19 September, 2013, Sydney, Australia*: 1223–6.

Briske, David D., Andrew J. Ash, Justin D. Derner, and Lynn Huntsinger. 2014. "Commentary: A Critical Assessment of the Policy Endorsement for Holistic Management." *Agricultural Systems* 125 (March): 50–3. https://doi.org/10.1016/j.agsy.2013.12.001.

Briske, D.D., J.D. Derner, J.R. Brown, S.D. Fuhlendorf, W.R. Teague, K.M. Havstad, R.L. Gillen, A.J. Ash, and W.D. Willms. 2008. "Rotational Grazing on Rangelands: Reconciliation of Perception and Experimental Evidence." *Rangeland Ecology and Management* 61 (1): 3–17. https://doi.org/10.2111/06-159R.1.

Carter, John, Allison Jones, Mary Brien, Jonathan Ratner, and George Wuerthner. 2014. "Holistic Management: Misinformation on the Science of Grazed Ecosystems." *International Journal of Biodiversity* 2014 (April): 1–10. https://doi.org/10.1155/2014/163431.

Department of Agriculture and Food. 2016. "What Is Soil Organic Carbon?" Government of Western Australia. 18 November 2016. https://www.agric.wa.gov.au/climate-change/what-soil-organic-carbon.

Doornbos, S., and P. Ampt. 2011. "Communities in Landscapes Project Benchmark Study of Innovators." Final Report. Wyong, New South Wales, Australia. http://www.lsln.net.au/naturalresourcesjspui/bitstream/1/3527/1/Ampt and Doornbos 2011.pdf.

Frith, Sheldon. 2017. "Holistic Management and Regenerative Agriculture." http://www.regenerateland.com/.

Hawkins, Heidi-Jayne. 2017. "A Global Assessment of Holistic Planned Grazing™ Compared with Season-Long, Continuous Grazing: Meta-Analysis Findings." *African Journal of Range and Forage Science* 34 (2): 65–75. https://doi.org/10.2989/10220119.2017.1358213.

Holistic Management International. 2017. "Why Holistic Management." https://holisticmanagement.org/holistic-management/.

– 2018. "Community Map – Directory." https://holisticmanagement.org/directory/.

Ketcham, Christopher. 2017. "Allan Savory's Holistic Management Theory Falls Short on Science." Sierra Club. 14 February 2017. http://www.sierraclub.org/sierra/2017-2-march-april/feature/allan-savory-says-more-cows-land-will-reverse-climate-change.

Liebig, M.A., J.R. Gross, S.L. Kronberg, R.L. Phillips, and J.D. Hanson. 2010. "Grazing Management Contributions to Net Global Warming Potential: A Long-Term Evaluation in the Northern Great Plains." *Journal of Environmental Quality* 39 (3): 799–809. https://doi.org/10.2134/jeq2009.0272.

Machmuller, Megan B., Marc G. Kramer, Taylor K. Cyle, Nick Hill, Dennis Hancock, and Aaron Thompson. 2015. "Emerging Land Use Practices Rapidly Increase Soil Organic Matter." *Nature Communications* 6 (April): 6995. https://doi.org/10.1038/ncomms7995.

Monbiot, George. 2014. "Eat More Meat and Save the World: The Latest Implausible Farming Miracle." *The Guardian*, 4 August 2014. https://www.theguardian.com/environment/georgemonbiot/2014/aug/04/eat-more-meat-and-save-the-world-the-latest-implausible-farming-miracle.

Rawls, W.J., Y.A. Pachepsky, J.C. Ritchie, T.M. Sobecki, and H. Bloodworth. 2003. "Effect of Soil Organic Carbon on Soil Water Retention." *Geoderma* 116 (1–2): 61–76. https://doi.org/10.1016/S0016-7061(03)00094-6.

Regeneration International. 2018. "Why Regenerative Agriculture?" https://regenerationinternational.org/why-regenerative-agriculture/.

Savory, Allan. 2013. *How to Fight Desertification and Reverse Climate Change*. Ted Talks. https://www.ted.com/talks/allan_savory_how_to_green_the_world_s_deserts_and_reverse_climate_change.

Savory, Allan, and Jody Butterfield. 1999. *Holistic Management: A New Framework for Decision Making*. Washington, DC: Island Press.

Simpkins, Graham. 2017. "Atmospheric Science: Guano Cools Arctic." *Nature Climate Change* 7 (1): 8. https://doi.org/10.1038/nclimate3196.

Smith, Abbey, and Spencer Smith. 2017. "Holistic Planned Grazing: Maximizing Forage Production, Livestock Gains." *Acres U.S.A.* Greely, CO: June 2017.

Soil Carbon Coalition. 2017. "Soil Carbon Change." SoilCarbonCoalition.org. July 2017. http://soilcarboncoalition.org/changemap.htm.

Strauch, A.M., A.R. Kapust, and C.C. Jost. 2009. "Impact of Livestock Management on Water Quality and Streambank Structure in a Semi-Arid, African Ecosystem." *Journal of Arid Environments* 73 (9): 795–803. https://doi.org/10.1016/j.jaridenv.2009.03.012.

Teague, W.R., S. Apfelbaum, R. Lal, U.P. Kreuter, J. Rowntree, C.A. Davies, R. Conser, et al. 2016. "The Role of Ruminants in Reducing Agriculture's Carbon Footprint in North America." *Journal of Soil and Water Conservation* 71 (2): 156–64. https://doi.org/10.2489/jswc.71.2.156.

Wang, Tong, W. Richard Teague, Seong C. Park, and Stan Bevers. 2015. "GHG Mitigation Potential of Different Grazing Strategies in the United States Southern Great Plains." *Sustainability* 7 (10): 13500–521. https://doi.org/10.3390/su71013500.

Weber, K.T., and B. Gokhale. 2010. "Effect of Grazing Treatment on Soil Moisture in Semiarid Rangelands." In *Final Report: Forecasting Rangeland Condition with GIS in Southeastern Idaho (NNG06GD82G)*, edited by K.T. Weber and K. Davis, 161–74. Pocatello, ID: Idaho State University.

6

Eco-Carnivorism in Garden Hill First Nation

Shirley Thompson, Pepper Pritty, and Keshab Thapa

As recently as a century ago, many Indigenous peoples in Canada relied exclusively on a local diet of wildlife and fish, as well as berries and other plants (LaDuke 2002; Kuhnlein et al. 2006; Paci, Tobin, and Robb 2002). Today, for many Indigenous people, particularly those living in remote communities, hunting, fishing, and gathering remains an integral part of their culture, food supply, and livelihood, which is local and small scale (Kuhnlein et al. 2006; Thompson et al. 2014). A common expression of Indigenous people in northern Manitoba is "Fishing and hunting is the farming of the north" (Thompson et al. 2012). The eco-carnivore food-shed encompasses all the food system components found in a regional setting, including harvesting, transporting, preparing, and eating food. The eco-carnivore foodshed reduces the distance that food travels dramatically, down to a tiny fraction of the thousands of kilometres that food travels in the global market (Thompson et al. 2014). In our view, the label "eco-carnivore" is applicable to the diet of Indigenous people who rely on a diet of sustainably harvested meat and fish.

This chapter maps the traditional land use within the foodshed of Garden Hill First Nation in Manitoba to demonstrate the sustainable character of eco-carnivore diets in that community. To be sustainable, an eco-carnivore foodshed must be regenerative, and the land and waters must be protected as they are the source of food (Friedmann 2014). We argue that Garden Hill's eco-carnivore foodshed is sustainable through the lens of social, economic, and environmental measures; we further identify how this foodshed is being protected while under attack from various political and corporate interests. Further, we use the case study of the Garden Hill foodshed to demonstrate how an eco-carnivore diet is one that operates in harmony with Indigenous values, culture, health, and the environment (Debassige 2010).

The Setting

Garden Hill First Nation is an isolated Indigenous community in northeast Manitoba without connecting roads to urban centres. This community, which is one of four Island Lake communities, requires travel by ice road and airplane to access urban centres. Winnipeg is a fifteen- to twenty-hour drive by ice road, depending on ice road conditions, and approximately 610 km away (380 miles) by plane. The community population is young, with a median age of 20.2 years (Statistics Canada 2016), and it grew by 46.3 per cent in eleven years: from 1,898 in 2006 to 2,776 in 2016. The community has largely preserved its language, culture, traditions, and territory, with most people (75 per cent) identifying either Oji-Cree or Cree (6 per cent) as their mother tongue (Statistics Canada 2016). As well as having a culture of hunting, fishing, and trapping, a history of gardening is evident from the Oji-Cree name for this community, *Kistiganwacheeng*, which translates to "Garden Hill."

Contemporary hunters and trappers habitually travel a constant route to check and set their traps, which requires traversing remote terrain and expertise in the geography of the area. During the fur trade era, the colonial government assigned trapline areas based roughly on family hunting grounds to maximize the number of furs trapped and traded to the Hudson Bay Company. The land of Garden Hill has discontinuous permafrost, poor soils, and a short growing season at the northern edge of the boreal forest with temperatures dipping to below –40 degrees Celsius in winter. Nevertheless, berries as well as some root and other vegetables grow here. Recently, gardening was re-established through Meechim Farm (Thompson et al. 2015), with youth employment workers growing potatoes, apples, tomatoes, beans, cabbages, and other vegetables, as well as raising layer and broiler chickens, through a youth employment program.

Surveying Garden Hill's Eco-Carnivore Foodshed

Shirley Thompson, along with community members Zack Flett and Ivan Harper, undertook a survey to examine traditional land use, including the wild meat and fish harvesting work of thirty-four people, which resulted in thirty-four map biographies. Admittedly, this small sample represents only a tiny portion of all the active hunters and harvesters in Garden Hill.

Map 6.1 is a summary of the entire foodshed for this community compiling the data from thirty-four map biographies of women and men. The map shows clearly that the Garden Hill ancestral territory is extensively used for hunting, trapping, and fishing. Garden Hill people travel to bush camps at Beaver Hill Lake, Sakkink Lake, Goose Lake, Kookus Lake, York Lake, Coccos Lake, and many others. This large area where people harvest represents the space required for an eco-carnivore diet for this community. Also, the map shows the vast distances people travel to their bush camp, despite the lack of roads to connect them. Garden Hill community members travel to the west 80 kms, crossing the Ontario border, and 70 kms to the northeast, and lesser distances to the south and east, as these directions represent the traplines of Wasagamack and St Theresa Point First Nations. This distance requires a skidoo or float plane trip if one does not have a week available to paddle a canoe there and another week to canoe back, which is still done. For example, two Elders canoe each year from Garden Hill to a camp past Red Sucker Lake.[1]

Map 6.2 shows all the wildlife hunted. A total number of 242 moose sites were identified by thirty-four people in Garden Hill. Map 6.2 shows the moose harvest sites, along with seventy other mammal harvesting sites by hunting (not trapping) (Thompson et al. 2015). Since moose consume plants that members of the community use for medicinal purposes, the moose meat is itself considered a special medicine, and the meat is typically shared among family members. In the fall, moose are the staple food that many people hunt to feed their families over the long winter.

Map 6.3 shows the trapping sites established at key spots to harvest a number of species, including beaver, muskrat, and other fur-bearing animals. As well as hunting beaver for their furs, people consider beaver and muskrat meats to be powerful medicines. Beaver tail is considered a particular delicacy in Oji-Cree culture.

Map 6.4 shows the many different birds harvested as well as egg harvesting sites. A lot of this activity occurs on Island Lake. Finally, map 6.5 illustrates how Garden Hill people depend on many kinds of fish to feed their families. Fish is harvested from different lakes for subsistence, including walleye, trout, white fish, and sucker fish.

Taken together, these four maps demonstrate a diverse and local eco-carnivore diet of moose, caribou, muskrat, beaver, rabbit, bear, duck, geese, grouse, swan, bird eggs, and fish. Further, the maps show how a traditional territory extends beyond provincial boundaries and beyond the government created trapline boundaries. This type of land-use mapping incorporates traditional knowledge of sacred sites as well as past experiences of hunting and fishing, and simultaneously provides data for land-use planning.

The maps of moose and other animal harvesting sites clearly demonstrate that the lakes and rivers are of primary importance, both as a food source and for culture. As a result, protecting the Hayes Watershed is essential to safeguarding the source of the community's food and culture. The mapping exercise shows how expansive a rural foodshed area is for the thirty-four study participants; yet this underestimates the overall community's foodshed and the amount of wildlife being hunted, which is much greater given the growing population, close to 3,000 people. Map 6.6 shows the estimated foodshed based both on Garden Hill First Nation traplines, harvest, and catch habitat. The watershed is also considered in map 6.6, as contamination or damming anywhere in the watershed could affect the animals throughout.

Is the Eco-Carnivore Foodshed Sustainable?

To be sustainable, an eco-carnivore foodshed of the type characterized in Garden Hill *must* be regenerative (reproducing the flora and fauna to replace those hunted year after year). As such, the protection of the watershed and forest habitat is of paramount importance. The Brundtland Report (World Commission on Environment and Development 1987) defines sustainability as "development that meets the needs of the present without compromising the ability of future generations to meet their own needs." The sustainability of eco-carnivorism in the Garden Hill First Nation traditional territory is defined based on future generations being able to continue to undertake traditional activities and live off the land and "to continue this traditional behavior indefinitely." We further examine the sustainability of the eco-carnivore foodshed through the three pillars of social, environmental, and economic sustainability (World Commission on Environment and Development 1987).

Social Sustainability

Mino bimaadiziwin is a term related to social sustainability, meaning "a good life" in the Oji-Cree language (Debassige 2010). For eco-carnivorism to be socially sustainable the community must be able to achieve mino bimaadiziwin, which necessitates healthy, sufficient, and culturally appropriate food (Daly 1990). Food for Indigenous communities is not merely a commodity but a celebration of culture and a relationship with the environment, spirit, land, and animals (Cidro 2015; Wilson 2003).

Indigenous food systems maintain reciprocal relations between Indigenous peoples through the sharing of food, and regenerate the earth through stewarding and harvesting the land (LaDuke 2002). Access to country foods is contingent on not only the ecological integrity of the land but the cultural foundation of the people (Cidro 2015). This cultural foundation includes the knowledge of wildlife behaviours in their habitats, as well the protocols, including ceremonies, required to hunt, fish, trap, gather, and live on the land. This Indigenous knowledge system is transferred through stories embedded in language and the land: "The land holds many layers of stories, not in time, but also with peoples who occupy that time and place in a past, present and future context. Indigenous languages enable this multi-dimensionality to merge cohesively into each generational experience; however, without language we detract from its nuances" (McLeod 2014, 18). The language therefore operates as a code that tells about the medicinal properties of various animals and plants. For example, *Otehimin* is the Oji-Cree word for strawberry, which means "the heart berry" – it being a heart medicine.

The eco-carnivore diet offers excellent health outcomes, contributing to social sustainability. Kuhnlein et al. (2006) suggest that significant pharmacological and therapeutic benefits result from a diet of wild meat and fish. This diet is rich in high-quality complete proteins as well as other nutrients, while being low in *unhealthy* fats, sodium, carbohydrates, and sugar (Batal et al. 2018). Other physiological benefits are found in the aerobic and muscle-building activities involved in the harvesting, gathering, and preparing of food. This activity provides a "health shield" against a host of chronic diseases such as diabetes, cardiovascular diseases, obesity, cancer, and many other negative health conditions that youth face today (Thompson et al. 2012). The healthy benefits of an eco-carnivore diet are evident from the archeological evidence of ancient Indigenous skeletons having good dental health and lacking any signs of arthritis despite reaching advanced ages (Price 1939).

Kuhnlein et al. (2006) identified hunting and fishing as well as community gardening and the production of local food (including livestock and poultry) as effective ways to regain Indigenous food sovereignty and food security (and thus restore dietary health). As noted above, Garden Hill people are engaged in poultry production, which has become an important source of local meat. Also, poultry production serves as an employer of youth and a dependable source of food (Klatt and Thompson 2016; Malay 2017). Similarly, fishing is both a source of sustenance for most families, through ice or fall fishing, and also the largest employer in the community for its short season, bringing $250,000 of cash into the community per year from exports. The fishing income pays for community members to fly out in the fall to their traplines to get moose and fish for the family.

With the transition from traditional diets in the community to commercial foods, the community has been plagued by food insecurity, diabetes, and other chronic diseases (Batal et al. 2018). Commercial foods require little or no preparation work, allowing sedentary lifestyles, compared to traditional foods which require active harvesting as well as preparation to cut the fish or meat. Commercial food is known to have lower nutritional values for vitamin A, potassium, and protein, and higher unhealthy fat and sugar contents (Batal et al. 2018). This dietary transition in many Indigenous communities resulted in dental caries, lowered resistance to infection, and higher rates of obesity, diabetes, and chronic diseases (Willows et al. 2012). Currently 85 per cent of Indigenous children in Canada aged three to five experience dental decay and 80 per cent of Indigenous children aged six to eleven have dental caries (Mathu-Muju et al. 2016). Indigenous people in Canada have higher rates of most chronic and infectious diseases, as well as a lower life expectancy rate than other Canadians (Statistics Canada 2011).

Regarding food security, in 2009 88 per cent of Garden Hill First Nation households reported being food insecure, which is approximately ten times the Canadian average (Thompson et al. 2012). The concept of food security is essentially about equality, considering the sharing of resources and power to deliver this basic human need to access food (Sen 1986). The food security survey largely focuses on retail food and access to money to buy food. Clearly, with such high rates of food insecurity, the retail food market is not sharing its resources and power to deliver a basic human need to remote First Nation communities, who are without economic wealth and power. The selection of healthy foods is very limited in Garden Hill's commercial outlets, and what healthy food is available is often too costly for most families to afford. The only full-scale grocery store in the area was located on an island across from Garden Hill, adding a $12 boat trip to the already high cost of food, until the store finally moved to the mainland in 2018 (Thompson et al. 2012).

Economic poverty and the lack of government support for travel and equipment costs to hunt and fish both challenge Indigenous peoples' food security in Canada, in the face of high-priced foods from one corporate monopoly supplying commercial food called the Northern Store (Ford et al. 2013). The federal government subsidizes corporate foods through the Nutrition North program in the Northern Store – but these financial policies exclude support for wild food. Indigenous peoples' local subsistence activities are in competition with subsidized commercial foods. As well, wild meat is illegal to sell, and illegal to provide in public venues (Thompson et al. 2012). This uneven playing field, we argue, has undermined eco-carnivorism and food security in Garden Hill First Nation.

Economic Sustainability

Economic sustainability, as applied to eco-carnivorism, not only implies being able to *afford* to consume meat, fish, and other resources indefinitely at renewable levels, but also means enabling food producers (including hunters and gatherers) to make a reliable income from their work harvesting, preparing, and/or selling foods (Daly 1990). The people from Garden Hill community, in this research, called for community-led economic development, requesting programs for Indigenous food sovereignty and home-building with local trees. Their rejection of industrial development and embrace of sustainable livelihoods contrasts with modernity. Around the globe, mining and other modern industrial development have over-extracted resources, devastated Indigenous cultures, and undermined the food sovereignty of Indigenous people (Thompson et al. 2011; Price, Roburn, and MacKinnon 2009).

Considering the sacredness of nature, biodiversity, and traditional uses and culture, intact ecosystems hold a higher value than gold to community people. However, Garden Hill's territory is on ancient Precambrian shield that is labelled greenstone, and under Manitoba's Land Use Planning Act Regulation (Regulation 81/2011, 38), "the best and only use" of greenstone belts is mining. Regulation 81/2011 states that greenstone cannot be protected and conserved for traditional uses: "greenstone belts ... must be identified and protected from conflicting surface land uses that could interfere with access to the resources" (Manitoba Government 2011, 38). This idea of protection is an oxymoron, as mining typically destroys landscape and water quality, rather than protecting or conserving land. The government has demonstrated that mineral and oil resources trump environmental and cultural integrity: the regulation is designed to shield "economically valuable mineral, oil and natural gas resources from land uses that would preclude exploration, extraction and development" (Manitoba Government 2011, 38). The lack of consultation on Regulation 81/2011 undermines the constitutional right for First Nation consultation (McGregor 2013; McIlwraith and Cormier 2016). Recently, after their airborne geophysical survey in Island Lake, Wolfden Resources Corporation announced a diamond drill program (Manitoba Government 2016). Similarly, Yamana Gold Inc. has an aggressive exploration drill program, after finding gold and tungsten in the nearby Twin Lake deposit (Manitoba Government 2016) with "indicated mineral resources" of 1.8 million ounces of gold and an equal amount of "inferred mineral resource" (Manitoba Government 2016). However, while the mineral deposits in the area are worth billions of dollars, the communities nearby have hardly benefitted from this exploration, remaining economically poor and without basic infrastructure. Further, the exploration activities and the potential for expansive extraction projects threaten the aquatic and forest habitats for the community's traditional diet. As such, the push to grow the extractive sector in the region threatens the environmental and public health of the community.

Environmental Sustainability

For harvesting to be *environmentally* sustainable, the wildlife, fish, and other renewable resources must be used at a rate that is replaceable, without negative impacts (e.g., pollution or depletion) (Daly 1990). By living off the land, many hunters, fishers, and gatherers are acutely aware of changes and disturbances to the regional ecosystems and thus respond to protect the resource when it is threatened (Ballard 2012), with the view that the land is sacred (Hughes 1978; Harper and Harper 1987). A welcome sign on the outskirts of Garden Hill reserve speaks to the importance of the integrity of the land for their culture. It reads:

> All of our rights originate from our connection to the land.
> Our lives, our beliefs and our presence as First Nations people
> are validated to the land, inhabited by our ancestors since time
> immemorial. Our land is sacred. It is the living body of our
> sanctity. The teachings and our customs are implicit and practiced
> through the integrity that protects and warrants our survival. .

Clearly, this sign shows the importance of ecological integrity to the culture and spirituality in Garden Hill. In discussions about land use, community members stress the need for their traditional territory to be preserved in a natural state, unsullied by industrial development such as mining and hydro development, as a means of protecting their culture (Harper, Klatt and Thompson 2017). Clearly, most Garden Hill residents want their territory preserved so that future generations can live off the land and practise their hunting, trapping, and fishing culture. This deep spiritual connection that many people have with the land is voiced in a video called *Visions for the Land: Garden Hill First Nation* (Harper, Klatt, and Thompson 2017). Within the film, one resident explains the need to save the land from mining and other development for community traditional uses: "I'm trying to save my land. We use it for lots of purposes like hunting, trapping, fishing, collecting berries, and collecting Indian medicine. It is really important to us and I would like to see our people to continue in these ways of life" (harvester in Harper, Klatt, and Thompson 2017).

In the film another resident similarly describes how the community wants to manage their ancestral land for food and community development: "I would like to see our people have control over the land. They know not to destroy it. We are supposed to be the caretakers of the land. What we are given is everything but we can't touch it because of the government. That is why we are so poor ... The most important thing is we have to get the people back eating off the land [again]. Not store foods" (Harper in Harper, Klatt and Thompson 2017). As these quotes demonstrate, many members of Garden Hill and neighbouring communities connect their food system with their active role as land stewards to ensure healthy natural ecosystems.

Island Lake is not only pristine but occupied almost exclusively by Indigenous people, with most speaking Oji-Cree language fluently (Statistics Canada 2016). Island Lake is in the Hayes Watershed, which is unlike all the other major watersheds in Manitoba because the latter are dammed (Thompson 2015). In the Hayes watershed, the Garden Hill First Nation territory of lakes has virgin boreal forests (WNO, 2010), naturally flowing rivers, and abundant wildlife.

The pristine, sovereign nature of Island Lake was described in 1907 in the marking of a historic event. In 1907 soldiers travelled with dog teams through Island Lake to arrest an Oji-Cree Indigenous leader, described as a "powerful" shaman, who after his trial by the Dominion of Canada was executed: "In the frost sun-up of May 9th, James Kirkness takes the soldiers, O'Neill and Cashman, southeast on Island Lake [Baskwinaksiing] ... It is a territory that soldiers have never before penetrated. It is a territory that has never seen a permanent western settler. Territory that has not been ceded to the Canadians" (Fiddler and Stevens 2012, 72). Less than a century ago, most people in Island Lake lived and ate from the land, in family groupings at their family camp area, until the 1950s required mandatory schooling. Then the children found in family camps were taken away to residential schools by police officers in float planes.

Until float planes, the remoteness shielded the regional ecosystems and communities from some of these pressures. Although legally confined to a small reserve, most people in northern Manitoba continued to live off the land by hunting, gathering vegetation, fishing, trapping, and gardening; in this isolated area, there was no competition for territory with settlers (Thompson et al. 2012). To this day, a number of Indigenous people in remote communities still depend heavily on hunting and fishing as an integral part of their livelihood and culture (Thompson et al. 2012; Tough 1997).

Stewardship and living off the land are part of Garden Hill's education and culture. Training of local Island Lake teachers through the Brandon University Native Teacher Education Program (BUNTEP) allowed Island Lake people to earn a university teaching degree in Island Lake. These teachers received a credited course in Nopimink, which is Oji-Cree for learning from the land, at Stevenson River with Elders: "The class travelled by boat using the old freight route between Island Lake and Norway House. They shot and butchered a moose ... during the course students were introduced to herbal medicines, rabbit snaring, traditional values and traditional teaching ways ... They set nets and preserved fish. They learned to play traditional camp games" (Harper and Harper 1987, 2.2). A student teacher, Cliff Flett, wrote a reflective piece to meet the course requirements: "The land is the teacher of my people. It is through the land that my elders gained their wisdom. It is the land that taught them how to live. It is the land that showed them how to appreciate who they are. It taught them to respect, not only each other, but also the animals, the trees and the water" (in Harper and Harper 1987, 2.16). The twelve Elders who participated had traditional teachings unimpacted by the residential school system, as these Elders had not been to residential school or any colonial school.

Conclusion

The foodshed maps of Garden Hill community members tell a radically different story from the typical modern industrial food system narrative. The maps document Indigenous peoples' efforts to steward the land and harvest food for their communities. Like a watershed, the foodshed needs protecting but is more difficult to map and plan around, as the boundary is a social artifact rather than a natural one.

At different times throughout the year, families engage in traditional activities at bush camps that need to be accessed by canoe, float plane, or skidoo. Similarly, Elders' workshops and Nopimink school with sacred and important teachings are shared amongst Elders and youth, requiring access by float planes or by canoe to traverse portages, rivers, and lakes. The summary map (map 6.1) shows that land use in Garden Hill First Nation involves not only Island Lake but also areas such as Beaver Lake and many other lakes and rivers in all directions.

The maps show that Garden Hill people continue to live off their territory's land and gain tremendous sustenance from the land. In their large territory and at great distances from the reserve, community members harvest beaver, duck, geese, moose, muskrat, and fish, as well as berries and medicines, which is undertaken within a complex social system requiring ceremonies, stewardship, and protocols. Garden Hill families actively go out to harvest in all seasons. These traditional pursuits are current activities that feed and keep families and the community healthy and nourish their culture. Their traditional land-use maps show that Garden Hill's claim and connection to land covers a more extensive area than its designated area under the registered trapline for sustenance activities. The yield is sustainable, but regenerative practices could improve the carrying capacity and diversity through native fish nurseries and more widespread cultivation of wild rice to feed wild ducks and geese that are then hunted (Friedmann 2014). As well, poultry and livestock production using local feed or grazing could improve food security further by supplying additional locally sourced low-input nutrition.

Garden Hill's eco-carnivore diet was found to be "sustainable" in social, economic, and environmental terms, but it is threatened by attacks from political and corporate interests. Mining, industrial development, and settlers risk the land's sustainability. Preserving Garden Hill's foodshed to harvest locally is considered key to both food security and sovereignty as well as cultural preservation. Evidently traditional food harvesting and sharing in an intact ecosystem (Power 2008) is important to culture, but so is stewarding the land (Settee, 2013).

Indigenous stewardship of traditional territory needs recognition from government beyond consultation and funding for Indigenous people to carry out conservation of their territory. Government needs the ability to control the resources in their traditional territory (Palmater 2014; Settee 2013). In order to move forward effectively, government policies must acknowledge the importance and relevance of Indigenous peoples' individual and community rights to access, harvest, and steward resources. Community-led land-use planning of the foodshed and watershed of Garden Hill for cultural priorities, including hunting, fishing, and gathering, offers significant potential to restore the food security and health of the people versus the negative impacts of industrial-scale development. Reclaiming an eco-carnivore diet requires preserving traditional territory and promoting healthy practices that sustained Indigenous populations prior to colonization, based on Indigenous knowledge systems.

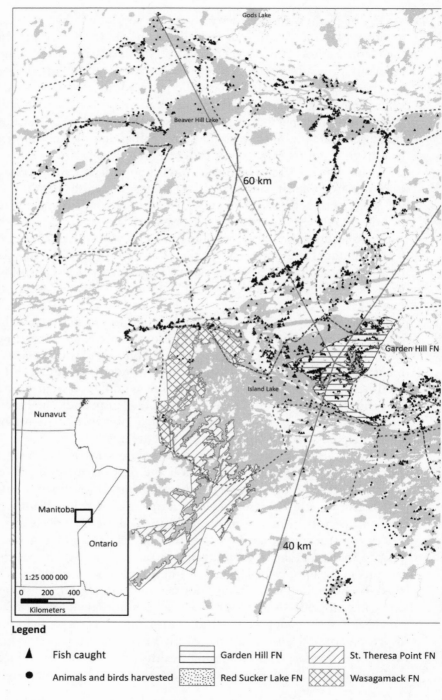

Legend

▲   Fish caught

●   Animals and birds harvested

Garden Hill FN

Red Sucker Lake FN

St. Theresa Point FN

Wasagamack FN

Map 6.1   Summary map of all wildlife harvesting sites showing aerial distance travelled

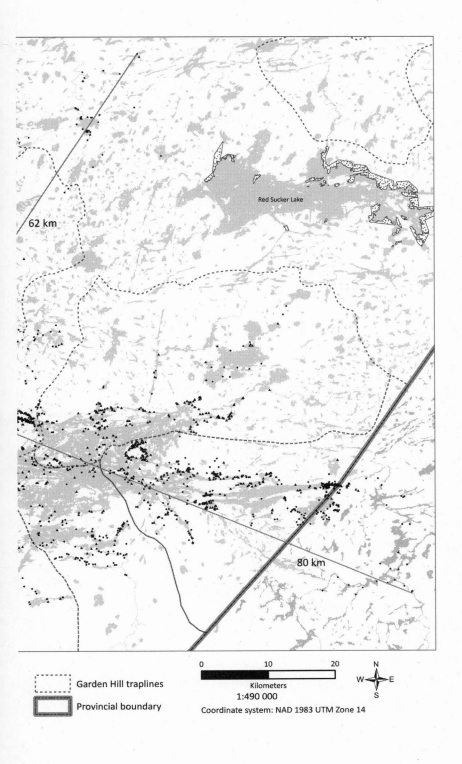

62 km

Red Sucker Lake

80 km

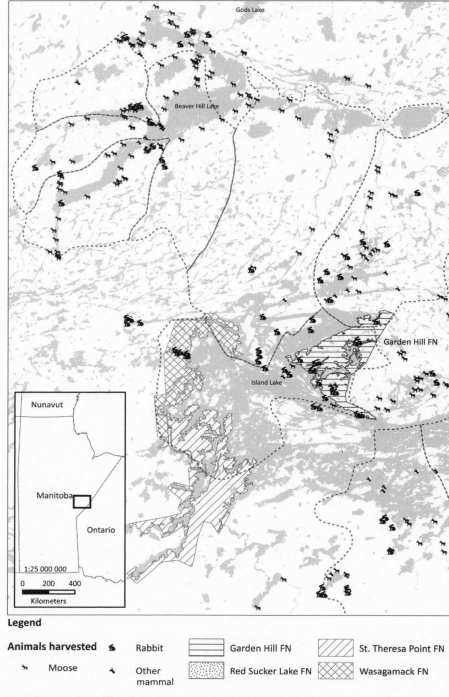

Gods Lake

Beaver Hill Lake

Garden Hill FN

Island Lake

Nunavut

Manitoba

Ontario

1:25 000 000

0   200   400

Kilometers

Legend

Animals harvested   Rabbit   Garden Hill FN   St. Theresa Point FN

Moose   Other
mammal   Red Sucker Lake FN   Wasagamack FN

Map 6.2   Garden Hill First Nation's moose and other mammal harvest sites
of 34 community hunters

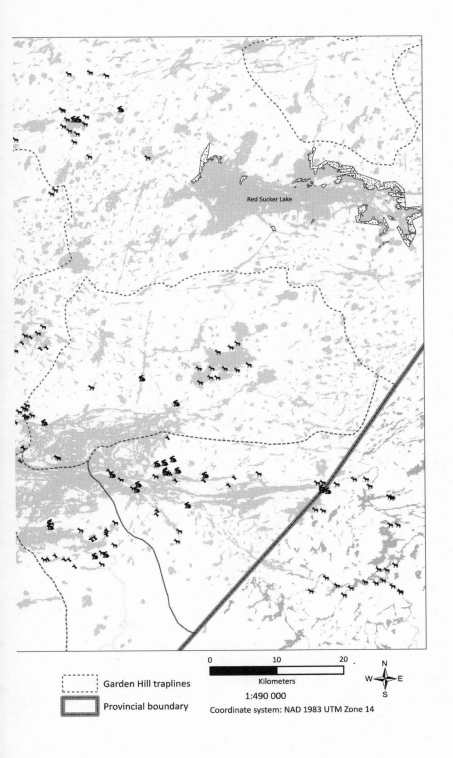

Red Sucker Lake

0   10   20
Kilometers
1:490 000
Coordinate system: NAD 1983 UTM Zone 14

N
W ⬦ E
S

Garden Hill traplines
Provincial boundary

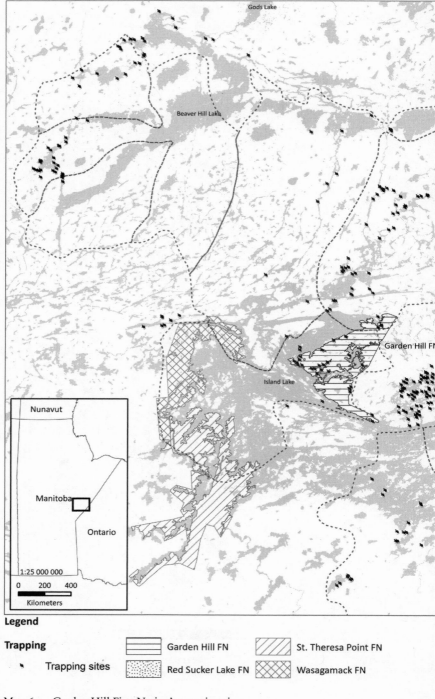

Legend

Trapping

⸲ Trapping sites

☰ Garden Hill FN	⧄ St. Theresa Point FN
⣿ Red Sucker Lake FN	⧉ Wasagamack FN

Map 6.3   Garden Hill First Nation's trapping sites

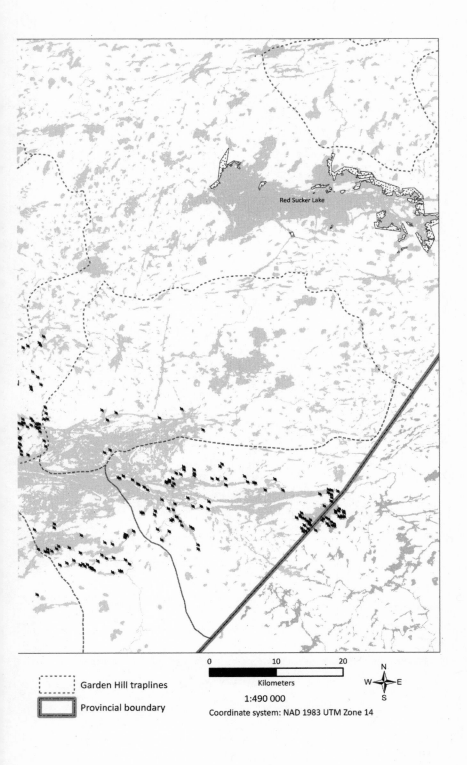

Red Sucker Lake

```
  0           10           20
  ▰▰▰▰▰▱▱▱▱▱
        Kilometers
```

1:490 000
Coordinate system: NAD 1983 UTM Zone 14

N
W——E
S

Garden Hill traplines

Provincial boundary

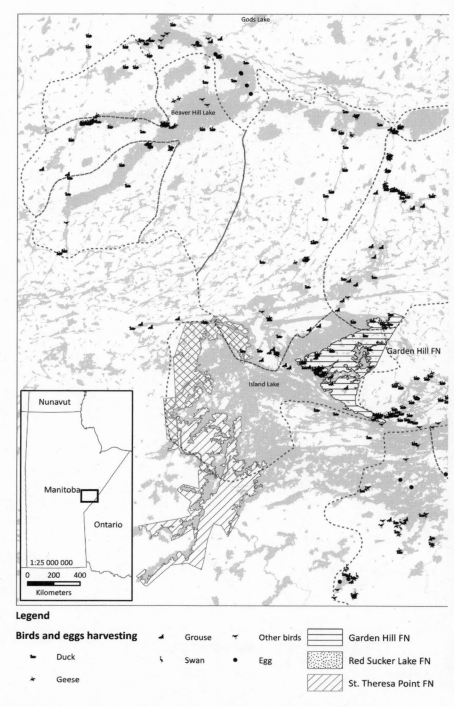

Map 6.4   Harvesting sites for birds and eggs in the traditional territory of Garden Hill First Nation

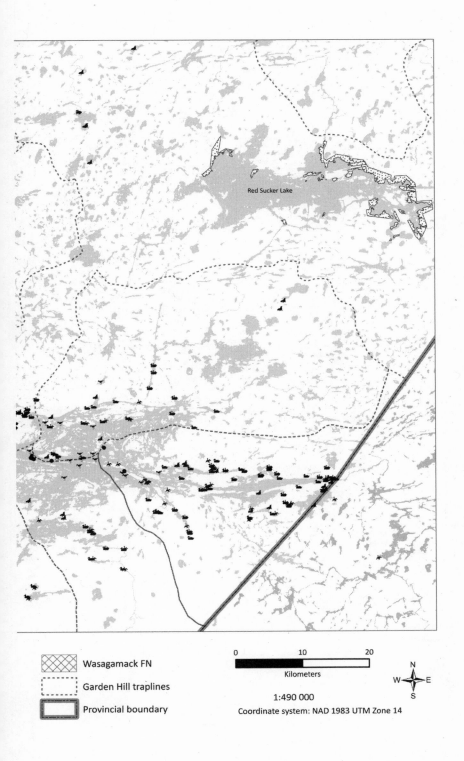

Red Sucker Lake

Wasagamack FN

Garden Hill traplines

Provincial boundary

0   10   20
Kilometers

N
W   E
S

1:490 000
Coordinate system: NAD 1983 UTM Zone 14

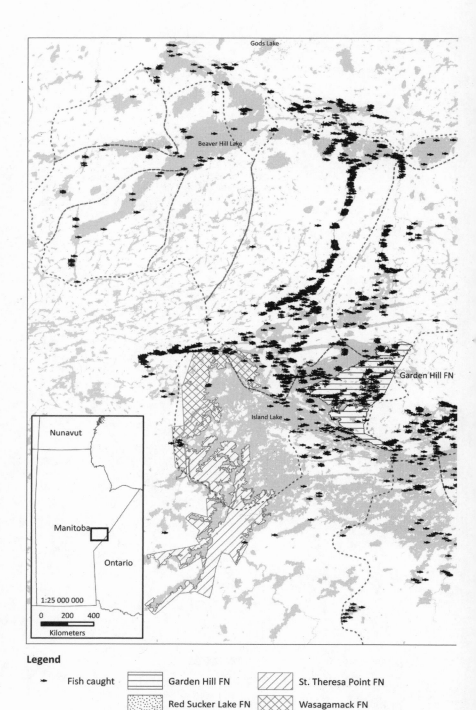

Map 6.5   Catch sites for fish for sustenance in the traditional
territory of Garden Hill First Nation

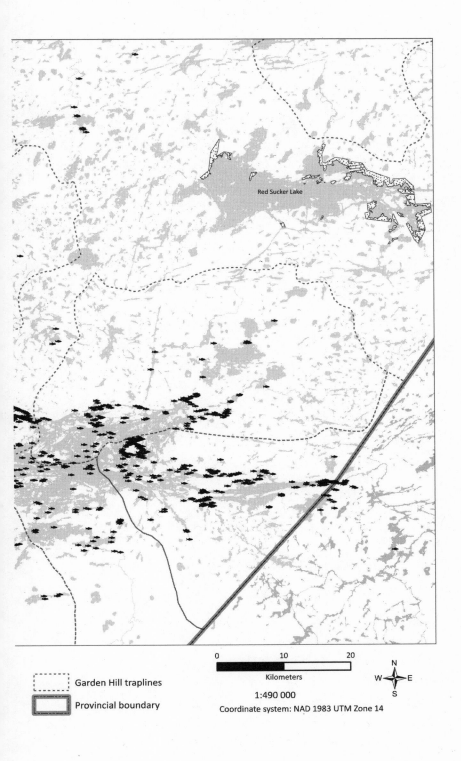

Red Sucker Lake

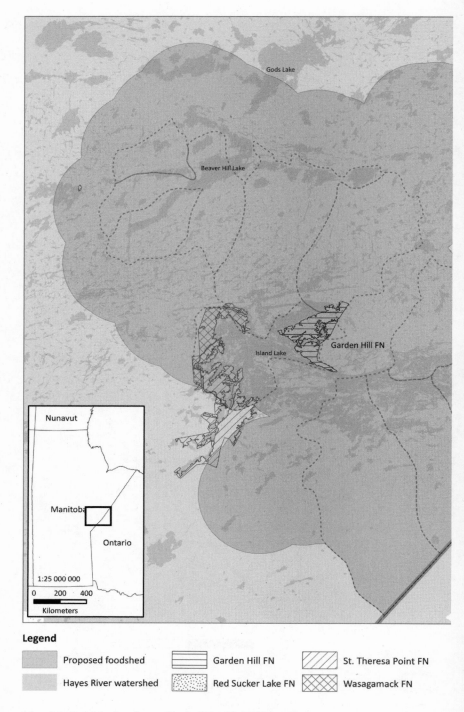

Map 6.6   Foodshed and watershed of Garden Hill First Nation

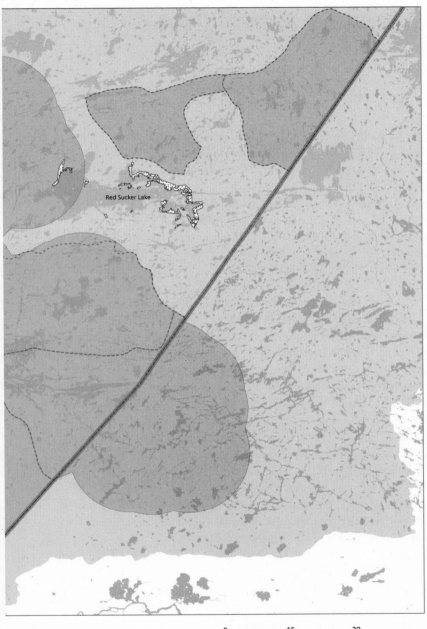

Red Sucker Lake

- - - - - Garden Hill traplines

▭ Provincial boundary

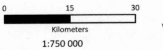

0   15   30

Kilometers

1:750 000

Coordinate system: NAD 1983 UTM Zone 14

N
W ✦ E
S

Notes

1 Motor boats cannot traverse the rapids or be carried over long portages. Thus, canoes or float planes to provide quick access.

References

Batal, M., L. Johnson-Down, J.C. Moubarac, A. Ing, K, Fediuk, T. Sadik … and N. Willows. 2018. "Quantifying Associations of the Dietary Share of Ultra-Processed Foods with Overall Diet Quality in First Nations Peoples in the Canadian Provinces of British Columbia, Alberta, Manitoba and Ontario." *Public Health Nutrition*, 21 (1): 103–13.

Blum-Evitts, S. 2009. "Designing a Foodshed Assessment Model: Guidance for Local and Regional Planners in Understanding Local Farm Capacity in Comparison to Local Food Needs." MRP thesis, University of Massachusetts, Amherst. http://scholarworks.umass.edu/theses/288.

Cidro, J. 2015. "Beyond Food Security." *Canadian Journal of Urban Research* 24 (1): 24–43.

Daly, Herman E. 1990. "Toward Some Operational Principles of Sustainable Development." *Ecological Economics* 2 (1): 1–6. https://doi.org/10.1016/0921-8009(90)90010-R.

Debassige, B. 2010. "Re-Conceptualizing Anishinaabe Mino-Bimaadiziwin (the Good Life) as Research Methodology: A Spirit-Centered Way in Anishinaabe Research." *Canadian Journal of Native Education* 33 (1): 11–28.

Elliott, B., D. Jayatilaka, C. Brown, L. Varley, and K.K. Corbett. 2012. "'We Are Not Being Heard': Aboriginal Perspectives on Traditional Foods Access and Food Security." *Journal of Environmental and Public Health* 2012: 130945. http://dx.doi.org/10.1155/2012/130945

Fiddler, T. and J. Stevens. 2003. *Killing the Shamen: Cree Legends of Sandy Lake, No. 2*. Newcastle: Penumbra Press.

Ford, J.D., M.P. Lardeau, H. Blackett, S. Chatwood, and D. Kurszewski. 2013. "Community Food Program Use in Inuvik, Northwest Territories." *BMC Public Health* 13 (1): 970.

Friedmann, Harriet. 2014. "Reflections on Foodsheds in Three Continents." *Canadian Food Studies / La Revue Canadienne Des Études Sur l'alimentation* 1 (1): 4–9. https://doi.org/10.15353/cfs-rcea.v1i1.35.

Harper, I., R. Klatt, and S. Thompson. 2017. "Visions of the Land: Garden Hill First Nation." https://www.youtube.com/watch?v=guQZikivBSo.

Harper, V., and E. Harper. *The Nopimink Project (Formerly Bear Lake/Stevenson River Project)*. Island Lake Tribal Council: Winnipeg.

Hughes, K. 1979. *Jackson Beardy – Life and Art*. Winnipeg: Canadian Dimension.

Kuhnlein, H., B. Erasmus, H. Creed-Kanashiro, L. Engelberger, C. Okeke, N. Turner, and L. Bhattacharjee. 2006. "Indigenous Peoples' Food Systems for Health: Finding Interventions That Work." *Public Health Nutrition* 9 (08): 1013–19.

LaDuke, W. 2002. *The Winona LaDuke Reader: A Collection of Essential Writings*. McGregor, MN: Voyageur Press.

Manitoba Government. 2011. *Provincial Planning Regulation 81/2011*. https://web2.gov.mb.ca/laws/regs/current/081.11.pdf.

– 2016. "Minerals Policy and Business Development: Exploration and Development Highlights 2016." http://www.manitoba.ca/iem/busdev/exp-dev/index.html.

Mathu-Muju, K.R., J. McLeod, M.L. Walker, M. Chartier, and R.L. Harrison. 2016. "The Children's Oral Health Initiative: An Intervention to Address the Challenges of Dental Caries in Early Childhood in Canada's Indigenous and Inuit Communities." *Canadian Journal of Public Health / Revue Canadienne de Santé Publique* 107 (2): e188–93.

McGregor, D. 2014. "Traditional Knowledge and Water Governance: The Ethic of Responsibility." *AlterNative: An International Journal of Indigenous Peoples*, 10 (5), 493–507. https://doi.org/10.1177/117718011401000505.

McIlwraith, Tad, and Raymond Cormier. 2016. "Making Place for Space: Land Use and Occupancy Studies, Counter-Mapping, and the Supreme Court of Canada's Tsilhqot'in Decision." BC *Studies* 188: 35–53.

McLeod, N., ed. 2014. *Indigenous Poetics in Canada*. Waterloo, ON: Wilfrid Laurier University Press.

Paci, C., A. Tobin, and P. Robb. 2002. "Reconsidering the Canadian Environmental Impact Assessment Act: A Place for Traditional Environmental Knowledge." *Environmental Impact Assessment Review* 22 (2): 111–27.

Palmater, P. 2014. "Genocide, Indian Policy, and Legislated Elimination of Indians in Canada." *Aboriginal Policy Studies* 3 (3): 27–54.

Power, E.M. 2008. "Conceptualizing Food Security for Aboriginal People in Canada." *Canadian Journal of Public Health* 99 (2): 95–7.

Price, K., A. Roburn, and A. MacKinnon. 2009. "Ecosystem-Based Management in the Great Bear Rainforest." *Forest Ecology and Management* 258 (4): 495–503.

Price, W. 1939. *Nutrition and Physical Degeneration: A Comparison of Primitive and Modern Diets and Their Effects*. New York: Hoeber.

Sen, A. 1986. *Poverty and Famine: An Essay of Entitlement and Deprivation*. Oxford: Clarendon Press.

Settee, P. 2013. *Pimatisiwin: The Good Life, Global Indigenous Knowledge Systems*. Vernon, BC: J. Charlton Press.

Statistics Canada. 2011. "NHS Aboriginal Population Profile, Garden Hill First Nation, 1RIManitoba, 2011." https://www12.statcan.gc.ca/nhs-enm/2011/dp-pd/aprof/details/page.cfm?Lang=E&Geo1=CSD&Code1=4622048&Data=Count&SearchText=Garden%20Hill%20First%20Nation&SearchType=Begins&SearchPR=01&A1=All&B1=All&GeoLevel=PR&GeoCode=4622048&TABID=1.

Thompson, S. 2015. "Flooding First Nations and Environmental Justice in Manitoba: Case Studies of the Impacts of 2011 Flood and Hydrodevelopment in Manitoba." *Manitoba Law Journal* 38 (2): 220–59.

Thompson, S., T. Clahane, A. Gulruhk, and U. Nwanko. 2014. "Growing Gardens, Youth and Food Security in Canada's Boreal Forest." *International Journal of Biodiversity Watch* 4 (3): 65–88. https://biodiversity-watch.com/issue/Biodiversity_Watch_Vol-4.pdf.

Thompson, S., A. Gulruhk, M.A. Alam, and J. Weibe. 2012. "Community Development to Feed the Family in Northern Manitoba Communities: Evaluating Food Activities Based on Their Food Sovereignty, Food Security, and Sustainable Livelihood Outcomes." *Canadian Journal of Nonprofit and Social Economy Research* 3 (2): 43–66.

Thompson, S., A. Gulrukh Kamal, M. Ballard, B. Beardy, D. Islam, V. Lozeznik, and K. Wong. 2011. "Is Community Economic Development Putting Healthy Food on the Table? Food Sovereignty in Northern Manitoba's Aboriginal Communities." *Journal of Aboriginal Economic Development* 7 (2): 15–40.

Thompson, S., M. Rony, J. Temmer, and D. Wood. 2014. "Pulling in the Indigenous Fishery Cooperative Net: Fishing for Sustainable Livelihoods and Food Security in Garden Hill First Nation, Manitoba, Canada." *Journal of Agriculture, Food Systems, and Community Development* 4 (3): 177–92. http://dx.doi.org/10.5304/jafscd.2014.043.016.

Tough, Frank. 1997. *As Their Natural Resources Fail: Native Peoples and the Economic History of Northern Manitoba, 1870–1930*. Vancouver: UBC Press.

Treaty Commission of Manitoba. 2017. "The Numbered Treaties." http://www.trcm.ca/wp-content/uploads/29627-treaty_poster_map_2017-web.pdf.

Willows, N.D., A.J. Hanley, and T. Delormier. 2012. "A Socioecological Framework to Understand Weight-Related Issues in Aboriginal Children in Canada." *Applied Physiology, Nutrition, and Metabolism* 37 (1): 1–13.

Wilson, K. 2003. "Therapeutic Landscapes and Indigenous Peoples: An Exploration of Culture, Health and Place." *Health and Place* 9 (2): 83–93.

World Commission on Environment and Development. 1987. *Our Common Future*. Oxford and New York: Oxford University Press.

7

The Practice of Responsible
Meat Consumption

Alexandra Kenefick

Eating meat is a contentious issue. From religious dogma and medical doctrine, cultural ritual and nutrition, to inquiries about the sentience of animals and the ethics of killing, heated debate over meat consumption has surged for centuries (Spencer 2002; Preece 2009; Zaraska 2016). While echoes of these old debates still reverberate, there are new dimensions to the conversation. Today we contemplate, for example, whether or not meat consumption is even necessary in a world where technology can make similar foods and comparable nutrition from different materials, such as seitan, tofu, or even cell-cultured meat (Ghosh 2013). Today's unique context has made the debate over meat consumption seem more intense given the wide range of ethical and environmental concerns surrounding industrial food production (Walsh 2013; Foer 2009; Lymbery 2014; and see this volume, chapter 2). Finally, the global population's steady increase has intensified the spotlight on earth's limited natural resources, a great volume of which are instrumental in industrial meat production, thus raising questions about whether plant-based proteins offer a more efficient use of what resources remain. This has sparked discourse over whether a shift towards "plant-based diets" might be a way of meeting the food needs of the 9 billion people expected to populate the earth by mid-century (Godfray et al. 2010; Poore and Nemecek 2018). In response, scholars and activists alike assert that centuries of arguing has run its course, and that the health and sustainability of the earth are now at stake. Many of these proponents have initiated a call to action, and suggested a worldwide reduction in meat consumption as a means of quelling the damage (Machovina, Feeley, and Ripple 2015; Walker et al. 2005). One method of potentially achieving this reduction can be found in the private- and public-sector efforts that have made plant-based diets successful and accessible through food science, medicine, and new product developments.

Yet the consumption of meat has played an important role in human cultural and physiological development throughout the evolution of our species (Stanford 2001). Notably, individuals and various cultures far and wide continue to eat meat. To contextualize this, only 5 per cent of the world's population is vegetarian (Economist 2017). Given this trend, it is realistic that meat consumption will continue in some capacity for the foreseeable future (Zaraska 2016; Hodgson and Helvenston 2006; Winkelman 2010; Smil 2002). Consequently, to eliminate meat consumption would suggest dramatically changing deeply embedded practices that underpin everyday life, important cultural rituals, holiday feasts, and the livelihoods of countless people. As such, despite the ostensible ideal of universal vegetarianism, I call for the reader to imagine the deep cultural importance of meat across the world, and to consider why ending its consumption is not only challenging, but potentially damaging to the fundamental socio-cultural infrastructures of many people. For great numbers of people, consuming meat is a way of life that demonstrates responsibility to their community, to their environment, and to themselves (Fiddes 2004).

The question of whether humans *should* eat meat provokes strongly charged responses (Smil 2013; PETA n.d.; Cordain 2012; Eaton and Konner 1985). Captive between the debate are North American consumers, many of whom face a daily moral conflict: wanting or needing to consume meat, but harbouring anxieties about contributing to the unhealthy or unsustainable consequences of doing so. Such people struggle to find a reasonable middle approach that benefits their need to eat meat while supporting the health of the planet. This chapter considers whether there is an approach to meat consumption that is responsible. For example, is there a means to meat consumption that is environmentally sustainable, humane in its treatment to animals, and supports public health and the local economy? Is it possible to eat less meat while staying true to long-standing cultural traditions, relationships, and community? As both a scholar and consumer concerned with the effects of my decisions, my argument below is that meat consumption can be responsible. Of course, it is true that what constitutes "responsible" behaviour is highly subjective. Therefore, what follows is grounded in my own praxis-based research, education, and experience. I align this work with Wakefield's (2007) discussion of praxis that is connected to activism and an engagement in our everyday lives. Specifically, I draw upon the year I spent living strictly as a carnivore and immersing myself in the theories I was encountering about responsible meat production and consumption. The purpose of this chapter is to demonstrate the complexity of meat consumption and the agency of the consumer to make ethical choices. It provides a reflexive take on the challenges and opportunities one faces in one's exploration of responsible meat consumption and one's relationship to eating animals.

Thinking about Production, Delving into Praxis

Responsible meat consumption begins with an individual addressing concerns they have about the impacts of its production. Years ago, as an environmentally minded and animal-loving young person, I felt that the only way to show responsibility to the earth and its creatures was to become a vegan. I had seen *Supersize Me* (Spurlock 2004), read *Silent Spring* (Carson 2002), *Diet for a Small Planet* (Lappé 2010), and enough of *Adbusters* (n.d.) to be confident that there was a lot of unsettling activity in the food system that went undisclosed to consumers. I was also reasonably confident that there was not much I could do about it. If this was *the* way meat was produced, and I wanted to be a responsible consumer, what choice did I have but *not* to eat it?

A plant-centric lifestyle had a reputation for being the most earth-friendly choice for its various positive effects, such as its smaller carbon footprint, and the advantageous immuno-supportive properties of phytonutrients (Marlow et al. 2009; Leitzmann 2003). However, veganism posed a range of material and conceptual challenges for me, such as the uncertainty about whether synthetic alternatives like plastic leather were any better for the environment, or the unclear level at which killing became taboo (e.g., was killing plants, insects, or microbial organisms any less bad than killing animals?). And while a cornerstone of the vegan praxis was to abstain from consuming goods that caused suffering to animals, what of the human labour required to produce such goods? Were fellow humans (animals too, it seems important to remember) suffering in their efforts to fill my vegetarian plate in their exposure to unhealthy working environments, dismal pay, and emotional or psychological abuse (Reed 2013)? As a vegan, was I supposed to unquestionably oppose the captive possession of companion animals, and their euthanasia when old and sick? Was I to argue against wildlife conservation efforts that necessitated the culling of invasive or overpopulated species (Fearnley-Whittingstall 2004)? Lastly, did veganism evoke a sense of colonialism by identifying meat-eaters as lesser moral beings and issuing imperious directives (Reed 2013)?

As a vegan, I could not help but feel that by eating *around* meat, avoiding it, and pretending it was not there, I was similarly avoiding the greater issues which had originally deemed it destructive or unhealthy. It was an unavoidable reality that somewhere people would eat meat, many of whom were aware of its politics, and many of whom were not. I reasoned that there needed to be better choices for such people, and if there were already better choices, consumers deserved better accessibility to them so that everyone could actively contribute to a healthier, more sustainable, and more responsible food system – even carnivores.

A certain amount of awareness toward vegetarian recidivism had piqued my interest at this point as well. In the West, vegetarianism has a troubled reputation of gathering on-again/off-again supporters. This recidivism has been thought to occur for a number of different reasons (Norris 2014; Hecht 2011), from fears of social ostracization to nutritional deficits incurred by dietary mismanagement. Such frequent backsliding was enough to signal to me that I was not alone in experiencing the conflicts that arose from choosing *not* to eat meat. It also highlighted that such indecision itself was conflicted: people wanted good health, social acceptance, and to respect the environment. They just could not resolve the best way to do it.

Plenty of films and literature have exposed the generally destructive nature of industrialized meat production (the film *Food Inc.* [Kenner 2009] comes to mind). While such exposure indirectly pointed consumers toward some alternative, I felt that there was not enough focus on *how* to be an ethical consumer. I wanted to know more about alternative choices that could realistically be articulated, and what additional practices or information were needed to execute responsible meat consumption. This realization was the result of a year of praxis-based research that culminated in my master's thesis. Fundamentally, my observations of meat consumption were that, generally speaking, theory and action on the subject existed independently of each another. My approach sought to better unite the two, with emphasis on using the agency of individual consumers to do so. I sought to cultivate a unique type of activism that bridged daily life with scholarship and built a practice that was replicable for other consumers.

Because of this work, I decided to make my life about meat. My objective was to generate the most extensive understanding of the choices available for consumers by learning all I could about the human relationship with animal flesh, including how meat was produced. Mostly, I was interested in the choices that could foster healthy and sustainable relationships. My project included sourcing ethically minded producers and exploring how and why they considered themselves to be less harmful alternatives to industrial animal agriculture. I conducted interviews with these producers, visited slaughterhouses, and participated in the work where I was permitted. This included interning with local butcher shops, which even led to an apprenticeship in the trade following my degree.

I was also interested in learning more about the nutrition of meat to address the tensions around its reputation as "unhealthy" during my experiment. For this reason I ate a strictly carnivorous diet for approximately a year. Making meat a necessity of survival forced me to be mindful about the quality of my nutritional health, learning what meats would sustain me, how to cook them, and what was too much or unnecessary. The objective of my meat-centric diet was not to say that we needed more meat, but to question what was beneficial about eating meat, what was lacking, what amount of meat was extraneous, what amount was reasonable, and how to ethically satisfy the amount that might be needed. The culmination of my research was a deepened understanding of the complexity of meat and how we might approach its consumption and production more responsibly.

My approach started with reflection on what I was getting myself into – an assessment of the options available while weighing their potential outcomes. As such, I sought to observe the direct and indirect connections between myself and my meat so as to best quantify and understand what responsible choices were available given the geographical specificities of my situation. What I learned from this praxis-based approach was that, in the end, responsible behaviour isn't about making the *absolutely ideal* decision, it's about making the *best* decision as per one's unique situation and specific context.

Doing One's Homework, Making Informed Choices

My approach posed one ultimate question: What was responsible meat consumption? It was a broad, contentious query that involved some homework and introspection. It involved spending time researching who and what was directly connected to my meat choices: considering what animals, producers, consumers, and environments were affected, and asking how my actions could support their health and sustainability. Many consumers might object that there is not enough transparency in their food system to know how their decisions will affect such actors, and to make informed decisions. It is likewise important to recognize the conditions of consumers who are presented with extreme limitations – financial, geographical, or otherwise – that may delimit their choices. Such scenarios raise the question of whether exercising responsible consumer behaviour is indeed universally possible.

There will certainly be scenarios that exhibit an absence of responsible purchasing options. However, *responsible meat consumption* as a practice is not defined by the literal purchase of a meat product. It can be in fact that the most responsible choice is to choose something else – another product, another protein, another method of food acquisition – or to vocalize an opinion, or even do nothing at all.

While these limited situations pose difficulties for great numbers of people, such extremes show the need for greater transparency within North American food systems. They expose the prevalent obfuscation surrounding the conditions of food production, the often exiguous space many consumers have within which to act responsibly, and greater concerns such as food security and sovereignty present throughout the continent. In these circumstances, the fundamental question of whether or not responsible consumption is something everyone can exercise demands consideration. It summons us to evaluate our positions as consumers, and to exert and vocalize our right to food that supports our personal health and sustainability, as well as that of our environment and our community. Ultimately, this means doing the best we can do within our conditions; and it means that while many can vote for responsible behaviour with their dollar, others cannot.

Finding the most responsible choice in your unique situation first demands researching your eating/purchasing choices, and asking: Will my decision support the health and sustainability of the environment? In my experience with meat production, there was a consensus among ethically responsible producers that the environment comes first, and the rest follows (Gliessman 1990; Salatin 2011). Likeminded producers focused on a uniform understanding of the interdependency of their product and the environment. In other words, the health of one being affected the health of another, and so such producers were attentive to the nutritive stability of the surrounding environment so as to better ensure the health of their animals. Scholars have written at length about the mutually beneficial relationships between animals and their environment in farming scenarios. They have also written about how fostering a biodiverse habitat encourages a nutrient-dense and healthier ecosystem that can support itself with little human intervention, such as the use of potentially toxic synthetic pesticides (Carson 2002; Chappell and LaValle 2011; Mäder et al. 2002; Thrupp 2000; Tscharntke et al. 2012). In contrast, meat production methods that cause harm to the environment will result in nutritionally poor foods that produce unhealthy animals and unstable ecosystems (Cribb 2016).

Prioritizing finding meat producers who strive to build a robust environment via their hunting or farming practices is one characteristic of a responsible decision. This could involve supporting farmers who enable biodiversity by using integrated farming techniques that permit the earth's biophysical systems to replenish the nutrients in the soils, waters, and atmosphere (Tscharntke et al. 2012). It could also be sourcing from hunters who, by gathering only what is necessary to feed themselves and their families/communities, permit wild animal populations to replenish (Gadgil, Berkes, and Folke 1993; see also chapter 6). It could mean looking for packaging materials that are recyclable or biodegradable. One could seek producers who strive for a minimal carbon footprint through the use of renewable energy sources, or by implementing fully sustainable closed-loop systems, such as Australia's Blue Smart Farms (Blue Smart Farms 2018). One could also support cattle producers who take a holistic approach to grazing (see chapter 5). Many choices will not be comprehensively environmentally sustainable, and so consumers must ask themselves which choice is best – or whether the most responsible decision is to abstain from any purchase. Prioritizing the environment in one's approach to responsible meat consumption also makes the decisions that follow substantially easier, since what is healthy and sustainable for the environment is the same for the animals we eat and human consumers as well.

Supporting Healthy Animals, Thinking Compassionately

One might combine considerations of the environment with the health and sustainability of the animals harvested: Are they mutually supportive? Does the animal's environment permit its access to an existence that is naturally and biologically appropriate for its species? This includes considering the animal's freedom to move and exercise to their preferable capacity, their access to natural, untampered whole foods suitable to their physiology, access to shelter and activities, and freedom to breed when seasonally appropriate (Blokhuis et al. 2003; Fearnley-Whittingstall 2004; Ghione et al. 2013; Webster 2001). Animals who consume their natural diet of diverse grasses and forage digest with greater ease, consequently emit less greenhouse gas, and produce meat with denser and more diverse nutritional profiles (Daley et al. 2010; Niman 2004). It is also worth questioning whether the animal's environment permits them to grow and live at their own pace. Does

the environment invite fear or distress? Likewise, how is the health of
the surrounding environment affected by the presence of animals? Do
the waste or grazing habits of these animals overwhelm surrounding
ecosystems through excessive grazing and trampling, or do the livestock
provide just-adequate fertilization and have enough pasture-space to eat
from while allowing grasses to regrow (Fleischner 1994; D.R. Edwards
and Daniel 1992)?

A significant controversy surrounding meat production and
consumption is the slaughter of animals – a practice that is forever
contentious for different reasons in different cultures around the world
(Herzog 2010; Francione and Charlton 2013; Foer 2009; Pollan 2006).
From a personal place, my query into responsible meat consumption
stemmed from the idea that the hyper-commodification of meat, and
measures taken to shield consumers from the visceral reality of slaughter,
had eroded the link between *meat* and *animal* for these consumers. That
meat and *animal* should exist in unrelated isolation, I felt, subverted the
gravity of what it meant to eat meat by eliminating the crucial step that
came between them. For me, compassion for animals was not only to
love them for being alive, but to also respect them for being dead; that
death contributed to food and human survival, and as such, deserved
a certain reverence and attention to what it was. Here my approach to
activism was to attempt a deeper understanding of animal slaughter in
the most objective manner I could manage, which meant to observe and
see reason in as many facets of the conversation as possible.

Slaughter is almost always considered a resolutely harmful action,
and even the concepts of "compassionate killing," assisted dying, euthanasia, and humane slaughter are contested (Kapleau 1981; Rachels 1987;
Yeats 2010). Such discourse arguably renders the concept of compassionate animal slaughter an oxymoron. The word *humane* is often
used synonymously with compassion, and whether or not it is indeed
a benchmark for the most *thoughtful* form of killing, it also serves as a
reminder that we can only understand our efforts at compassion as far as
"humanly" possible. It reminds us that unless we could experience death
as another animal, we can only exert compassion in the ways we would
expect it to be given and received as humans. Paul Nadasdy (2007)
explores the concept of animal sentience and personhood from the
perspective of the Kluane people in his essay "The Gift in the Animal."
In their struggles with life and death in hunting they acknowledge other
animals as persons for this reason. Likewise, many farmers argue that
outfitting meat-animals with a life that allows them to freely exercise,
sleep, and eat when and how they desire; experience sociality with

members of their and other animal species; be routinely fed nutritious feed; and be sheltered from weather and predators is an enviable life that neither wild nor human animals could access. Such an observation urges us to consider whether providing animals a good life can justify killing them (Fearnley-Whittingstall 2013; Niman 2004; Reed 2013).

Nonetheless, recent concern for animal welfare has contributed to the creation of industry standards for what is considered humane animal slaughter, and thus given the latter term some objective, though contestable, conditions (Grandin 2010). Many writers on the subject argue that killing an animal oneself enlists a particular kind of empathy that helps in better evaluating the "humanity" of killing animals (Foer 2009; Pollan 2006; Lymbery 2014; Ozeki 1999; Gross 2018). It would seem that a deeper understanding of the experience of killing an animal enables us to make more responsible decisions as eaters. At the same time, one cannot rely on hearsay and text alone to understand what is humane or responsible. It becomes the consumer's responsibility to reflect on their relationship with animal slaughter, and to evaluate their personal ethos of killing and eating the flesh of another being. While reflection may seem cosmetic in light of such a serious procedure, I believe that a humane system begins with the consideration of the suffering of animals.

Labour and the Production Context

Understanding the circumstances of producers can help in creating a healthy and sustainable meat consumption/production ecosystem. In other words, your purchasing decision can ultimately support ethical or unethical production conditions, and it serves to be aware of which ones you are supporting. This involves researching the challenges faced by producers and what ultimately makes for a positive work environment. Meat production entails a great deal of people within its supply chain; knowing everyone's role and unique situation is therefore unrealistic. However, striving for better workplace policies across all industries is a matter of being more aware of the social dimensions underpinning the production process. Are there human rights issues within the system? Are workers being hired and treated with equality? One would like to imagine health in meat production outfits as reflected in the working environment itself. This would include the wellness of labourers safe from the use of hazardous or unnatural substances, unsanitary surroundings, or exposure to physically and psychologically damaging situations (Foer 2009; Dillard 2007). Observing the sustainability of producers, within the context of this chapter, means that workers are supported by appropriate pay for their time, their labour, and the resources used in their work.

To further this, it is important to recognize the historical struggle between producers and local communities, wages, land, resources, rights, and respect (La Via Campesina 2018). For example, multiple unfortunate conditions result from the aggressive purchasing of vast amounts of arable land by big agribusinesses – otherwise known as "land grabbing" (Cochrane 2011; Daniel 2011). Here, not only are small communities, nomadic tribes, and Indigenous peoples often stripped of their ancestral lands and native food sources – thus jeopardizing their food security and sovereignty – but monoculture crops end up devastating the biodiversity and health of local environments (Thrupp 2000; Tscharntke et al. 2012). "Big AG" certainly does employ farmers to work their crops; however, the use of cheap resources combined with the large scale of industrial production permits such businesses to sell their product cheaply while paying workers minimally. This subjects farm workers to poverty without an adequate way to leave the industry to find other work (Lobao 1990). Joel Salatin has written as a farmer about the often unrealistic and destructive conditions faced by industrial farmers with many tongue-in-cheek publications, such as *Everything I Want to Do Is Illegal* (2007). Ultimately, while it may cost more to purchase meat produced by independent farmers, it is a huge support for the rights of famers everywhere.

Conscious Eating, Avoiding Waste

Living carnivorously forced me to learn how to use meat to sustain my body. This provided me a renewed perspective on the nutritive qualities of different meat cuts, different animals, different fats, different proteins, and even different cooking techniques (Health Canada 2016; McGee 2007; Williams 2007). Health and sustainability were not acquired by simply eating steak every night. They were attained through consuming a variety of meats that collectively supplied the nutrition needed to sustain me. Various studies have substantiated the traditional knowledge of focally carnivorous Indigenous communities worldwide, showing that raw meat provides many vitamins otherwise obtained from plants, and that fat serves as a powerful source of energy (Fediuk et al. 2002; Pereira and Vicente 2013). As such, a carnivorous diet could provide all the necessary vitamins, minerals, proteins, and energy needed to survive (Stefansson 2016), but it requires attention to a variety of meats that fall outside of conventional supermarket staples. Steaks and similarly lean meats like skinless chicken breast are indeed excellent sources of protein, vitamin B12, and iron (Pereira and Vicente 2013), but compared to nutrient-dense organ meats, steaks and chicken breasts were simply inadequate for nutrition as dietary staples.

Organ meats were the most important products on my plate. Though initially unattractive, it is my belief that a conscious eater will come to love offal (that is, the liver, heart, and other organs of an animal). Fortunately, when I undertook my project I was living in a small rural town in Italy where meat was a proud fixture in local fare, and there were many butcher shops that sold organ meats. Offal-focused dishes were plentiful, as they were traditional in the area. I was easily persuaded to the ways of consuming organ meats, charcuterie, and raw sausage thanks to the helpful recipes and suggestions of my friends and neighbours. There, offal was a delicious and everyday meal. It was affordable and easy to find, talk about, cook, and serve. I can fondly recall a meal with friends, surrounded by their children and grandchildren, all eating tripe soup, and sucking the marrow from bones with pleasure.

Offal is an uncommon item in North American supermarkets, with a reputation for triggering disgust and hesitation. Restaurants featuring offal are often considered avant-garde. Those who eat offal are often considered bold or anachronistic (N. Edwards 2013). Animal by-products, principally offal, account for roughly 30–44 per cent of carcass weight in pigs and cattle. If the by-products are not used in pharmaceuticals, pet foods, or textiles, they are simply disposed of (American Meat Science Association 2015). Likewise, the meat cutting industry produces a lot of "leftovers" and "off-cuts" that are difficult to market and sell, which consequently become further components of this waste (C. Walsh 2014). The stigma surrounding the buying and selling of organ meats, as well as the enormous amount of wasted offal, ultimately calls attention to the problematic attitudes North Americans bring to respective animal products over others. Essentially, it is a somewhat puzzling endeavour to enlist such great amounts of time, money, and resources to grow steer, pig, or poultry in entirety, only to harvest a limited section of their bodies. It is especially tragic that the offal that is wasted is not only delicious, but full of valuable nutrition. Perhaps the rate of meat production could be reduced if we raise animals for better-quality meat, so we can eat more of the animal bodies we raise, and learn to enjoy offal. This could also result in a more conscientious use of resources, which would lead to a more sustainable meat production system that is healthier to boot. This has been Slow Food's ethos toward meat for a long time now (Slow Food 2015).

Conclusion

One's decision to eat meat has a significant impact on many things: labour, time, resources, life, death. This makes the path to responsible consumption all at once controversial, optimistic, disheartening, clear, and confusing. The actors and systems discussed here demonstrate the incredible thing it is to consume meat as we do in North America. It is staggering to realize the vast network on which we are dependent to source the food we eat. Producers, consumers, animals, and environments aside, this chapter only touches on the complex set of key intermediaries involved in selling meat, such as distributors, drivers, marketers, designers, and retailers. Is it even possible to be accountable for every process, every actor, every detail? Probably not, but that is precisely the point of this chapter. The scope of meat production has become so large that we no longer feel able to take responsibility for our food choices. Issues of health and sustainability feel beyond the reach of consumer choice. However, there are a few remaining ways to be responsible that I have detailed above – all of which are orchestrated by holding fast to one's right to choose access to healthy food. There are more than 7 billion of us. Even if everyone made one step toward responsible meat consumption, that's more than 7 billion paces forward.

References

Adbusters. n.d. "Adbusters Media Foundation: Journal of the Mental Environment." Accessed 27 November 2018. https://www.adbusters.org/.

American Meat Science Association. 2015. "What Are Animal Byproducts?" 20 November 2015. https://meatscience.org/TheMeatWeEat/topics/raising-animals-for-meat/article/2015/11/20/what-are-animal-byproducts.

Berton, Pierre. 1988. *The Arctic Grail: The Quest for the North West Passage and the North Pole, 1818–1909*. New York: Viking.

Blokhuis, H.J., R.B. Jones, R. Geers, M. Miele, and I. Veissier. 2003. "Measuring and Monitoring Animal Welfare: Transparency in the Food Product Quality Chain." *Animal Welfare* 12 (4): 445–55.

Blue Smart Farms. 2018. "Blue Smart Farms." http://www.bluesmartfarms.com/.

Carson, Rachel. 2002. *Silent Spring*. Boston, MA: Houghton Mifflin Harcourt.

Chappell, Michael Jahi, and Liliana A. LaValle. 2011. "Food Security and Biodiversity: Can We Have Both? An Agroecological Analysis." *Agriculture and Human Values* 28 (1): 3–26. https://doi.org/10.1007/s10460-009-9251-4.

Cochrane, Logan. 2011. "Food Security or Food Sovereignty: The Case of Land Grabs." *The Journal of Humanitarian Assistance*, 5 July 2011. https://sites.tufts.edu/jha/archives/1241.

Cordain, Loren. 2012. AARP *The Paleo Diet Revised: Lose Weight and Get Healthy by Eating the Foods You Were Designed to Eat*. Hoboken, NJ: John Wiley and Sons.

Cribb, Julian. 2016. *Surviving the 21st Century: Humanity's Ten Great Challenges and How We Can Overcome Them*. Cham, Switzerland: Springer.

Daley, Cynthia A., Amber Abbott, Patrick S. Doyle, Glenn A. Nader, and Stephanie Larson. 2010. "A Review of Fatty Acid Profiles and Antioxidant Content in Grass-Fed and Grain-Fed Beef." *Nutrition Journal* 9 (March, article 10). https://doi.org/10.1186/1475-2891-9-10.

Daniel, Shepard. 2011. "Land Grabbing and Potential Implications for World Food Security." In *Sustainable Agricultural Development: Recent Approaches in Resources Management and Environmentally-Balanced Production Enhancement*, edited by Mohamed Behnassi, Shabbir A. Shahid, and Joyce D'Silva, 25–42. Dordrecht: Springer Netherlands. https://doi.org/10.1007/978-94-007-0519-7_2.

Dillard, Jennifer. 2007. "A Slaughterhouse Nightmare: Psychological Harm Suffered by Slaughterhouse Employees and the Possibility of Redress through Legal Reform." SSRN Scholarly Paper ID 1016401. Rochester, NY: Social Science Research Network. https://papers.ssrn.com/abstract=1016401.

Eaton, S. Boyd, and Melvin Konner. 1985. "Paleolithic Nutrition." *New England Journal of Medicine* 312 (5): 283–9. https://doi.org/10.1056/NEJM198501313120505.

The Economist. 2017. "What Percentage of the World Is Vegetarian?" https://www.youtube.com/watch?v=oFGqGpJrIs8.

Edwards, D.R., and T.C. Daniel. 1992. "Environmental Impacts of On-Farm Poultry Waste Disposal – A Review." *Bioresource Technology* 41 (1): 9–33. https://doi.org/10.1016/0960-8524(92)90094-E.

Edwards, Nina. 2013. *Offal: A Global History*. London: Reaktion Books.

Fearnley-Whittingstall, Hugh, and Simon Wheeler. *The River Cottage Meat Book*. London: Hodder and Stoughton, 2004.

Fediuk, Karen, Nick Hidiroglou, René Madère, and Harriet V. Kuhnlein. 2002. "Vitamin C in Inuit Traditional Food and Women's Diets." *Journal of Food Composition and Analysis* 15 (3): 221–35. https://doi.org/10.1006/jfca.2002.1053.

Fiddes, Nick. 2004. *Meat: A Natural Symbol*. Boston, MA: Routledge.

Fleischner, Thomas L. 1994. "Ecological Costs of Livestock Grazing in Western North America." *Conservation Biology* 8 (3): 629–44.

Foer, Jonathan Safran. 2010. *Eating Animals*. Boston, MA: Little, Brown.

Francione, Gary Lawrence, and Anna E. Charlton. 2013. *Eat Like You Care: An Examination of the Morality of Eating Animals*. New York: Exempla Press.

Gadgil, Madhav, Fikret Berkes, and Carl Folke. 1993. "Indigenous Knowledge for Biodiversity Conservation." *Ambio* 22 (2/3): 151–6.

Ghione, Jacopo, Anne Marie Matarrese, Raffaella Ponzio, and Piero Sardo. 2013. "Slow Food Policy Paper on Animal Welfare: A Survey of European Slow Food Members." Bra, Italy: Slow Food Foundation for Biodiversity. https://www.slowfood.com/sloweurope/wp-content/uploads/ING_sondaggio_benessere.pdf.

Ghosh, Pallab. 2013. "World's First Lab-Grown Burger Eaten." BBC.com. 5 August 2013. https://www.bbc.com/news/science-environment-23576143.

Gliessman, S.R. (1990). "Agroecology: Researching the Ecological Basis for Sustainable Agriculture." In *Agroecology*, 3–10. New York: Springer.

Godfray, H. Charles J., John R. Beddington, Ian R. Crute, Lawrence Haddad, David Lawrence, James F. Muir, Jules Pretty, Sherman Robinson, Sandy M. Thomas, and Camilla Toulmin. 2010. "Food Security: The Challenge of Feeding 9 Billion People." *Science* 327 (5967): 812–18. https://doi.org/10.1126/science.1185383.

Grandin, Temple. 2010. "Auditing Animal Welfare at Slaughter Plants." *Meat Science* 86 (1): 56–65. https://doi.org/10.1016/j.meatsci.2010.04.022.

Gross, Terry. 2018. "Food Writer Becomes a Butcher to Better Understand the Value of Meat." NPR.org. 24 July 2018. https://www.npr.org/sections/thesalt/2018/07/24/631845582/food-writer-becomes-a-butcher-to-better-understand-the-value-of-meat.

Health Canada. 2008. *Nutrient Value of Some Common Foods*. Ottawa, ON: Health Canada. https://www.canada.ca/en/health-canada/services/food-nutrition/healthy-eating/nutrient-data/nutrient-value-some-common-foods-booklet.html.

Hecht, Jaime Deborah. 2011. "The Vegetarian Social Movement: An Analysis of Withdrawal and Backsliding." MA thesis, Florida State University, Orlando. https://stars.library.ucf.edu/etd/2049.

Herzog, Hal. 2010. *Some We Love, Some We Hate, Some We Eat: Why It's So Hard to Think Straight About Animals*. New York: Harper Collins.

Hodgson, Derek, and Patricia A. Helvenston. 2006. "The Emergence of the Representation of Animals in Palaeoart: Insights from Evolution and the Cognitive, Limbic and Visual Systems of the Human Brain." *Rock Art Research* 23 (1): 3–40.

Kapleau, Phillip. 1981. *To Cherish All Life: A Buddhist View of Animal Slaughter and Meat Eating*. Rochester, NY: Zen Centre.

Kenner, Robert. 2009. *Food, Inc.* http://www.imdb.com/title/tt1286537/.

La Via Campesina. 2018. "Via Campesina – Globalizing Hope, Globalizing the Struggle!" Via Campesina English. https://viacampesina.org/en/.

Lappé, Frances Moore. 2010. *Diet for a Small Planet: The Book That Started a Revolution in the Way Americans Eat*. New York: Random House Publishing Group.

Latour, Bruno. 2005. *Reassembling the Social: An Introduction to Actor-Network-Theory*. Oxford: OUP.

Leitzmann, Claus. 2003. "Nutrition Ecology: The Contribution of Vegetarian Diets." *The American Journal of Clinical Nutrition* 78 (3, supplement): 657S–9S. https://doi.org/10.1093/ajcn/78.3.657S.

Lobao, Linda M. 1990. *Locality and Inequality: Farm and Industry Structure and Socioeconomic Conditions*. Albany, NY: SUNY Press.

Lymbery, Philip. 2014. *Farmageddon: The True Cost of Cheap Meat*. London: Bloomsbury.

Machovina, Brian, Kenneth J. Feeley, and William J. Ripple. 2015. "Biodiversity Conservation: The Key Is Reducing Meat Consumption." *Science of the Total Environment* 536 (December): 419–31. https://doi.org/10.1016/j.scitotenv.2015.07.022.

Mäder, Paul, Andreas Fliessbach, David Dubois, Lucie Gunst, Padruot Fried, and Urs Niggli. 2002. "Soil Fertility and Biodiversity in Organic Farming." *Science* 296 (5573): 1694–7. https://doi.org/10.1126/science.1071148.

Marlow, Harold J., William K. Hayes, Samuel Soret, Ronald L. Carter, Ernest R. Schwab, and Joan Sabaté. 2009. "Diet and the Environment: Does What You Eat Matter?" *American Journal of Clinical Nutrition* 89 (5): 1699S–1703S. https://doi.org/10.3945/ajcn.2009.26736Z.

McGee, Harold. 2007. *On Food and Cooking: The Science and Lore of the Kitchen*. New York: Simon and Schuster.

Nadasdy, Paul. 2007. "The Gift in the Animal: The Ontology of Hunting and Human-Animal Sociality." *American Ethnologist* 34 (1): 25–43.

Niman, Nicolette Hahn. *Defending Beef: The Case for Sustainable Meat Production*. Chelsea, VT: Chelsea Green, 2014.

Norris, Jack. 2014. "Humane Research Council Survey on Vegetarian Recidivism." *Vegan Outreach* (blog). 15 December 2014. https://veganoutreach.org/humane-research-council-survey-on-vegetarian-recidivism/.

Ozeki, Ruth L. 1999. *My Year of Meats*. London: Penguin.

Pereira, Paula Manuela de Castro Cardoso, and Ana Filipa dos Reis Baltazar Vicente. 2013. "Meat Nutritional Composition and Nutritive Role in the Human Diet." *Meat Science* 93 (3): 586–92. https://doi.org/10.1016/j.meatsci.2012.09.018.

PETA. n.d. "People for the Ethical Treatment of Animals (PETA): The Largest Animal Rights Organization in the World." PETA. Accessed 27 November 2018. https://www.peta.org/.

Pollan, Michael. 2006. *The Omnivore's Dilemma: A Natural History of Four Meals*. London: Penguin.

Poore, J., and T. Nemecek. 2018. "Reducing Food's Environmental Impacts through Producers and Consumers." *Science* 360 (6392): 987–92. https://doi.org/10.1126/science.aaq0216.

Preece, Rod. 2009. *Sins of the Flesh: A History of Ethical Vegetarian Thought*. Vancouver: UBC Press.

Rachels, James. 1987. "The End of Life: Euthanasia and Morality." *Ethics* 97 (4): 878–9.

Reed, Berlin. 2013. *The Ethical Butcher: How Thoughtful Eating Can Change Your World*. New York: Soft Skull Press.

Salatin, Joel. 2007. *Everything I Want to Do Is Illegal*. Swope, VA: Polyface.

– 2011. *Folks, This Ain't Normal: A Farmer's Advice for Happier Hens, Healthier People, and a Better World*. New York: Center Street.

Slow Food. 2015. "Slow Meat." *Slow Food International* (blog). https://www.slowfood.com/what-we-do/themes/slow-meat/.

Smil, Vaclav. 2002. "Eating Meat: Evolution, Patterns, and Consequences." *Population and Development Review* 28 (4): 599–639. https://doi.org/10.1111/j.1728-4457.2002.00599.x.

– 2013. *Should We Eat Meat? Evolution and Consequences of Modern Carnivory*. Hoboken, NJ: John Wiley and Sons.

Spencer, Colin. 2002. *Vegetarianism: A History*. New York: Four Walls Eight Windows.

Spurlock, Morgan. 2004. *Super Size Me*. http://www.imdb.com/title/tt0390521/.

Stanford, Craig B. 2001. *The Hunting Apes: Meat Eating and the Origins of Human Behavior*. Princeton, NJ: Princeton University Press.

Stefansson, Vilhjalmur. 2016. *The Fat of the Land*. London: Macmillan.

Thrupp, Lori Ann. 2000. "Linking Agricultural Biodiversity and Food Security: The Valuable Role of Agrobiodiversity for Sustainable Agriculture." *International Affairs* 76 (2): 283–97. https://doi.org/10.1111/1468-2346.00133.

Tscharntke, Teja, Yann Clough, Thomas C. Wanger, Louise Jackson, Iris Motzke, Ivette Perfecto, John Vandermeer, and Anthony Whitbread. 2012. "Global Food Security, Biodiversity Conservation and the Future of Agricultural Intensification." *Biological Conservation* (Advancing Environmental Conservation: Essays in Honor of Navjot) 151 (1): 53–9. https://doi.org/10.1016/j.biocon.2012.01.068.

Wakefield, Sarah E.L. 2007. "Reflective Action in the Academy: Exploring Praxis in Critical Geography Using a 'Food Movement' Case Study." *Antipode* 39 (2): 331–54. https://doi.org/10.1111/j.1467-8330.2007.00524.x.

Walker, Polly, Pamela Rhubart-Berg, Shawn McKenzie, Kristin Kelling, and Robert S. Lawrence. 2005. "Public Health Implications of Meat Production and Consumption." *Public Health Nutrition* 8 (4): 348–56.

Walsh, Bryan. 2013. "The Triple Whopper Environmental Impact of
    Global Meat Production." *Time*, 16 December 2013. http://science.time.
    com/2013/12/16/the-triple-whopper-environmental-impact-of-global-
    meat-production/.
Walsh, Christine. 2014. "The Use of Animal By-Products." EBLEX,
    May 2014, 74.
Webster, A.J. 2001. "Farm Animal Welfare: The Five Freedoms and the Free
    Market." *Veterinary Journal* 161 (3): 229–37. https://doi.org/10.1053/
    tvjl.2000.0563.
Williams, Peter. 2007. "Nutritional Composition of Red Meat." *Nutrition &
    Dietetics* 64 S113–19. https://doi.org/10.1111/j.1747-0080.2007.00197.x.
Winkelman, Michael. 2010. *Shamanism: A Biopsychosocial Paradigm of
    Consciousness and Healing*. Santa Barbara, CA: ABC-CLIO.
Yeates, J. (2010). "Ethical Aspects of Euthanasia of Owned Animals."
    In Practice, 32 (2): 70–3.
Zaraska, Marta. 2016. *Meathooked: The History and Science of Our 2.5-Million-
    Year Obsession with Meat*. New York: Basic Books.

8

A Feminist Multi-Species Approach to Green Meat

Gwendolyn Blue

No community works ... without eating together.
This is not a moral point, but a factual, semiotic,
and material one that has consequences.

Donna Haraway 2008, 294

Introduction

Following a presentation that I gave to a local scientific organization on the importance of interpretive frameworks for how we collectively respond to climate change, I was approached by an audience member who chastised me for neglecting to consider the role of meat consumption as a significant source of greenhouse gas emissions. He asked pointedly: If scientists truly care about climate change, should not they advocate that people stop eating meat and especially beef?

His provocation is understandable given efforts – such as the United Nations Food and Agriculture Organization's report *Livestock's Long Shadow* (Steinfeld 2006), the promotion of numerous climate-friendly diets (Geagan 2009; Heyhoe 2009; Harrington 2008; Wellesley, Froggat, and Happer 2015), popular documentary films such as Kip Anderson's *Cowspiracy* (2014), and recent policy recommendations from the Intergovernmental Panel on Climate Change (ipcc) (Schiermeier 2019) – to link the consumption of meat and particularly red meat to anthropogenic climate change. In various ways, these interventions respond to the unsustainable nature of the dominant resource-intensive global food system by highlighting the significant although often overlooked role of individual diets in global environmental change (Clapp 2013; Weis 2015).

While I am supportive of individual and collective efforts to connect consumption to health and environmental sustainability, my concern lies with the conceptual limitations and political implications of recommendations that posit a reduction in meat consumption as a solution for climate change. In part, this concern stems from an interpretive framework – defined here as a shared way of making sense of the world – on which such recommendations typically rest. Framing is a normal and inescapable part of communication. While framing cannot be avoided, taking into consideration a range of different frames and worldviews can assist with decision-making by opening multiple avenues for action (Blue 2015). One dominant frame that is shared by policy-makers, scientists, activists, and citizens alike positions climate change as a global environmental problem defined in terms of quantitative GHG emissions. While linking individual diets with global processes can make the unwieldy scale of global climate change easy to understand and digest, the solutions offered, such as "eat less meat to save the planet," can be reductionist and, in some cases, politically and ethically problematic. As environmental lawyer turned cattle rancher Nicolette Hahn Niman puts it, "efforts to minimize greenhouse gases need to be much more sophisticated than just making blanket condemnations of certain foods" (Niman 2009; see also Niman 2014).

Alternative interpretive frameworks that move beyond a metrics-oriented understanding of and response to the challenges of climate change are available and have already been applied to issues such as climate governance (Bee, Rice, and Trauger 2015) and food sovereignty (Martens et al. 2016). Central to these efforts is a recognition that human and non-human species and the environments they inhabit are constitutive of and constituted by continuous dynamic interactions that are not captured by static quantitative metrics. Feminist interventions in particular have productively opened climate change to multiple perspectives and values, making possible a range of holistic approaches to promote justice and well-being (Bee, Rice, and Trauger 2015; Haraway 2015; Isreal and Sachs 2012). Drawing on these insights, this chapter proposes a framework that puts meat consumption and climate change into broader contexts. This framework seeks a "multispecies ecojustice, which can also embrace diverse human people" (Haraway 2015, 161). A key feature of this framework is the recognition that consumption is an inescapable feature of living (Haraway 2008). Elsewhere, I have referred to a multi-species approach to human-environment interactions as "gastro-ethical encounters," a contextual, place-based, pragmatic, and inherently messy ethical stance that acknowledges three inescapable conditions: humans need to eat, as do other living creatures; we eat in multi-species environments composed of different entities with conflicting tastes and bodily requirements; and eating and killing are intimately entangled, as are life and death (Blue 2006; Blue and Alexander 2015, 150–1). Although some feminist perspectives advocate for an animal-free diet (Adams 2015), the relational approach outlined in this chapter engages the tensions or, to use Haraway's terminology, "troubles" associated with consumption. Thinking relationally is a subtle but profound challenge to mainstream ways of approaching environmental issues, as it "requires us to ask much more about and elaborate in detail the specific mechanisms of connection that prevail in particular times and places" (Head 2008, 376). The goal of such experimental imaginings is to foster innovative connections and locate potential pathways for change (Gibson-Graham 2011).

This chapter first outlines the limitations of a metrics-oriented, quantitative frame of climate change and highlights how a feminist multi-species approach can provide an important counterbalance. Drawing on my own situated and necessarily provisional experiences with the production and consumption of beef, the next section provides an example of the dynamics, perspectives, and values that encompass the challenges inherent in advancing a multi-species framework to inform climate change responses. To conclude, I examine what stakes are raised by multi-species lines of questioning that unsettle reductionist ways of approaching climate change and entrenched divisions between nature-culture and humans-animals.

A Feminist Multi-Species Approach to Meat Consumption and Climate Change

Climate change belongs to a class of policy problems – including ozone depletion and biodiversity loss – that are typically framed as global in scale where the driving forces are invisible to the naked eye but are rendered materially real and politically tractable through science and technology. This dominant approach to climate change privileges statistical forms of reasoning over the ways in which people historically and culturally have made sense of environmental change (Demeritt 2006; Hulme 2009; Isreal and Sachs 2012; Taylor and Buttel 1992). Framing climate change as an inherently global issue subsumes complex social and ecological relations into elements, such as carbon dioxide and methane, that are quantifiable. While this approach enables a comparison of emissions across industries and regions, and in turn allows people to conceptualize the relationship between something as mundane as meat consumption and something as complicated as global warming, it has several practical limitations.

First, the focus on GHG emissions privileges technical experts who are ultimately positioned as the ones to determine which sectors, practices, and bodies are normal and which ones require correction (Ripple et al. 2013). Not only are the values and assumptions that experts bring to their analysis typically shielded from public scrutiny, the people who represent the sectors that are deemed problematic – in this case food systems – have not historically played a role in shaping climate policy. As such, their values, perspectives, and knowledge are not incorporated into the ways in which climate change is conceptualized and addressed in collective and individual decision-making.

Second, a global discourse of climate change conceals the uneven geographies of GHG emissions by removing them from the social contexts that produce and give them meaning. As early critics of the global climate regime argued, statistical approaches to GHG emissions hide, normalize, and ultimately reproduce unequal social relations (Agarwal and Narain 1991). Tensions between the universalism of a global statistical gaze and the particularity of regional, place-based practices are apparent when meat consumption is linked to climate change. For instance, while globally the consumption of red meat might be on the rise, this is not necessarily the case regionally. In Canada, beef consumption has declined over the past four decades due in large part to health and environmental concerns among consumers (Blue 2008, 2009). According to data from Statistics Canada, the per capita consumption of beef dropped from approximately 39 kilograms in 1980 to 24 kilograms in 2015, whereas the consumption of other forms of protein such as poultry increased over this same period (Agriculture and AgriFood Canada 2011). This data raises several questions, including why the consumption of red meat is disproportionately targeted as a problem in relation to other forms of animal-based protein. In turn, a focus on diet and consumption promotes individualistic responses to climate change that can divert attention away from the structural forces that drive emissions, such as state commitments to increasing economic growth and productivity through global agricultural trade (Paterson and Stripple 2014).

A third limitation of a global, quantitative frame of climate change lies with the ways in which it facilitates the depoliticization of environmental issues by pushing aside factors such as identity, meaning, and culture. People have deeply rooted cultural, emotional, material, and historical ties with the foods they produce and consume and with the animals and plants that provide food to eat. These ties are not readily nor necessarily wisely severed, and efforts to reduce GHG emissions through a focus on consumption should take these place-based relations into account.

A feminist multi-species perspective provides an important counter-balance to this dominant frame of climate change and its tendency to privilege statistical forms of analysis which ultimately serve to depolit-icize environmental change by removing GHG emissions from their contexts of production and consumption. The political, ecological, and ethical vantage point of a feminist multi-species frame begins with relations on the ground and in the flesh. It links the personal with the epistemological and the political, and situates the abstractions given by scientific and technical experts in their geographical, cultural, and historical contexts. Science is positioned as a powerful institution that – in some instances – can constrain collective decision-making to its tacit assumptions and values.

Central to a feminist multi-species perspective are efforts to challenge human exceptionalism – the tendency to position humans as distinct from and better than all other life on earth. *Homo sapiens* are one of millions of species on earth, each unique and exceptional in its own way. In response to human-induced climate change, many species are changing across various scales – at the level of the gene, the body, and the population (Scheffers et al. 2016). Species distribution modelling suggests that as global temperatures rise and existing habitats become less suitable for the organisms that currently occupy them, species will need to adapt, move, or face extinction (Synes et al. 2015). Existing practices and policies will have direct and indirect effects on the capacity of various species to adapt to climatic changes.

While feminist multi-species scholarship draws insight from the ecological sciences, it diverges in important ways. Scientific narra-tives of climate change and biodiversity loss often reinforce dualistic separations between nature and culture, in part a result of a deeply ingrained belief that the natural sciences speak for nature in ways that circumvent the politics of representation (Latour 2004). Rather than positioning nature and culture as separate, a feminist multi-species approach views these realms as relational, mutually reinforcing, and co-constitutive (Haraway 2008). In turn, while scientific methodolo-gies typically assume a separation between the subjects and objects of research, critical autobiography is a central part of feminist epistemol-ogy, as lived, subjective experience is considered an important aspect of feminist politics and ethics. In this regard, feminist epistemologies share similarities with Indigenous methodologies insofar as an explicit acknowledgement of how researchers are located in the research they do is significant (Martens et al. 2016).

A feminist multispecies perspective reframes the ethics and politics of meat consumption and climate change by locating "us" – broadly defined – decidedly within socio-ecological relations. The default assumption is that humans and non-humans are interconnected and co-constitute the world. As such, agency is not limited to human actors but is distributed across a range of bodies and entities. The result is a situated, embodied, and inherently fraught engagement with the "species assemblages" that make up what is otherwise called society and environment (Haraway 2008, 289). Here, the meanings given to species and the boundaries that separate groupings are not assumed in advance. As with other categories such as gender and race, the concept of species does not pre-exist its linguistic and social enactment in the world. For Haraway (2008; 2015), human evolution and development emerged in the context of cohabitation with "companion species," a term she coined to capture the ongoing processes of distinction and boundary-making that characterize provisional but influential formations of kin and kind. As Haraway intends it, "companion species" is an expansive term that encompasses a range of biotic creatures including plants, animals, and microbes, as well as abiotic elements such as greenhouse gases. For instance, in stating that "every species is a multispecies crowd" (2008, 165), Haraway signals the complex relations and interconnections among species, particularly at a genetic level, where the transfer and sharing of the basic material of life disrupts notions of clean separations, distinctions, and hierarchies. In turn, the concept of companion species acknowledges that lives are made and undone through the inseparable acts of eating and killing. Haraway insists that it is through the mundane, quotidian practices of producing, procuring, distributing, and consuming food that we contribute to processes that constitute identities and collective worlds.

Resisting moral dogmatism, epistemological monism, and facile consensus as desirable outcomes, Haraway encourages a commitment to "nourishing indigestion" by attending to divergent and irreconcilable views and practices that warrant respect but not necessarily resolution (2008, 299). As she states, taking divergent claims and practices centrally and seriously has the potential to "draw us into the world, make us care, and open up political imaginations and commitments" (2008, 300). The purpose of such an agonistic political stance is to envision new forms of world-making and kinship that avoid repeating the injustices of the past. The overarching intent of this political vision is to "stay with the trouble" of eating, killing, disagreeing, thriving, surviving, and dying on an increasingly depleted and damaged planet (Haraway 2015).

Situating Meat Consumption and Climate Change in a Feminist Multi-Species Framework

To offer a provisional example of what a feminist multi-species approach to (en)tangled questions about meat consumption and climate change entails, I turn to my current habitat (southern Alberta, Treaty 7 land, South Saskatchewan River Basin). Biogeographically, the climate of the semi-arid short grass prairies of southern Alberta is characterized by low precipitation, high winds, and extreme temperatures. This eco-cultural landscape has been indelibly shaped by ruminants and the creatures, human and otherwise, that eat them. My family has occupied this region for four generations, arriving as part of government-orchestrated resettlements of Europeans in the late-nineteenth century and drawing sustenance over the years largely from ranching, farming, and coal mining. My familial ties to cattle ranching have nurtured in me sufficient theoretical and ethical indigestion about the politics of meat consumption and production. While I recognize the value of cattle ranching for rural communities and while I enjoy the taste of bovine flesh, I am persuaded by the insights of those whose critical sensibilities and love of animals leads them to oppose meat-eating and livestock production (Adams 2015; Probyn-Ramsey 2015).

Delving into regional socio-natural politics reveals that grazing patterns in this part of the world have changed substantially over the past centuries, reflecting changes in human occupation of the land. Archeological evidence suggests that the transition from the icy Pleistocene to the inter-glacial Holocene was characterized by large-scale ecological transformation, as mammoths and mastodons went extinct; animals such as horses, camels, and sloths disappeared from the region; oxen moved further north; and existing bison populations were reduced to half the size of Pleistocene species (Kehoe 2017). Some claim that the First Peoples known to occupy what is now called the Canadian Prairies immigrated from Asia across the Bering Strait, although this claim is challenged by Indigenous scholars who argue for a more comprehensive analysis of ancestry and migration (Sterritt 2018). Regardless of origins, for centuries the material, cultural, and spiritual lives of these First Peoples were tied with bison. The use of fire as land management kept forests at bay and ensured productive grasslands as food for the vast bison populations that roamed the region (Isenberg 2000).

European exploration, colonization, and settlement led to other large-scale transformations in grazing patterns and land use. In the 1600s, the adoption of the horse, reintroduced to North America by Spanish settlers, increased the mobility of Indigenous and non-Indigenous peoples, and reshaped the ecological and political landscapes accordingly (Isenberg 2000). As European explorers and railways penetrated the Canadian and American West, eastern markets opened for bison hides and bones. Materially and symbolically, the treaty-making processes of the 1870s and the Canadian Dominions Lands Act of 1872 opened the grasslands to homesteaders and facilitated the segregation of Indigenous peoples onto reservations. As new settlers fenced and plowed the grasslands to fuel the economic engines of the global settler-colonial food regime (Friedman 2005) and the emerging nation-state of Canada, the migratory routes of the bison and the peoples who hunted them were significantly disrupted. By the late 1880s, bison populations were diminished to near extinction due to a combination of factors including targeted government policy, unregulated hunting, competition with domesticated grazers such as cattle and horses, and the fragmentation of habitat (Daschuk 2013). Settler colonialism in Canada institutionalized racism at the state level, facilitating the cultural genocide of Indigenous and Métis peoples (Mackey 2016). These interactions had dramatic and tragic implications for the ecological and cultural web of relations that sustained the region for centuries. The effects of this state-endorsed genocide continue to this day as the disappearance of the bison also dramatically shifted the relations between Indigenous groups and the state. As James Daschuk describes in his historical account of the Canadian Prairies, the slaughter of the bison and the depletion of food resources for Indigenous peoples was nothing short of a "state-sponsored attack on indigenous communities" whose effects "haunt us as a nation still" (2013, 186). The signing of the treaties themselves was viewed strategically by Indigenous leaders as "a bridge to a future without bison," and a transition to a difficult future of farming and ranching to avoid further food insecurity for Indigenous peoples (ibid., 21).

Over the past century, domesticated cattle have become the dominant grazer in the region. Currently, most of Canada's beef cattle are raised and processed in southern Alberta, which also houses the nation's largest cattle feeding networks and processing plants. Much of this production goes for export to the United States, Europe, and Asia. The beef industry is divided into two sectors: the agricultural sector, consisting of small-scale producers (farmers and ranchers), and the agribusiness sector, comprising feed lots, slaughterhouses, packing houses, chemical industries, marketing divisions, and retail outlets. As I have explored in more detail elsewhere (Blue 2008), ranchers and farmers are a small and increasingly vulnerable sector of the beef industry. The trend in Alberta and elsewhere in Canada is towards consolidation in the agricultural sector, resulting in larger but fewer farms. Ranchers and farmers suffer the vagaries not only of weather but also of land and commodity prices, and bear a disproportionate amount of the costs and risks associated with export-driven agricultural markets.

Throughout the twentieth century, rural regions in the Canadian Prairies were sustained largely by extractive industries such as agriculture, coal mining, forestry, and later oil and gas (Sheridan 2007). In recent years, urban, suburban, and ex-urban constituencies have encroached on rural landscapes, fostering what anthropologist Thomas Sheridan describes as "a cultural as well as political divide between the urban and rural [that] is growing ever deeper, with explosive political and ecological consequences" (2007, 123). One indication of this divide is that urban-based environmentalists tend to blame beef producers (and cows) for global environmental degradation, while beef producers see environmentalists as harbouring anti-rural sentiments (White 2015). In rural areas, terms like "climate change" are often associated with urban elites and can be politically divisive, such that policy-makers and citizens in these parts of the world use alternative frames to address environmental degradation (Tabuchi 2017; Wood, Hultquist, and Romsdahl 2014).

While farmers, ranchers, and others who occupy and work the rural landscapes of southern Alberta tend to disproportionately deny the existence of climate change (Mildenberger et al. 2016), they are important agents in conserving and maintaining biological diversity and ecological integrity in the region (Herrero, Wirsenius, and Henderson 2015; Holecheck et al. 2006; Horn 2016). Consider, for instance, that the small amount of ecologically rich prairie grassland that remains in southern Alberta has been preserved by cattle and bison producers, some of whom are returning cultivated agricultural land back to grasslands. This "re-grassing" of the land can help prevent soil erosion, provide habitat for numerous species, and act as a sink for carbon (White 2015). While overgrazing can decrease the capacity of the region's chernozemic soils to store carbon (Wang, VandenBygaart, and McConkey 2014), some grazing is necessary to keep the grasslands and the soils that sustain them vibrant and diverse (Holecheck et al. 2006). Much depends on the underlying values and assumptions that inform land-use practices. As Wendell Berry observes, "cattle ... can be used invasively, so that they overgraze the grass and trample too heavily the margins of the streams, or they can be managed considerately as components or members of the land's community of creatures" (Berry 2015, x). Less intensive grazing practices provide strategies that align with recent global initiatives to combat climate change such as the UNFCCC "Soils for Food Security and Climate" and the FAO's "Global Soil Partnership."

In addition to ruminants and the humans that depend on them for sustenance, nonhuman carnivores also actively shape the bio-cultural landscapes of southern Alberta. Conflicts among livestock, ranchers, and large carnivores such as grizzly bears and wolves are a long-standing feature of this region. Ranchers have historically controlled nonhuman carnivores by killing or removing them, often enrolling the services of the state. As historian Donald Worster once described, in Canada and the United States, ranchers' and farmers' hatred of large carnivores was "almost metaphysical" (Worster 1982, 60). These practices and cultural beliefs are changing in important ways, although slowly, as a small but growing movement of conservation-oriented agricultural producers is experimenting with efforts to coexist with large predators through monitoring and changes to prevailing attitudes and practices (Waterton Biosphere Reserve 2014). Coexistence on private land enables grizzlies and wolves to move from the mountainous regions of the province where they were pushed over the course of the twentieth century to the prairie landscapes on which they historically evolved. For example, the Cowboys and Carnivores project, a landowner-driven monitoring project spearheaded by the Drywood Yarrow Conservation Partnership and the Mistakiis Institute, uses motion-sensored trail cameras and other monitoring devices to better understand the movement and habits of large carnivores. Based on these findings, modifications have been made to farming practices such as changing grain bin doors and bottoms to reduce the attractants that draw large carnivores onto farmland. The partnership of renowned rancher, naturalist, and filmmaker Charlie Russell with provincial wildlife managers has resulted in innovative ranch management practices that involves intentionally leaving dead cows for bears to consume during calving season to prevent further predation (Willcox 2016). Other examples include using guardian animals, electric fences, and predatory-friendly certification as ways to encourage producers and consumers to shift to conservation-oriented ranching practices (Early 2012).

While it might seem a stretch to connect responses to climate change with changing assumptions and land-use practices that foster coexistence among humans, ruminants, and large carnivores, climates are connected in important ways with local land-use practices that necessarily comprise interactions among various species. Reducing climate change to greenhouse gas emission metrics glosses over such place-based, embodied, multi-species encounters. While not without problems and contradictions (Wuerthner 2016), conservation-oriented and predatory-friendly farming practices connect domesticated ruminants, wildlife, and people in potentially more salubrious and just relations than have previously been the case. In turn, silvo-pasturing combines agriculture, ranching, and forestry in innovative ways to sequester carbon, protect biodiversity, and provide food for humans and nonhumans alike (Toensmeier 2016). Another promising initiative is the recently signed Northern Tribes Buffalo Treaty that seeks to restore wild bison populations in the Canadian and American West (Locke 2015). By enrolling human and nonhuman species in creative responses to socio-environmental challenges, these initiatives align with a multi-species imaginary that seeks mutual flourishing for human and nonhuman species alike. Finding ways to support these initiatives through public awareness, policy directives, or financial subsidies can ensure their continued viability. More substantial transformations are also required that include fostering Indigenous food sovereignty in the region, in part through policies that recognize and incorporate Indigenous and Métis rights (Martens et al. 2016).

Conclusion

A feminist multi-species orientation provides a useful conceptual frame for addressing meat consumption in a carbon-constrained world. Inspired by Haraway's trope of companion species, I propose an approach that acknowledges from the outset the various interactions among species that are constitutive of nature and society. A provisional account of the alimentary ties that bind companion species – in this case Indigenous and settler peoples, ranchers, farmers, cows, bison, large carnivores, grass, and soil – highlights how routines of food production and consumption are deeply connected with identity, ecology, and politics. Reconciling the economic viability and cultural identity of agricultural producers with changing biophysical and political climates will present a major challenge in the twenty-first century. Developing guidelines for action based on reductionist and universalizing metrics might simplify solutions in the short term, but may also prove to be ecologically and politically wrongheaded in the long run. Challenges – perceived or actual – to multi-species relations can easily become flash points for organized political contestation and resistance precisely because they sever deeply rooted cultural and ecological ties (for potential political outcomes, see Cotton 2017).

The way forward is not to skirt complicated regional politics and practices, nor to ignore scientific information about rising GHG emissions, but to construct ethical approaches to environmental change capable of addressing complexity in and across regions and among species. As Haraway puts it, "we need stories (and theories) that are just big enough to gather up the complexities and keep the edges open and greedy for surprising new and old connections" (2015, 160). A framework of meat consumption and climate change informed by feminist multi-species scholarship does not lend itself to tidy, elegant slogans such as "eat less (or no) meat to save the climate." Indeed, it is more in line with advice to keep public issues complex (e.g. Stirling 2010). While this approach offers no generalizable bumper-sticker-ready answer, it aligns with calls for culturally and regionally sensitive solutions to GHG emission reductions. Ethically, politically, and epistemologically speaking, efforts to link meat consumption with environmental change are inescapably a place-based, multi-species, indigestion-inducing affair.

References

Adams, C.J. 2015. *The Sexual Politics of Meat: A Feminist-Vegetarian Critical Theory*. 25th anniversary ed. New York and London: Bloomsbury.

Agarwal, A., and S. Narain. 1991. "Global Warming in an Uneven World: A Case of Environmental Colonialism." *New Delhi: Centre for Science and Environment*.

Agriculture and AgriFood Canada. 2011. "Per Capita Disappearance." Centre for Science and Environment. http://www.agr.gc.ca/eng/industry-markets-and-trade/canadian-agri-food-sector-intelligence/poultry-and-eggs/poultry-and-egg-market-information/industry-indicators/per-capita-disappearance/?id=1384971854413.

Anderson, K., and K. Kuhn. 2014. *Cowspiracy: The Sustainability Secret*. AUM Films and Media.

Bee, B., J. Rice, and A. Trauger. 2015. "A Feminist Approach to Climate Change Governance: Everyday and Intimate Politics." *Geography Compass* 9 (6): 339–50.

Berry, W. 2015. "Introduction." In *The Age of Consequences: A Chronicle of Concern and Hope*, edited by C. White, ix–x. Berkeley, CA: Counterpoint.

Blue, G. 2008. "If It Ain't Alberta, It Ain't Beef: Local Food, Regional Identity, (Inter)National Politics." *Food, Culture, Society* 11 (1): 69–85.

– 2009. "Branding Beef: Marketing, Food Safety and the Governance of Risk." *Canadian Journal of Communication* 34 (2): 229–44.

– 2015. "Framing Climate Change for Public Deliberation: What Role for the Interpretive Social Sciences and Humanities?" *Journal of Environmental Policy and Planning* 18 (1): 67–84.

Blue, G., and S. Alexander. 2015. "Coyotes in the City: Gastro-Ethical Encounters in a More-than-Human World." In *Critical Animal Geographies: Politics, Intersections and Hierarchies in a Multispecies World*, edited by K. Gillespie and R. Collard, 149–63. London and New York: Routledge.

Clapp, J. 2013. "Eating and Surviving: The Case for More Government Support of Sustainable Food and Less Meat in Our Diets." *Literary Review of Canada*. http://reviewcanada.ca/magazine/2013/05/eating-and-surviving/.

Cotton, J. 2017. "France's Disillusioned Farmers Turn to Le Pen." Reuters. http://www.reuters.com/article/us-france-election-farmers-idUSKBN16627O?il=0.

Daschuk, J.W. 2013. *Clearing the Plains Disease, Politics of Starvation, and the Loss of Aboriginal Life*. Regina, SK: University of Regina Press.

Demeritt, D. 2006. "Science Studies Climate Change and the Prospects for Constructivist Critique." *Economy and Society* 35 (3): 453–79.

Early, M. 2012. "An Inquiry into Eco-Labeling: The Promise of Predator Friendly Certification." Unpublished. http://scholarworks.umt.edu/cgi/viewcontent.cgi?article=1156&context=etd.

Friedman, H. 2005. "Feeding the Empire: The Pathologies of Globalized Agriculture." In *The Empire Reloaded*, edited by L. Pantich, 124–42. Winnipeg: Fernwood Publishing.

Geagan, K. 2009. *Go Green Get Lean: Trim Your Waistline with the Ultimate Low-Carbon Footprint Diets*. New York: Rodale Books.

Gibson-Graham, J.K. 2011. "A Feminist Project of Belonging for the Anthropocene." *Gender, Place and Culture* 18 (1): 1–21.

Haraway, D. 2008. "Chicken." In *Animal Subjects: An Ethical Reader in a Posthuman World*, edited by J. Castricano, 33–8. Waterloo, ON: Wilfrid Laurier University Press.

– 2015. "Anthropocene, Capitalocene, Plantationocene, Chthulucene: Making Kin." *Environmental Humanities* 6: 159–65.

Harrington, J. 2008. *The Climate Diet: How You Can Cut Carbon, Cut Costs and Save the Planet*. New York: Routledge.

Head, L. 2008. "Is the Concept of Human Impacts Past Its Use-by Date?" *The Holocene* 18 (3): 373–7.

Herrero, M., S. Wirsenius, and B. Henderson. 2015. "Livestock and the Environment: What Have We Learned in the Past Decade?" *Annual Review of Environment and Resources* 40 (1): 177–202.

Heyhoe, K. 2009. *Cooking Green: Reducing Your Carbon Footprint in the Kitchen*. Boston, MA: Da Capo Lifelong Books.

Holecheck, J., T. Baker, J. Boren, and D. Galt. 2006. "Grazing Impacts on Rangeland Vegetation: What We Have Learned." *Rangelands Archive* (February): 7–13.

Horn, M. 2016. *Rancher, Farmer, Fisherman*. New York: W.W. Norton and Co.

Hulme, M. 2009. *Why We Disagree about Climate Change*. Cambridge: Cambridge University Press.

Isenberg, A. 2000. *The Destruction of the Bison: An Environmental History, 1750–1920*. New York: Cambridge University Press.

Isreal, A., and C. Sachs. 2012. "A Climate for Feminist Intervention: Feminist Science Studies and Climate Change." In *Research Action and Policy: Addressing the Gendered Impacts of Climate Change*, edited by M. Alston and K. Whittenbury, 33–51. London: Springer.

Kehoe, A. 2017. *North America before the European Invasions.* 2nd ed. New York and London: Routledge.

Latour, B. 2004. *Politics of Nature: How to Bring the Sciences into Democracy.* Cambridge, MA: Harvard University Press.

Locke, H. 2015. "Pledge to Restore Wild Buffalo Unites First Nations of North America." *National Geographic*, 18 August. http: blog. nationalgeographic.org/2015/08/18/pledge-to-restore-wild-buffalo-unites-first-nations-of-north-america.

Mackey, E. 2016. *Unsettled Expectations: Uncertainty, Land and Settler Decolonization.* Halifax and Winnipeg: Fernwood Publishing.

Martens, T., J. Cidro, M. Hart, and S. McLachlan. 2016. "Understanding Indigenous Food Sovereignty through an Indigenous Research Paradigm." *Journal of Indigenous Social Development* 5 (1): 20.

Mildenberger, M., P. Howe, J. Marlon, and A. Leiserowitz. 2016. "Yale Climate Opinion Maps – Canada." 2016. http://climatecommunication.yale.edu/visualizations-data/ycom-canada/.

Niman, N. 2009. "The Carnivore's Dilemma." *New York Times*, 30 October 2009. http://www.nytimes.com/2009/10/31/opinion/31niman.html.

– 2014. *Defending Beef*. White River Junction, VT: Chelsea Green.

Paterson, M., and J. Stripple. 2014. "Governing Subjectivities in a Carbon Constrained World." In *Culture, Politics and Climate Change: How Information Shapes Our Common Future*, edited by D. Crow and M. Boykoff, 189–202. London and New York: Earthscan.

Probyn-Ramsey, F. 2015. "Carbon Hoofprints: Should We Have a Vegetarian Campus?" 2015. http://sydney.edu.au/environment-institute/blog/the-universitys-carbon-hoofprint/.

Ripple, W., P. Smith, H. Haberl, and D. Boucher. 2013. "Commentary: Ruminants, Climate Change and Climate Policy." *Nature Climate Change* 4 (1): 2–5.

Scheffers, B., L. de Meester, T. Bridge, A. Hoffman, J. Pandolfi, R. Corlett, S. Buchart, et al. 2016. "The Broad Footprint of Climate Change from Genes to Biomes to People." *Science* 354 (6313): 719–30.

Schiermeier, Q. 2019. "Eat Less Meat: UN Climate-Change Report Calls for Change to Human Diet." *Nature* 572: 291–2.

Sheridan, T.E. 2007. "Embattled Ranchers, Endangered Species, and Urban Sprawl: The Political Ecology of the New American West." *Annual Review of Anthropology* 36 (1): 121–38. https://doi.org/10.1146/annurev.anthro.36.081406.094413.

Steinfeld, H. 2006. *Livestock's Long Shadow: Environmental Issues and Options.* Rome: Food and Agriculture Organization of the United Nations.

Sterritt, Angela. 2018. "B.C. Indigenous People React to the Resurfacing of 2 Migration Theories." CBC.ca. 10 January 2018. https://www.cbc.ca/news/canada/british-columbia/bc-indigenous-communities-react-to-the-resurfacing-of-two-migration-theories-1.4479632.

Stirling, A. 2010. "Keep It Complex." *Nature* 468: 1029–31.

Synes, N., K. Watts, S. Palmer, G. Bocedi, K. Barton, P. Osborne, and J. Travis. 2015. "A Multi-Species Modelling Approach to Examine the Impact of Alternative Climate Change Adaptation Strategies on Range Shifting Ability in a Fragmented Landscape." *Ecological Informatics* 30: 222–9.

Tabuchi, H. 2017. "In America's Heartland, Discussing Climate Change without Saying 'Climate Change.'" *New York Times*, 28 January 2017. https://www.nytimes.com/2017/01/28/business/energy-environment/navigating-climate-change-in-americas-heartland.html?_r=5.

Taylor, P., and F. Buttel. 1992. "How Do We Know We Have Global Environmental Problems? Science and the Globalization of Environmental Discourse." *Geoforum* 23 (3): 405–16.

Toensmeier, E. 2016. *The Carbon Farming Solution: A Global Toolkit of Perennial Crops and Regenerative Agriculture Practices for Climate Change Mitigation and Food Security.* New York: Chelsea Green.

Wang, X., A. VandenBygaart, and B. McConkey. 2014. "Land Management History of Canadian Grasslands and the Impact on Soil Carbon Storage." *Rangeland Ecology and Management* 67 (4): 333–43.

Waterton Biosphere Reserve. 2014. "Sharing the Range." http://www.sharingtherange.com/.

Weis, Tony. 2015. "Meatification and the Madness of the Doubling Narrative." *Canadian Food Studies* 2 (2): 296–303.

Wellesley, L., A. Froggat, and C. Happer. 2015. "Changing Climate, Changing Diets: Pathways to Lower Meat Consumption." London: Chatham House, Royal Institute of International Affairs. https://www.chathamhouse.org/publication/changing-climate-changing-diets%20.

White, C. 2015. *The Age of Consequences: A Chronicle of Concern and Hope.* Berkeley, CA: Counterpoint.

Willcox, L. 2016. "Cattle in Grizzly Country." *Grizzly Times*, 21 April 2016. http://www.grizzlytimes.org/single-post/2016/04/21/Cattle-in-Grizzly-Country.

Wood, R., A. Hultquist, and R. Romstadt. 2014. "An Examination of Local Climate Change Policies in the Great Plains." *Review of Policy Research* 31 (6): 529–40.

Worster, D. 1982. *Under Western Skies: Nature and History in the American West.*
   Oxford: Oxford University Press.
Wuerthner, G. 2016. "Why Predator-Friendly Beef Isn't So Friendly, After
   All." Counterpunch.org. http://www.counterpunch.org/2016/05/09/why-
   predator-friendly-beef-isnt-so-friendly-after-all/.

PART THREE

The Future of "Green Meat"

9

The Promise and Peril
of "Cultured Meat"

Lenore Newman

Animal husbandry is a central technology of the modern food system. Defined as the taming, keeping, and breeding of animals for human use, the practice of animal agriculture dates back at least 10,000 years, and was a central technological pillar of the Neolithic revolution. More recently (in human historical timescales), the use of animals in the food system has been challenged due to a range of ethical and socio-ecological concerns. The transition away from animal agriculture is hard to imagine from within, though the seeds of this transition, I argue, have already been planted. Anticipating the dynamics of a socio-technological transition is always fraught; ultimately, the success of a specific technological path is partially dependent on timing and luck. But can we even imagine a world where animals do not play a primary role in the food supply chain? This chapter delves into the rapidly evolving field of cellular agriculture, which offers the potential to create meat, dairy, and other animal products without the use of actual animals. I attempt here to sketch out a rough overview of the field and the literature, expose certain under-studied areas of thought, and highlight some of the emerging reactions to these technologies. Though replacement of all animal products with lab-grown analogues is likely very far away, the following pages illustrate that many of these products are quickly nearing the market, and many are already being used in our daily lives.[1]

The progression from one technological paradigm to a new one can be difficult to imagine, but Geels (2005) has modelled this transition using a parallel example, one that is useful for the discussion of cellular agriculture as a disruptive technology: the use of animals for labour and transportation. The horse, for instance, was a keystone of transportation right into the modern age, but the reality falls far short of any romantic image of animal-driven transportation. Horses led short and brutal lives in Victorian cities, created dangerous challenges to public health, and required specialized feed, stabling, and sanitation. The Victorian horse was above all an economic object, and as Turvey (2005) summarizes very well, that object was expensive and unpredictable. Horses stumbled, horses sickened, and horses died, and a smart businessman had to calculate the odds of each of these outcomes. Horses were "sold down" in society as they aged, first pulling the carriages of the rich and ending their days hauling waste among the poor. The world was ready for a better horse, but the transition away from the horse proceeded surprisingly slowly, particularly given that there were a number of emergent options (bicycle, car, tram), a phenomenon known as lock-in (Barnes, Gartland, and Stack 2004 give a good overview of this concept; horses were "locked into" the economy despite better options being available). To Geels, socio-technical systems consist of a cluster of elements, including technology, regulation, user practices and markets, cultural meaning, infrastructure, maintenance networks, and supply networks; all of these elements must shift for a paradigm change to take place. Several potential paths could have become reality, including a world of bicycles, a world of trains, or, as emerged in North America, a world of private cars. In the case of the horse, the shift occurred from roughly 1920 to 1950, by which time the road horse population had dropped 99.9 per cent from its peak.

The use of living animals for food displays an even more complex socio-technical system, with a correspondingly high component of lock-in. But could this change? It is likely that the world will have to come to terms with changing its approach to meat-eating, as the production of meat at a level necessary to allow all citizens of the planet to consume at North American levels is impossible (Datar and Betti 2010 address this; see also chapter 2 of this volume). The socio-technical system will then change as a result. This chapter outlines one potential technological path that could emerge in a world where meat-eating continues to grow. I begin with a discussion of why we are likely to continue to eat meat or "meat-like" foods; introduce the concept of cellular agriculture, in which sentient animals are removed from the food chain; discuss the plant-based alternatives to this model; explore the current state of cellular agriculture; and finally discuss some of the challenges and concerns cellular agriculture introduces.

The first question of interest is the continued growth in meat-eating, including in cultures where meat-eating was once rare. Why are plant-based alternatives not more successful as an alternative to meat? Roughly 5 per cent of the North American population is vegetarian and half of those are vegan, for reasons including religion, health, morality, and the environment. As argued in previous chapters, the environmental impact of animal products is still under debate, but clearly the possibility of producing non-animal meat is of interest to those who want to continue eating meat without the ecological impacts associated with rearing livestock. Similarly, there is the simple moral question that is immutably tied to animal agriculture: Should we continue to create, torture, and kill animals for food if the need to do so is removed? For many people the answer is a resounding "no," and for many others there is a sense of unease similar to that of Victorian writers decrying the horrors visited upon transport horses.

Despite these "ecological" and "moral" critiques, meat-eating has become strongly locked in. In a recent study, a large portion of those surveyed reported an attachment to meat based upon hedonism, affinity, entitlement, and dependence (Graça, Calheiros, and Oliveira 2015). This attachment is extremely difficult to break, and in some cases trends to an outright hostility towards vegans. Hennigan (2015) explains how vegans pose a moral threat to the meat-eater, provoking a response against both vegan food and vegans themselves. Though commentary on the internet and in the mainstream media can be juvenile, the same debate has long simmered in the academic literature, relating back to our moral dilemma over whether we should protect those sentient beings who lack the agency to protect themselves. From the classic arguments laid out in "Do Trees Have Standing" (Stone 1972), we come to arguments such as those Hsiao (2015) explores in his article "In Defense of Eating Meat." Hsiao argues that sentience is not sufficient for moral status, and that the needs of humans trump the interests of animals (a key flaw with this argument, as Bruers 2015 explains, is that if we abandon sentience as a measure of moral inclusion, we are in effect arguing against the rights of humans who lack agency, including children and the aged). At the end of the day, the specific nature of these ongoing debates suggests that, if technology was not a factor, it is unlikely that the planet would shift to vegetarian or vegan diets, or even towards reduced meat consumption. But what if instead we challenge Hsiao's last assertion by removing the need for animal husbandry, similarly to the way in which technology removed the need for the road horse? The field of cellular agriculture is poised to do exactly that.

Cellular Agriculture

Cellular agriculture is the production of agricultural products from cell cultures. Taken to its logical extreme, cellular agriculture could remove the need for sentient animals within the food chain, a shift whose significance could rival that of the domestication of animals itself.[2] Cellular agriculture has received a great deal of attention in the last five years, though research into cellular agriculture has much older roots. There are two major research directions within cellular agriculture: acellular production and cellular production. *Acellular* products consist of organic molecules such as proteins and fats, and include products such as biopharmaceuticals, artificial flavours, rennet, and the precursor materials for common foods such as milk. Most *existing* cellular agriculture products fall into this category. Cellular production involves a multistep process in which cells are grown on a scaffold in the presence of a serum to create muscles and organs; in the industry the four components of the process are described as cells, scaffold, media, and bioreactor. In terms of food production, cellular products such as *in vitro* meats have received almost all of the academic attention and popular press. This, in my view, is a great mistake: social scientists also need to pay attention to acellular products. Part of this uneven interest is due to Mark Post of Maastricht University, a leading innovator in the field of cellular agriculture (see, e.g., Post 2012) who garnered world-wide attention by creating the first *in vitro* hamburger and serving it in London on 13 August 2013. This prototype, described as being tasty but a touch lean, cost several hundred thousand dollars to create, and the global attention obscured the reality of the field of cellular agriculture. The production of meat *in vitro* both captivates and appalls, and it dominates the academic and non-academic literature for undeniably good reasons. A recent summary by Jönsson (2016), for example, highlights that by producing meat outside of animal bodies, food will be healthier, more environmentally friendly, and kinder to animals – a typical reaction that has elevated *in vitro* meat to a techno-logical "holy grail." *In vitro* meat could help to displace the 300 million tonnes of meat produced worldwide annually, a figure Jönsson notes is a 73 per cent increase since 1990. This production level requires over 30 billion animals, mainly chickens. So certainly the stakes are very high in terms of the replacement of meat. Yet world-shaking burgers aside, industrial-scale production is optimistically several decades away.

Cellular agriculture, however, is about far more than meat. Acellular products are orders of magnitude easier to create, and have been used in medicine and the food system for decades. Stephens and King (2018), for example, explore the potential for lab-grown blood replacements. The story really begins with insulin (see Nielsen 2013 for a much more technical explanation of this process). Developed in 1922 by Frederick Banting, Charles Best, and James Collip, replacement insulin was collected from pig or cattle pancreases. This method, though miraculous for those facing certain death, was problematic in several ways; it was expensive, created a product of varying quality, and could cause patients to develop allergies. In 1978, Riggs, Itakura, and Boyer inserted the gene for insulin creation into a bacteria, building on earlier work by Herbert Boyer and Stanley Cohen (Cohen et al. 1973), creating human insulin *in vitro*. Today almost all insulin is produced in this manner using either yeast or bacteria. In the case of yeast, the process is in effect a form of fermentation. Boyer and colleague Cohen are now credited with creating the field of genetic engineering, with insulin often hailed as one of the field's earliest ground-breaking successes.

Cellular agriculture's first and, to date, greatest success in the food system is surprisingly almost unknown and rarely discussed outside of a very large technical literature: the production of rennet for cheesemaking. Rennet is a set of enzymes found in the stomachs of ruminants, including chymosin, which curdles the casein in milk and thus renders cheesemaking possible. Throughout history rennet was produced by extraction from the mucus found in the fourth stomach of calves and other ruminants, a difficult and time-consuming process. In the 1970s the supply of rennet fell short of what was needed to support the rapidly expanding consumption of cheese, and several substitutes were explored. By 1980, bacteria and yeasts were being genetically altered to create rennet during the fermentation process. Almost all cheese is now made with such rennet, a fact that Ellahi (1996) found was very poorly understood by the public. Technically rennet is not a GMO. The yeast that produces the rennet is a GMO, as it has been altered to create rennet as a waste product (yeast creates alcohol and carbon dioxide as a waste product naturally, a process we exploit to happy effect in the production of alcoholic beverages; changing the genetic structure of the yeast leads to the production of different end products). Once a batch of rennet has been created by the modified yeast, the yeast itself is removed, leaving a non-GMO end product; artificial rennet was the first such enzyme to be allowed by the US Food and Drug Administration. Nielsen (2013) reports that about 90 per cent of all commercial cheese made in the US and Britain uses such rennet. Because of this, such cheeses may be considered vegetarian (and halal and kosher), provided that no animal-based feedstocks are used during chymosin production.

The step from rennet production to the production of the components of milk is one of volume only. Milk is composed of fats, minerals,
and the proteins casein and whey, and the latter two can be manufactured with genetically altered yeast. These two ingredients can then be
combined with plant fats and trace minerals to create milk without
the use of dairy cows. Perfect Day Foods, a company incubated by
cellular agriculture research institute New Harvest, originally planned
to have such dairy products on shelves by late 2017, but is now aiming
to commercialize their technology over the next few years (New Harvest
2016). They sold their first commercial product, ice cream, in a limited
run in the summer of 2019. The milk, of course, can be made into butter,
yogurt, cheese, and other dairy products. The academic literature has
so far been silent on this rapidly evolving technology, but the impact
could be very large. Total world dairy exports grew by 4.6 per cent
per year, on a milk equivalent basis, during 2010–2014 (Vitaliano and
IFAMR 2016), and total production is 240 billion litres annually. The
environmental impact of dairy production is of particular note. The
FAO highlights livestock as a source of climate-changing gasses (Gerber
et al. 2013); 14.5 per cent of total emissions are estimated to come from
livestock, and 65 per cent of these are from cattle. The total for dairy
cattle is about 2.9 per cent of humanity's total. Dairy cattle are also
water intensive, and produce difficult-to-manage liquid and solid waste
(Baskaran, Cullen, and Colombo 2009). Industrial dairy processes are
not entirely to blame for this rather heavy hoofprint. Capper, Cady, and
Bauman (2009) show through modelling that while more traditional
methods of dairy management might seem more environmentally
friendly, that is not true by volume. Eliminating the dairy industry
would also address a set of particularly difficult animal welfare issues.
Ventura, Von Keyserlingk, and Weary (2015) identified concerns over
lameness, cow comfort, disease, on-farm mortality, injuries, management
of calves, and restrictions of behavioural freedoms. I am highlighting
milk production before the much more charismatic meat products
because there is potential for rapid disruption of conventional dairy.
Around the globe, dairy farmers in temperate regions are struggling to
compete with dairies in tropical zones, and plant-based alternative milks
are already nibbling into market share, in part due to fairly common
reactions to lactose (which one can choose to leave out of milk made
in the lab). Perfect Dairy Foods is pursuing an optimistic launch date,
but it is likely that these products will be taking market share from
conventional dairy at some point during the 2020s.

Financing in the cellular agriculture space has scaled rapidly in
the last few years. Mouet (2018) provides a good overview of recent

developments, including Google co-founder Sergei Brin's funding of Mark Post's first cellular hamburger, support from Richard Branson and Bill Gates for Memphis Meats, and Li Ka-Shing's support for Perfect Day Foods. Tyson Foods, best known for production of chicken in a more conventional manner, has acquired a minority stake in a cellular agriculture start-up based in Israel.

Plant-Based "Meat"

Is the technology to grow meat in vats needed at all? Superiority Burger's vegan option has been rated as the best in the world by several reviewers; certainly the taste, look, and feel of the burger is similar to one made from animal products. It is a long way from the puck-like vegetarian patties of the twentieth century. However, Superiority Burger is no longer the most exclusive veggie burger in town. Consider the Impossible™ Burger; Fellet (2015) describes it as targeted at "hard core, uncompromising meat lovers." A meat burger contains myoglobin, which contains heme, a substance that gives meat a bloody, umami flavour. Impossible Foods uses leghemoglobin (a similar protein found in bean nodules) produced by cellular fermentation to give their burgers a meat-heavy flavour. Fellet also notes that California-based Beyond Meat is achieving similar results with chicken; *New York Times* columnist and food expert Mark Bittman claimed that he could not tell the difference between a wrap containing plant-based chicken produced by Beyond Meats and chicken from a live animal.

With such excellent plant-based substitutes, the question has been asked why we need *in vitro* meat at all. This is explored in the literature (Fudge 2010; Miller 2012) and is akin to asking why the development of the car should proceed when the train and tram already exist. However, if the goal is to completely end industrial husbandry (a goal stated by just about all of the current leaders in the field of cellular agriculture in their literature, websites, and public talks), cellular agriculture can take us farther than simple plant substitution can. Partly this comes down to cuisine, and may help explain the obsession with the *in vitro* hamburger. As Belasco (2006, vii) notes, food is our biggest industry, our greatest export, our most frequently indulged pleasure, and as Pierre Van den Berghe (1984) explains, we are food-sharing animals and use food to establish, express, and consolidate societies. The conflict over animal-based foods has the ability to interject tension into this process, partially explaining the unusual level of conflict found in debates over veganism outlined above. The hamburger in particular has emerged as an iconic object in the US, and has a surprisingly vibrant associated literature. In *The Hamburger: A History*, Ozersky (2009, 2) claims that "nothing says America like a hamburger," and in *Hamburger: A Global History*, Smith (2008) argues that the hamburger has adapted to local cultures and changed the world. Caldwell (2014) charts the rise of the gourmet hamburger, and discusses how this iconic dish has weathered the rise of foodie culture. In short, hamburgers matter, and they do seem to need to be made of meat to "count." Early vegetable burgers flew in the face of North American cuisine, and the tension between vegetarians and meat eaters exposes uncomfortable realities about cuisine's place in a culture. Cuisine may refer to the set of foods and practices common to a culture, the term descending from the Latin *coquina*, from *coquire*, "to cook." The word entered popular use in late-eighteenth-century France, but as Cook and Crang (1996) describe, cuisine emerges as extensive flows of food and people are mediated locally, creating geographical knowledges. But cuisine reflects place (Newman 2014), and "cuisines aren't just innocent concoctions but reflect the dominant ideologies of the societies in which they emerge." Vegetarian burgers, good as they might be, do not quite live up to what Appadurai (1986, 25) describes as the concept of authenticity; he argues that authenticity implies a timeless perspective on profoundly historical processes, stating that "authenticity measures the degree to which something is more or less what it *ought* to be. It is thus a norm of some sort." Debate is still heated over the question of meat's role in culture. Fudge (2010) argues that *in vitro* meat simply demonstrates the hegemony of meat, but other writers argue just as strongly that veganism is not an acceptable option for actual human societies, particularly where meat-eating is deeply culturally entrenched. Thus the real choice is between cultured meat and slaughtered meat (Hopkins and Dacey 2008). Sexton (2018) recently explored the issue of acceptance of both cellular agriculture and the eating of insects, and argued that the normalization of novel foods accelerates with adaptation. A study by Slade (2018) found that if offered the choice, 65 per cent of diners would choose conventional beef, 21 per cent would choose a plant-based burger, and 11 per cent a cellular burger,[3] suggesting that adoption for cellular agriculture is still in the early stages – but of course no such products are yet on the market. Another interesting aspect of this debate is the opinion that cellular agriculture is not actually a break from the brutality of animal agriculture, but is rather an extension of the sort of technologies that have bred pigs, chickens, and cows for efficiency at turning feed into pork, chicken meat, and beef, and that the logical conclusion of these technologies is meat production without animals (Driessen and Korthals 2012). While interesting, I disagree that the suffering of billions of sentient animals can be waved away. Cellular meat is a reasonable solution to a cultural dilemma.

From the *In Vitro* Hamburger to New Harvest

I attended the first conference on cellular agriculture in San Francisco to get a crash course in the field. The packed sessions did not disappoint, running the gamut from spider silk clothing (Spiber) prized for toughness and feel, vegan gelatin made from mastodon DNA (Gelzen) and shaped into gummy bears for show, *in vitro* leather (Modern Meadow), and egg white (Clara Foods), to specialty coffee (Afineur), among others. Beer made with *in vitro* hops was available for tasting, reminding the drinker that plant products can also be created in the lab (vanillin is another such product). There were several sessions on cellular agriculture and meat, including updates from Mark Post on the potential for *in vitro* burgers. The mood was highly optimistic, focused on the future, and determined. A fair number of journalists attended, and there were representatives from major agricultural companies present to assess the state of the science. There was little to no talk about any potential downsides to these technologies, and a conspicuous lack of farmers in this future of food. This suggests a potential role for the social scientist in these emerging fields; start-up culture by necessity is focused on delivering a product to market; there is a need for academia to provide critique and analysis of the social impacts of these technologies.

The conference was arranged by New Harvest, a research institute with the mission "to build and establish the field of cellular agriculture" and a vision to create "a strong foundation of accessible, public, fundamental cellular agriculture research, upon which we can build a post-animal bioeconomy, where we harvest animal products from cell cultures, not animals, to feed a growing global population sustainably and affordably" (New Harvest 2016). New Harvest funds research into cellular agriculture, educates the public, incubates start-ups, and generally does in a very small way what the animal agriculture industries spends hundreds of millions of dollars on: lobbying. The conference was an upbeat, energetic presentation about a possible future of food. And, as with the literature, it gave ample time to the preparation of *in vitro* meat.

A good starting point for those interested in a technical introduction to *in vitro* meat should refer to Datar and Betti (2010), which gives an overview of the process involved. Isha Datar is now the CEO of New Harvest, and views *in vitro* meat as a humane, safe, and environmentally beneficial alternative to slaughtered animal flesh. She and Betti argue that such meat would have a reduced need for water, energy, and land, would be faster than conventional growth, and could be produced in vertical farms, lowering the footprint of the agricultural industry. And, of course, the product would be cruelty free. Bonny et al. (2015) give a good overview of the regulatory and consumer-preference aspects of *in vitro* meat, and present the idea that once the technology improves it may push conventional agriculture to the premium end of the market. This is an intriguing idea, tinged with the hint of fear that "authentic" food will be reserved for the rich, an attitude found in the popular press with regards to the meal replacement "Soylent."[4] Bonny et al. (ibid., 255) do see cellular agriculture as one answer to a problem that must be addressed; as they comment, "the meat industry cannot respond to increases in demand by ever increasing resource use." This idea of alternate pathways (explored in previous chapters) is also captured by Van der Weele and Driessen (2013), who describe the future of meat as an ontological void that can be filled in various ways. The optimism of the proponents of *in vitro* meat is certainly not matched within agricultural circles, who either doubt the ability of the technology to meet demand or feel that the conventional system is simply too big to disrupt. One of the best summaries of this point of view is presented by Ford (2011), who feels that animals play too big a role in landscape dynamics to be ignored. However, the idea of a landscape populated by grazing animals that are not routinely slaughtered does challenge this opinion somewhat.

The issue of variety has also been raised; as Gelzen's mastodon gels attest, one doesn't have to play in the usual barnyard with cellular agriculture. As Mark Post (2012, 298) comments, stem cells from probably any mammalian source can be used as a basis for "hitherto unimaginable meats." This sort of language has evoked fear of this "free range" future, but the cellular agriculture movement calms the worried diner with visions of village makerspaces and cottage laboratories. The creation of *in vitro* meat has even been likened to the microbrewing industry (van der Weele and Tramper 2014). Several authors have grappled with the problem of customer acceptance, and have considered how cellular agriculture might change our relationship with nature (e.g., van der Weele and Tramper 2014).

The Joy (and Unease) of a Farm in a Bottle

Though there is reason to be optimistic that cellular agriculture will address the moral and environmental costs of animal husbandry, it is unlikely that this particular future will arrive as quickly or as painlessly as one might hope. Though I am optimistic that in the near future acellular production of milk and milk products and egg products will occur, *in vitro* meat will emerge more slowly, and with more heated debate. One site of active debate over such meat products is in the vegan community; though organizations such as New Harvest stress that the products they hope to encourage are designed for current meat eaters rather than vegans, the latter community is a ready sounding board for the acceptability of meat in a vat. Not all vegan scholars are convinced; critiques include the charge that techno-optimism is being mapped onto the future of veganism (Simonsen 2015), and that cellular agriculture represents a designer ethic which means that there is no need to engage in a more difficult normative struggle to alter social practices (Haraway 2008; Dilworth and McGregor 2015). As the ecological impact of cellular agriculture is poorly understood (in part because there are so many distinct and evolving methods of production), the ethical argument remains a key driver of early development.

There is also the lingering disquiet around GMO technologies to consider. Understanding the actual safety of GMOs is an open question that is beyond the scope of this essay (Hilbeck et al. 2015 provides a good overview); in general these studies stress that no scientific assessments to date have conclusively shown that GMOs are harmful, but neither has scientific study shown that GMOs are conclusively safe. There is a measurable disquiet around GMOs that Scott, Inbar, and Rozin (2016) describe as ranging from mild to an absolute moral opposition. The ultimate acceptance of cellular agriculture will partly hinge on the evolution of society's comfort level with genetic technologies, and/or more solid scientific work supporting the safety of these technologies. For example, the genetically modified components of the Impossible Burger have yet to win FDA approval, though this did not prevent the adoption of the burger by the White Castle chain of restaurants.

Two other elements of cellular agriculture provide reasons for caution; first, an under-studied impact of the creation of industrial cellular agriculture is the demand for feedstock. Second, fermentation processes consumer sugar as an input, and the industrial production of sugar has a well-documented impact on sensitive tropical environments. A full discussion of this aspect of cellular agriculture is beyond the scope of this paper; Goldstein et al. (2015) provide a very complete overview of sugar and its impacts, and Macinnis (2002) remains a personal favourite of mine for its engaging discussion of this issue. Feedstocks are also needed to transform cellular products into familiar foodstuffs such as butter and cheese, including fats. Tan et al. (2009) provide a good overview of why palm oil in particular is problematic. There is a real danger that cellular agriculture might shift production from cool grazing climates of low biodiversity to tropical regions of high biodiversity, and this danger must be considered, though the environmental benefits are likely still orders of magnitude greater. The energy and material inputs of this very new field are poorly understood, and will require careful study to ensure that the technology can scale without damaging delicate ecosystems. Additionally, no real work has been done on the potential impact of laboratory production of food on the rural landscape. This is an area for further study.

The question of the actual environmental impact of cellular agriculture will need more study as well. The technology has not developed far enough to allow for a field-to-plate analysis of it, leaving the environmental benefits, which are much advertised, in the realm of the hypothetical (Lee 2018 explores this issue). Stephens et al. (2018) highlight several potential environmental challenges to the technology that remain unknown; the creation of feedstock, water use, potential waste streams, carbon footprint, and the continued domination of Northern economies over the Global South. All of these issues will need to be studied in depth as the technology matures. In short, environmental benefit at this stage is assumed, but unproven.

Conclusion

To understand cellular agriculture, one must pull back from the debate over whether burgers should be grown in a lab. Cellular agriculture's techniques are already being used to produce both pharmaceuticals and food products such as rennet. Many other products are close to market, including gelatin, leather, milk, and cheese. These latter two pose the potential for major disruption to traditional agricultural economies, and once milk and cheese can be produced in a lab for the same price as traditional products, cellular agriculture could very well vault into the average consumer's conscience. Substitutes for meat are likely farther off into the future, but if one considers the average hamburger or chicken finger, the substitution will likely occur rather seamlessly for at least some products once quality and economic concerns are addressed.

Though moral arguments will be a selling feature for these products, their development and adoption will ultimately rest on much more banal features. Cellular products will be adopted because they are cheaper, because they can be manipulated easily for optimum health outcomes, and because they will easily allow for almost infinite variety. While such products are certainly not "impact free" in an ecological sense, most indications suggest that the impact is significantly smaller than that of commensurate animal-based products. In this light they represent the endgame of a very long series of agricultural innovations, beginning with animal domestication, continuing with cross-breeding and hybridization, and transitioning into the age of global supply chains, factory farms, and genetic modification. The ultimate implications of the farm in a vat, and the potential positive and negative impacts of such technologies, will depend greatly on larger social and political movements rather than intrinsic qualities of the technologies themselves.

Notes

1   Cellular agriculture is evolving quickly; this discussion is current as of writing but is subject to rapid change, and should be taken as an introductory guide.
2   This shift would largely eliminate the pain and suffering associated with the use of sentient beings for food, as cellular cultures lack an organized nervous system.
3   One assumes the other 4 per cent don't enjoy burgers.
4   I've enjoyed Soylent, and though not exciting, exactly, it is perfectly serviceable.

References

Appadurai, Arjun. 1986. "On Culinary Authenticity." *Anthropology Today* 2 (4): 25.

Barnes, William, Myles Gartland, and Martin Stack. 2004. "Old Habits Die Hard: Path Dependency and Behavioral Lock-In." *Journal of Economic Issues* 38 (2): 371–7.

Baskaran, Ramesh, Ross Cullen, and Sergio Colombo. 2009. "Estimating Values of Environmental Impacts of Dairy Farming in New Zealand." *New Zealand Journal of Agricultural Research* 52 (4): 377–89.

Belasco, W. 2006. *Meals to Come: A History of the Future of Food*. Oakland: University of California Press.

Bonny, Sarah P.F., Graham E. Gardner, David W. Pethick, and Jean-François Hocquette. 2015. "What Is Artificial Meat and What Does It Mean for the Future of the Meat Industry?" *Journal of Integrative Agriculture* 14 (2): 255–63.

Bruers, Stijn. 2015. "In Defense of Eating Vegan." *Journal of Agricultural and Environmental Ethics* 28 (4): 705–17.

Caldwell, Mark. 2014. "The Rise of the Gourmet Hamburger." *Contexts* 13 (3): 72–4.

Capper, Jude L, R.A. Cady, and D.E. Bauman. 2009. "The Environmental Impact of Dairy Production: 1944 Compared with 2007." *Journal of Animal Science* 87 (6): 2160–7.

Cohen, Stanley N., Annie C.Y. Chang, Herbert W. Boyer, and Robert B. Helling. 1973. "Construction of Biologically Functional Bacterial Plasmids *In Vitro*." *Proceedings of the National Academy of Sciences* 70 (11): 3240–4.

Cook, Ian, and Philip Crang. 1996. "The World On a Plate Culinary Culture, Displacement and Geographical Knowledges." *Journal of Material Culture* 1 (2): 131–53.

Datar, Isha, and Mirko Betti. 2010. "Possibilities for an *In Vitro* Meat Production System." *Innovative Food Science and Emerging Technologies* 11 (1): 13–22.

Dilworth, Tasmin, and Andrew McGregor. 2015. "Moral Steaks? Ethical Discourses of *In Vitro* Meat in Academia and Australia." *Journal of Agricultural and Environmental Ethics* 28 (1): 85–107.

Driessen, Clemens, and Michiel Korthals. 2012. "Pig Towers and *In Vitro* Meat: Disclosing Moral Worlds by Design." *Social Studies of Science* 42 (6): 797–820.

Ellahi, Basma. 1996. "Genetic Modification for the Production of Food: The Food Industry's Response." *British Food Journal* 98 (4/5): 53–72.

Fellet, Melissae. 2015. "A Fresh Take on Fake Meat." *ACS Central Science* 1 (7): 347–9.

Ford, Brian J. 2011. "Impact of Cultured Meat on Global Agriculture." *World Agriculture* 2 (2): 43–6.

Fudge, Erica. 2010. "Why It's Easy Being a Vegetarian." *Textual Practice* 24 (1): 149–66.

Geels, Frank W. 2005. "The Dynamics of Transitions in Socio-Technical Systems: A Multi-Level Analysis of the Transition Pathway from Horse-Drawn Carriages to Automobiles (1860–1930)." *Technology Analysis and Strategic Management* 17 (4): 445–76.

Gerber, Pierre J., Henning Steinfeld, Benjamin Henderson, Anne Mottet, Carolyn Opio, Jeroen Dijkman, Allessandra Falcucci, and Giuseppe Tempio. 2013. *Tackling Climate Change through Livestock: A Global Assessment of Emissions and Mitigation Opportunities*. New York: Food and Agriculture Organization of the United Nations (FAO).

Goldstein, D., S. Mintz, M. Krondl, and L. Mason. 2015. *The Oxford Companion to Sugar and Sweets*. Oxford: Oxford University Press.

Graça, João, Maria Manuela Calheiros, and Abílio Oliveira. 2015. "Attached to Meat? (Un) Willingness and Intentions to Adopt a More Plant-Based Diet." *Appetite* 95: 113–25.

Haraway, Donna. 2008. "Chicken." In *Animal Subjects: An Ethical Reader in a Posthuman World*, vol. 8, edited by Jodey Castricano, 33–8. Waterloo, ON: Wilfrid Laurier University Press.

Hennigan, Paul. 2015. "Is Vegan Food Really that Bad? The Relation between Moral Identity Threat and Flavor Preference." Honours thesis, Salem State University.

Hilbeck, Angelika, Rosa Binimelis, Nicolas Defarge, Ricarda Steinbrecher, András Székács, Fern Wickson, Michael Antoniou, Philip L. Bereano, Ethel Ann Clark, and Michael Hansen. 2015. "No Scientific Consensus on GMO Safety." *Environmental Sciences Europe* 27 (1): 1.

Hopkins, Patrick D., and Austin Dacey. 2008. "Vegetarian Meat: Could Technology Save Animals and Satisfy Meat Eaters?" *Journal of Agricultural and Environmental Ethics* 21 (6): 579–96.

Hsiao, Timothy. 2015. "In Defense of Eating Meat." *Journal of Agricultural and Environmental Ethics* 28 (2): 277–91.

Jönsson, Erik. 2016. "Benevolent Technotopias and Hitherto Unimaginable Meats: Tracing the Promises of *In Vitro* Meat." *Social Studies of Science* 6 (5): 725–48.

Lee, Angela. 2018. "Meat-ing Demand: Is In Vitro Meat a Pragmatic, Problematic, or Paradoxical Solution?" *Canadian Journal of Women and the Law* 30 (1): 1–41.

Macinnis, P. 2002. *Bittersweet: The Story of Sugar*. Sydney: Allen and Unwin.

Miller, John. 2012. "*In Vitro* Meat: Power, Authenticity and Vegetarianism." *Journal for Critical Animal Studies* 10 (4): 41–63.

Mouat, Michael J., and Russell Prince. 2018. "Cultured Meat and Cowless Milk: On Making Markets for Animal-Free Food." *Journal of Cultural Economy* 11 (4): 315–29.

New Harvest. 2016. Accessed 10 December 2016. www.newharvest.com.

Newman, Lenore. 2014. "Blackberries: Canadian Cuisine and Marginal Foods." *Cuizine: The Journal of Canadian Food Cultures / Cuizine: Revue des cultures culinaires au Canada* 5 (1).

Nielsen, Jens. 2013. "Production of Biopharmaceutical Proteins by Yeast: Advances through Metabolic Engineering." *Bioengineered* 4 (4): 207–11.

Ozersky, J. 2009. *The Hamburger: A History*. New Haven, CT: Yale University Press.

Post, Mark J. 2012. "Cultured Meat from Stem Cells: Challenges and Prospects." *Meat Science* 92 (3): 297–301.

Scott, Sydney E., Yoel Inbar, and Paul Rozin. 2016. "Evidence for Absolute Moral Opposition to Genetically Modified Food in the United States." *Perspectives on Psychological Science* 11 (3): 315–24.

Sexton, Alexandra E. 2018. "Eating for the Post–Anthropocene: Alternative Proteins and the Biopolitics of Edibility." *Transactions of the Institute of British Geographers* 43 (4): 586–600.

Simonsen, Rasmus R. 2015. "Eating for the Future: Veganism and the Challenge of *In Vitro* Meat." In *Biopolitics and Utopia*, edited by Patricia Stapleton and Andrew Byers, 167–90. New York: Springer.

Slade, Peter. 2018. "If You Build It, Will They Eat It? Consumer Preferences for Plant-Based and Cultured Meat Burgers." *Appetite* 125: 428–37.

Smith, A.F. 2008. *Hamburger: A Global History*. London: Reaktion Books.

Stephens, Neil, Illtud Dunsford, Lucy Di Silvio, Marianne Ellis, Abigail Glencross, and Alexandra Sexton. 2018. "Bringing Cultured Meat to Market: Technical, Socio-Political, and Regulatory Challenges in Cellular Agriculture." *Trends in Food Science and Technology* 78: 155–66.

Stephens, Neil, Emma King, and Catherine Lyall. 2018. "Blood, Meat, and Upscaling Tissue Engineering: Promises, Anticipated Markets, and Performativity in the Biomedical and Agri-Food Sectors." *BioSocieties* 13 (2): 368–88.

Stone, Christopher D. 1972. "Should Trees Have Standing? Toward Legal Rights for Natural Objects." *Southern California Law Review* 45: 450.

Tan, K.T., K.T. Lee, A.R. Mohamed, and S. Bhatia. 2009. "Palm Oil: Addressing Issues and towards Sustainable Development." *Renewable and Sustainable Energy Reviews* 13 (2): 420–7.

Turvey, Ralph. 2005. "Horse Traction in Victorian London." *The Journal of Transport History* 26 (2): 38–59.

Van den Berghe, Pierre L. 1984. "Ethnic Cuisine: Culture in Nature." *Ethnic and Racial Studies* 7 (3): 387–97.

Van der Weele, Cor, and Clemens Driessen. 2013. "Emerging Profiles for Cultured Meat; Ethics through and as Design." *Animals* 3 (3): 647–62.

Van der Weele, Cor, and Johannes Tramper. 2014. "Cultured Meat: Every Village Its Own Factory?" *Trends in Biotechnology* 32 (6): 294–6.

Ventura, B.A., M.A.G. Von Keyserlingk, and D.M. Weary. 2015. "Animal Welfare Concerns and Values of Stakeholders within the Dairy Industry." *Journal of Agricultural and Environmental Ethics* 28 (1): 109–26.

Vitaliano, Peter, and IFAMR. 2016. "Global Dairy Trade: Where Are We, How Did We Get Here and Where Are We Going?" *International Food and Agribusiness Management Review* 19: 27–36.

Weis, A.J. 2013. *The Ecological Hoofprint: The Global Burden of Industrial Livestock*. London: Zed Books.

10

The Structural Constraints on Green Meat

Abra Brynne

Almost 150 years ago, a few large companies organized the meat packing industry to favour large-scale and high-volume operations and, as this chapter will show, that history has had lasting repercussions for sustainable livestock production and meat processing. In what follows, I explore how the early days of the North American meat sector affected how meat is produced and consumed today. It has affected how most domestic animals are raised, where and how most consumers obtain their meat, the regulatory regimes governing the entire sector, and the profitability of the businesses involved. By demonstrating the significant scale, regulatory, and economic constraints tied to commercial meat production, this chapter makes the case that a truly sustainable meat system also involves people, in the sense that it is founded on the social and economic needs of the people who work in the sector, in addition to animal welfare and environmental objectives. Yet as this chapter argues, the structure of the North American meat sector, including regulatory, scalar, and economic constraints, limits a truly sustainable meat system.

The structural mould for North America's meat industry was set more than a century ago in the US Midwest by the "Chicago Four," and continues to this day. Today, as in the past, just four corporate giants – Tyson, Cargill, JBS, and National Beef – control 84 per cent of America's beef slaughter industry (PBS 2014). The North American meat processing industry has a long history of relying on income streams *other* than meat for profits. This includes government subsidies and supply chain control through consolidation. This history has driven a public policy that privileges the very large, very few processors that dominate the sector. As a consequence, smaller-scale producers have continued to struggle to compete, or have altogether been driven out of the market.

This chapter examines the barriers to and opportunities for a sustainable meat system. A truly sustainable meat regime is one that addresses social and economic concerns relating to livestock farmers, and community health and resilience. It aims to convey that the ethical decision about meat need not resort to the extremes of either veganism or the industrial meat systems – there are alternatives located in between. Cultural and policy shifts will be necessary in order to achieve sustainable meat. In this chapter I outline how historical and structural manifestations have created barriers to "green meat" in North America. I then reflect on lessons learned from working closely with abattoir operators from 2006 to 2012 in British Columbia, Canada. I hope to contribute to an enhanced understanding of the constraints on sustainable meat production in Canada by explaining the development of meat sector policy regimes. A more nuanced understanding of these issues may lead conscientious consumers to seek out and value meat from provincially licensed abattoirs and sustainably raised livestock producers.[1]

Origins of the Mould: The Early Days of the North American Meat Industry

Before the development of new transportation and refrigeration technologies in the late nineteenth century, early North American settlers relied on place-based diets for any meat they consumed. As Gordon (1984, 246) explains, the constraints of transportation and perishability shaped the geography of meat processing: "Before the 1870s and 1880s firms could exercise control over little more than the most immediate area. The reason was simple: freshly slaughtered meat was highly perishable. Sending it far away was not expensive, it was impossible." Nevertheless, where a critical mass of people resided, small-scale businesses slaughtered and processed the animals that fed their meat supply, and the numbers reflect this. In 1892, "there were 1,950 wholesale and retail butchers in Chicago alone and some 80,000 nationwide" (Libecap 1992, 246), at a time when the US population was only 63 million!

Chicago was a key hub for the grain and meat sectors in the nineteenth and early twentieth centuries. In *Nature's Metropolis: Chicago and the Great West*, William Cronon documents a key shift that would ever-after mould the structure of the North American meat sector. The latter was transformed from a sector where every community had local abattoirs and multiple butchers to one dominated by a handful of large corporations and long supply chains. By the 1860s, quickly expanding railroad infrastructure radiated out from Chicago to facilitate aggregation of agricultural products and other resources extracted from the hinterlands. Its location on Lake Michigan also enabled those goods – sometimes further processed or refined in Chicago – to travel by water on to key markets on the east coast of the US and onwards to Great Britain and Europe (Cronon 1992). Chicago became the site of a large meat processing infrastructure that became the mould for industrial-scale meat processing, marketing, and distribution. This was due to its location in relation to the grain surplus of the plains, livestock, and the transportation that delivered the animals and then sent them out to markets after being processed.

Onto this stage strode George H. Hammond, Gustavus Swift, Philip D. Armour, and Nelson Morris, who together became known as the "Chicago Four" (Gordon 1984, 246). By the early twentieth century, they were collectively slaughtering and marketing millions of cattle, sheep, and pigs a year. These early tycoons contributed to the structural foundations for the North American meat sector that continues to this day. The Chicago Four were able to process, market, distribute, and profit from the production and sale of meat thanks to economies of scale and proximity to the necessary specialty processing infrastructure. Swift perfected displaying and marketing less desirable cuts of meat to wholesale and individual buyers (Cronon 1991, 237). Hammond applied and perfected shipping fresh meat to distant markets with ice packs (Gordon 1984, 246) – which was later replaced with mechanical refrigeration, to "store winter" and move meat during the warm months of the year (ibid., 230–5). These marketing and transportation advances were soon taken up by Armour and Morris as well, who completed this powerful quartet.

The Chicago Four also applied and refined the "disassembly line" model first invented in the pork packing plants of Cincinnati. The line mechanically moved carcasses past a series of workers who each disassembled it into smaller cuts. As Cronon explains, this "division of labor allowed packers to accelerate the rate at which workers handled hogs [and later, cattle] and led to specialized ways of dealing with each constituent body part. The enormous volume of animals meant that even body parts that had formerly been waste now became commercial products: lard, glue, brushes, candles, soaps" (ibid., 229). Frederick Law Olmsted expressed his awe at the pace of the disassembly line: thirty-five seconds, from the moment when one hog touched the table until the next occupied its place (ibid.).

The Chicago Four were able to profit from animal slaughter in new ways. In short, the income from the by-products offset the losses incurred from a deliberately distorted pricing model that privileged large operations and marginalized small-scale ones. The testimony given in 1889 by Philip Armour before the Senate Select Committee on the Transportation and Sale of Meat Products, commonly referred to as the Vest Committee (ibid., 251) demonstrates loss from the processing and sale of the meat from one beef carcass. What is important to note here is that a net profit was only achievable through the sale of by-products.[2] As Cronon points out, this often came at the expense of the quality of meat produced: "By shrewdly manipulating bone and offal and even spoiled meat in myriad ways, Chicago companies could convert them into substances which had all the appearance of human food" (ibid., 252). However, as noted above, this was an unsustainable business model for small operators who were unable to transform these by-products for *commercial* purposes. In contrast, sheer volume made this entirely workable for the members of the Chicago Four. In the year 1904, for instance, Swift and Company alone had sales of approximately $200,000,000, with a profit of 19 per cent or $3,850,000 (Walker 1906, 501).

The advantages of economies of scale and the large processing infrastructure, particularly for the by-products, were used to derive additional income for the bigger producers. The Chicago Four, like all mass producers who quickly saturate local markets, looked further afield to move the large volumes of meat they were producing, resulting in the undercutting of "mom and pop" operators across northeastern US (Cronon 1991, 243). Part of their strategy to achieve this end was to collude to keep cattle prices down and to drive competition out of the market by selling below the cost of production (Walker 1906; Gordon 1984). By 1890 these firms controlled 89 per cent of the US-dressed meat trade and had created a year-round market for meat (Gordon 1984, 246).

Government attempts to regulate the Chicago Four, also known as the Beef Trust, began in the late nineteenth century. As Libecap (1992, 242) explains, these efforts and the resulting acts (the Interstate Commerce Act of 1887, the Sherman Act of 1890, and the Meat Inspection Act of 1891) represented "a significant break from what had previously been considered an appropriate role for the federal government ... providing a new and permanent mandate for government regulation in the market economy." As early as 1888, the US Senate examined possible collusion in the sector and its impact on beef and cattle prices. The Vest Report, issued two years later, found that the Beef Trust fixed beef prices, divided territories and business amongst themselves, and compelled retailers to purchase only from them (Azzam and Anderson 1996, 15). Senate testimony described how packers sold products from diseased animals. It also illustrated how it was "therefore less healthy than locally slaughtered beef" (Libecap 1992, 255). Based on the investigation of the

Vest Committee and its report, the Meat Inspection Act – the first in North America – was passed in 1891, created to constrain the power of the Beef Trust oligopoly. As Libecap suggests, the act was primarily intended as anti-trust legislation, with the concern over human health serving as a popular justification: "The disease issue was stressed by local slaughterhouses in an effort to limit or redirect the economic effects of the introduction of refrigeration. Similarly, the midwestern farmers, who blamed the Beef trust for low cattle prices and who had other concerns about trusts and low agricultural prices, were the most active lobbyists for state and federal anti-trust legislation" (Libecap 1992, 259).

Despite high hopes for the Meat Inspection and Sherman Anti-Trust Acts, they appear to have done little to constrain or change the practices of the Chicago Four. Attorney General Knox filed the federal suit against the Beef Trust in May of 1902, in a case known as *Swift and Co. v. United States*. In 1905 the court found that the Trust had colluded in contravention of the Sherman Act. Nevertheless, disputes over the ruling continued into the 1920s, and failed to end litigation against the Beef Trust or their control of the meat sector (Gordon 1984, 278).

Additional attempts at government oversight in the early twentieth century also failed to significantly curtail the power of the Beef Trust. Upton Sinclair's 1906 novel, *The Jungle*, portrayed some of the worst offences of the Chicago meat sector based on first-hand interviews of workers in the slaughterhouses. The novel raised concerns in the public about food safety. It is widely credited for contributing to the introduction in that same year of the US's Meat Inspection and Pure Food and Drugs Act. It is also credited to some extent for the creation of Canada's 1907 Meat and Canned Foods Act (Ostry 2006, 15–16). Nonetheless, well-intentioned legislation has done little to prevent the sector's consolidation in the hands of few large players, which continues today.

Meat Inspection in Canada: The British Columbia Experience

Allow me to now travel north across the border and focus on a more recent example with which I am intimately familiar. Just as early industrialization of US meat production had layers of consequences for smaller-scale sustainable producers, so too have recent Canadian federal and provincial regulations contributed to reshaping the contemporary meat processing sector in British Columbia. Specifically, I argue that the regulatory framework and governance of meat inspection in the province has negatively affected small and medium abattoirs and those that depend on them. Regulations have implications for whether or not sustainable meat can be processed, distributed, and consumed. I gained a privileged perspective on this sector and the struggle of many small-scale abattoirs and livestock farmers as a member of the five-person "meat team" associated with the province's Meat Industry Enhancement Strategy (MIES) between 2006 and 2012. The meat team was tasked with assisting abattoir operators to achieve licensing under the new provincial regulations introduced in 2007. Here, I explore how meat inspection regulation in British Columbia affected local abattoirs and how the meat team's strategies sought to support and build a more sustainable meat sector.

Meat Inspection in Canada is divided between the federal and provincial/territorial governments. The federal government provides inspection for facilities constructed and operated to meet the Federal Meat Inspection Act requirements that apply to products destined for inter-provincial trade or export out of Canada. The provincial or territorial government determines the form and level of oversight for meat destined for markets within the province or territory in which the animal is slaughtered. In British Columbia, inspection at abattoirs commenced in 1966 and was restricted to designated "meat inspection areas," which were generally pockets of higher (human) population density. Meat inspection of provincially licensed abattoirs started in and around Victoria, the provincial capital, and then expanded to include the Greater Vancouver region, the city of Vernon, a portion of the Peace River District, and southern sections of the Sunshine Coast. In these areas, abattoirs were required to have continuous inspection while operating and were subject to prescriptive physical infrastructure requirements. The remaining and vast majority of the province, geographically speaking, fell under the oversight of local health authorities. These latter abattoirs operated without continuous inspection and had no specific infrastructure requirements.

Eventually, this dual meat inspection regime was viewed by political authorities as a threat to export market access. As such, successive federal governments worked to bring "a more internally coherent food safety regime," starting with the Mulroney government in the 1980s and followed by the Chrétien government in the 1990s (Skogstad 2006, 192).

In 1994, these efforts resulted in the creation of the Blueprint for the Canadian Food Inspection System, which "was signed by federal/provincial/territorial agriculture ministers and subsequently by their health and fisheries counterparts," along with an accompanying guidelines document (Skogstad 2006, 163). Ironically, more than a century after small-scale American processors were proposing meat inspection to ensure that small and medium-scale producers could survive, larger-scale producers in Canada promoted meat inspection to *retain* their access to markets.

The Canadian Food Inspection System Implementation Group – an interdepartmental and intergovernmental group – was tasked with implementing the Blueprint but had limited success. British Columbia had representation on the Canadian Food Inspection System Implementation Group, which was undoubtedly the impetus behind changes in BC's meat inspection regulations introduced in 2004 and brought fully into force with the Meat Inspection Regulation of 2007. The changes sought to harmonize provincial standards to federal ones, to impose them across the entire province. They were mostly opposed by small and medium-sized abattoirs because of the associated cost of capital investments to comply with them, and the potential impact on their market boundaries (Skogstad 2006, 164).

The introduction of the 2007 regulations also created a new set of problems for many of the smaller abattoirs because it forced the slaughter sector out of the barn, off the farm, and into the public eye. Prior to the province-wide meat inspection regime in British Columbia, many abattoirs were based on farms and, as such, were just one part of the complex business enterprise of raising livestock.[3] However, with the new regulations, slaughter was no longer regarded as simply one among diverse farm activities, and the sector experienced a backlash. Many abattoirs were suddenly no longer a welcome part of the local food system, though paradoxically the demand for local, sustainable meat did not diminish. In some communities, the abattoirs faced profound and prolonged opposition especially to their ancillary activities, such as the rendering or composting of offal – the very activities that often are the difference between making a profit or not. Livestock and its associated markets declined in most areas. For example, on Salt Spring Island there was an estimated loss of almost 50 per cent of the sheep population and its iconic high-quality lamb meat sought by foodies and restaurateurs alike (Reichert and Thomson 2010, 4). In the heavily populated North Okanagan, a 2008 report documented the pre-Meat Inspection Regulation of local custom slaughter for farmers and estimated the impact on the local economy was in excess of $5 million (Johnson 2008).

Abattoir operators who declared the intention of obtaining a licence found themselves under the scrutiny of government agencies at all levels. Diverse agencies and ministries each considered the practices and implications of the slaughter of animals from the perspective of their respective mandates. This resulted in a series of changes to policy, regulation, and a cumulative regulatory burden on the abattoir operators. The meat team witnessed new regulations applied to waste, the introduction of the Canadian Food Inspection Agency's Enhanced Feed Ban related to the incidence of bovine spongiform encephalopathy (BSE, or mad cow disease), and changes to some abattoir owners' tax classifications, from farm to commercial or industrial, resulting in a significantly higher annual tax burden. Restrictions on activities in BC's Agricultural Land Reserve also impacted abattoirs. Specifically, this was related to the sources of livestock being processed and the handling of specified risk material. Business planning and the financial viability of existing and prospective small-scale abattoir operators could not help but suffer under that degree of uncertainty, change, and additional regulatory requirements (see table 10.1 for a timeline of regulatory changes in the sector). The transition was complicated by the new regulatory requirements, including construction or renovation costs associated with compliance. Abattoir owners were encouraged to model their upgraded or new abattoirs after a template provided in the BC Centre for Disease Control's (2005) *Plant Construction, Equipment and Operation Guidelines*, which recommended finishing materials and equipment that were not strictly necessary in the regulation. If followed, the template would add significant expenses that few could afford or felt matched their operational requirements and needs. At the same time, local governments, civil society, and grassroots movements fought to keep local abattoirs in operation and to mitigate the regulatory and financial burden imposed by the new meat inspection regulations. Boucher (2008, 1) describes how the new regulations threatened food security and sovereignty in the isolated Bella Coola Valley: "In rural areas where the infrastructure and resources for regulatory compliance are not as vast as they are in urban areas, taking away the right of the small-scale farmer to sell a dozen sides of beef to his neighbors is ruining cultural identity, food security and a sense of sovereignty over local resources." The costs and the effects of the new meat sector regulations were starting to affect local community's food security.

In 2006, the government established a program to assist the industry in making the transition to licensing, full inspection, and the accompanying facility requirements. The province contracted the BC Food Processors Association to manage a capital grant and loans program, as well as the meat team – five staff located across the province to assist with the licensing under the Meat Inspection Regulation of 2007. The meat team adopted two key strategies to try to ease the transition and regulatory requirements. The first strategy was to prove that humane and safe practices could be achieved in small abattoirs, reducing the construction or renovation costs associated with compliance. I and my colleagues on the meat team identified inconsistencies in what

Table 10.1   Timeline of regulatory interventions impacting abattoirs

Year	Agency	Regulatory Intervention
2004	Ministry of Health Services	Meat Inspection Regulation introduced
2006	Ministry of Health Services	Meat Inspection Regulation initial implementation deadline
2007	Ministry of Environment	Organic Matter Recycling Regulation, Waste Discharge Regulation both amended to include abattoir operations and waste
2007	Ministry of Health	Meat Inspection Regulation implemented
2007	Canadian Food Inspection Agency	Enhanced Feed Ban (related to mad cow disease)
2008	Agricultural Land Commission	Information bulletin: slaughter plants and handling red meat waste in the ALR
2008	Ministry of Environment	Code of Practice for the Slaughter and Poultry Processing Industry
2009	Interior Health Authority	Meat Inspection Guide for Facility Operations
2010	Ministry of Healthy Living and Sport	Meat Inspection Regulation amended, Class D and E introduced
2014	Ministry of Agriculture	BC Abattoir Inspection System

abattoir operators were being told and what was actually required in the regulations. The regulations were trumpeted as "outcomes based." This, in theory, is supposed to mean that they could be met in different ways. We were able to advocate effectively on behalf of the operators, in part because it was not our livelihoods that were at stake in the dialogue with the agency granting the licences. The second meat team strategy was to insist on geographically distributed processing that aligned with the needs of communities. It was crucial to locate licensed abattoirs in areas where the volume of livestock (across the species) warranted a facility, and in turn this would help to ensure that both the livestock and abattoir operators were viable.

Over time, as the negative impact of the regulatory changes manifested in community after community across the province, the regulations were amended and grants to assist with regulatory compliance were increased. Among the regulatory amendments was the creation of a novel graduated licensing system that provided viable options for rural and remote regions, with a reduced oversight and financial burden in regions where the business case for a conventional abattoir could simply

Table 10.2   Licences available under the Graduated Licensing System

Licence type	Activities permitted	Sales permitted	Geographic scope	No. of animal units*	Oversight
Class A	Slaughter and cut and wrap	Retail and direct to consumer	BC	Unlimited	Pre- and post-slaughter inspection of each animal
Class B	Slaughter only	Retail and direct to consumer	BC	Unlimited	Pre- and post-slaughter inspection of each animal
Class D	Slaughter only (own and other people's animals	Retail and direct to consumer	Sales restricted within the regional district where meat is produced	1–25	Periodic site assessments and audit of operational slaughter records
Class E	Slaughter only (own animals only)	Direct to consumer only	Sales restricted within the regional district where meat is produced	1–10	Periodic site assessments and audit of operational slaughter records
Personal use – no licence required	Slaughter only	None	For producer only	Unlimited	None

Source: BC Ministry of Agriculture
* One animal unit is equivalent to 1,000 pounds (one steer or the equivalent volume by weight of pigs, sheep, or poultry).

not be made (BC Ministry of Agriculture 2018; see table 10.2). The grant amounts made available to abattoirs were also increased over time. The initial offering was $50,000 per abattoir, unless it was a communal effort; in such cases the grant was up to $150,000. As abattoir operators began the process of upgrading or creating new builds to obtain licensing, it became clear that the average investment would be in excess of $250,000. This frequently did not include the cost of either liquid or solid waste infrastructure, which could double the bill. The grant amount available to individual operators was eventually increased to $150,000 and low-interest loans were also arranged through the MIES program.

The meat team estimated that before the change in regulations, there were well in excess of 300 abattoirs operating across the province. Immediately following the implementation of the changes, that number dropped to thirteen provincially licensed abattoirs and fourteen federally

Table 10.3   Sampling of livestock numbers before the introduction and after the implementation of the Meat Inspection Regulation

Species	Regional District Central Kootenay		Regional District Okanagan-Similkameen		Salt Spring Island	
	2001	2011	2001	2011	2005	2008
Cattle	11,500	7,401	31,528	16,117	219	123
Pigs	349	148	329	102	26	16
Chickens	22,580	10,854	10,541	7,316	4,000	1,829
Sheep	685	729	1,391	1,228	2,342	1,302

Sources: RDCK data – author; RDO-S data – *Agriculture in Brief*; Salt Spring Island data – Reichert and Thomson

registered plants (see table 10.3). What had been a vital link in the local meat supply chain, an important contributor to the food security of (particularly rural and remote) regions, and a long-held cultural practice in many communities suddenly required licensing (or it became a criminal activity). Those who opposed the regulatory changes on multiple grounds proved correct: farmers lost a key source of income, vacant pastures became overgrown, and the community lost access to locally produced meat and organic manure (essential for soil fertility).

By the time the meat team folded in 2012, there were fifty abattoirs with full Class A or B licences (though in excess of seventy proponents had dropped out of the licensing process) and more than seventy Class D and E licences in designated remote regional districts. During the years that the team worked directly with the industry as it adjusted to the new demands, it became clear that the financial viability of Class A or B licensed abattoirs depends on a zero or negligible debt load and, ideally, on income streams from further processing in addition to slaughter fees. However, even combination slaughter and processing abattoirs struggle with razor-thin profit margins. This is largely for the same reasons that plagued the competitors of the Chicago Four over a century ago: the ability to charge the *true* cost of meat, including the cost of raising the livestock, is rarely afforded to the sector. This is the result of more than a century of consumer expectations of low meat prices.

Meat is not a low-cost item to produce. Animals raised outdoors in Canada experience four distinct seasons, which impacts their growth rates and reproductive cycles, as well as the availability and cost of feed. To stay afloat, the industry looks to the potential value found in by-products, as established by the cutthroat business strategies of the Chicago Four in the late nineteenth century. To derive income from these same by-products, however, there must be access to the necessary infrastructure. This can include tanneries, wool mills, and rendering plants. But these too have been lost across the Canadian landscape at the same time as the demise of small-scale abattoirs. With no means to transform the portions of the animal that are not suitable for human consumption,[4] they amass quickly and become a true waste. This results in considerable operational and expense implications for the abattoir operator and the livestock farmer alike.

Red Herrings and Food Safety

Legitimately or otherwise, "food safety" has been used for over a century in North America as the primary rationale for regulating the meat sector. In the late nineteenth century the Chicago Four's oligopoly faced increasing opposition from workers, livestock producers, and consumers. Rather than promoting fundamental changes, the newly introduced regulations targeted food safety. Cronon (1991, 242) elaborates, stating that, "in a pattern that became typical of meat industry controversies from this time on, public health was a convenient way of putting the best face on a deeper and more self-interested economic issue." For example, the 1906 enactment of the Meat Inspection and Pure Food and Drugs Act was an attempt to protect the public good in the form of safe, unadulterated food rather than break the control of the Chicago Four.

More than a century later the meat industry in Canada has been partnering with the government of Canada on food safety.[5] This was done to ensure that export market requirements are met with the same ostensible public good in mind. The *Blueprint for the Canadian Food Inspection System* designed a food safety protocol where the federal government determines the outcomes and standards, while the industry determines the means to meet them. This protocol is especially important for exported meat that must be processed through federally registered plants. The capital and operating costs of federal plants are very high and necessitate a high-volume throughput to justify the investment in the large facilities and auditing protocols.

The introduction of the Hazard Analysis and Critical Control Point (HACCP) program into the North American meat sector delegated food safety standards to food processors, food manufacturers, and farmers (Skogstad 2008). In federal plants, HACCP programs are relied upon to identify and manage hazards. The role of government is then "to focus on the provision of scientific and technical advice to industry, possibly some on-site inspection, and auditing industry records to verify compliance" (Skogstad 2006, 165). The decision by the United States to require HACCP in their federal plants and for any imported meat led Canada to follow suit and adopt it in 1998 to secure the large export market (ibid., 165–6). The use of HACCP reduced inspection costs and shifted some of the expense of food safety oversight to the private sector. The problem with HACCP is that it is very expensive to implement and equally expensive to operate, especially for smaller operators.

Risk, rather than danger, dominates food safety discourse and oversight for supply chains that aggregate and distribute meat, and HACCP is no guarantee of safe meat. Recalls from full HACCP plants across North America appear regularly in the media. For example, Food Safety News (2016) documented the recall of 47 million pounds of meat and poultry products in the US in 2016 alone. One of the most notorious recalls in Canada occurred in 2012, involving XL Foods, whose Brooks, Alberta plant was the subject of the largest meat recall in Canadian history. It received wide media coverage. Meat with an estimated value of $40 million was recalled from across Canada, the US, Mexico, Egypt, and Japan (D'Aliesio 2013). These examples provided community members in BC with some evidence to help push back against changes in the meat inspection regulation. They pointed out that there was no evidence that anyone had ever become sick from meat from the *smaller* abattoirs. But as the axiom goes, an absence of evidence is not evidence of absence.

Provincially licensed abattoirs do not rely on the HACCP-based audits. Provincially licensed abattoirs employ an organoleptic ("sight and smell") method in which inspectors visibly inspect each carcass and the corresponding organs for signs of disease or contamination. The inspection of each carcass, every key organ, and every poultry cavity is the basis of safe meat. Where there is cause for concern, the carcass is isolated and held until it can be inspected by a veterinarian or other qualified professional. The risk of food-borne illness outbreaks is mitigated because of the small numbers and the limited reach of the product. Provincially licensed plants are limited by provincial boundaries – there is no inter-provincial trade permitted for meat produced at provincially inspected abattoirs.

This limitation extends to whether or not the handful of large grocery chains that dominate Canadian food outlets will purchase meat from provincially licensed abattoirs. Grocery chains move products across provincial boundaries, a problem that large suppliers such as Cargill and JBS (two of the world's largest processors of meat) can easily overcome, and at the same time facilitate purchasing by retailers with a "one-stop shop." Unfortunately, sourcing meat from large scale operations generally means sourcing meat from confined animal feeding operations (CAFOS) and feedlots.

The meat sector is dominated by today's version of the Chicago Four. When something goes wrong at one plant, the wide – frequently global – distribution of the meat results in millions of pounds of tainted products. Ironically, such recalls tend to result in calls for *more* inspection and stricter controls that are to be imposed on *all* abattoirs and meat processors due to the public's legitimate fear of contaminated food. This unsustainable vicious cycle is built into the structural mould of a meat processing sector dominated by a few very large processing corporations. Consequently, potential solutions to support sustainably produced meat need to be found outside the dominant meat supply chains.

As Waltner-Toews (2009, 209) has written, "the globalization of the food supply has simply accentuated the fault lines that already existed in the agrifood system." In other words, the global agrifood system deals in undifferentiated commodities and the link between the producer, the field, the animal, and the eater has been severed. In such a system, the average consumer cannot possibly know how the animal was raised, the quality of its feed, or what its final days or moments may have been like. With large abattoirs processing upwards of 5,000 animals per week, and processors producing hamburger patties that may contain meat from thousands of animals, not only can the life circumstances of each of those animals not be known, but "the risks are magnified through mass production systems" (ibid., 210). Sustainable production, distribution, and consumption of meat are constrained by the present business and regulatory models.

Thinking Outside the (Knock) Box: Creative Responses to the Needs of Small and Medium-Scale Abattoirs

The mould of the meat sector has sidelined small and medium-sized abattoirs, and limited access to sustainable meat. Creative responses are needed to build and support an infrastructure that enables sustainable livestock rearing and slaughter, and meat consumption. This includes appropriate abattoir regulations, humane animal rearing and slaughter, and meat consumption that values the people who raise, butcher, and prepare our food. Sustainable meat production is context-specific and founded on values and ethics supported by local communities. Steps are being taken to address the varying contexts of where and how meat is produced and distributed.

In January 2014, the BC government took over inspection of provincially licensed abattoirs from the Canadian Food Inspection Agency. This shift initiated a process that began to address abattoir operators' concerns about the regulations. The BC Ministry of Health sought input from abattoir operators, conducted a review of the existing inspection system, and developed terms of reference for a new provincial system prior to setting up its own inspectorate. The culture of inspection under the Canadian Food Inspection Agency resembled a "command and control" relationship in which abattoir operators had little or no voice in the resolution of production issues, perceived or real. BC's new inspectors work with abattoir operators to problem-solve when issues arise, which has changed the culture of oversight. As Martin, Mundel and Rideout (2016, 184) have stated: "It is a delicate yet important task to recognize that rules and regulations exist for good reasons but that regulators will apply them somewhat differently in different contexts. A standard equation for mitigating risk in all situations is not realistic, but a framework that shows how and why discretion is used could support context-specific risk assessments. Flexibility and consistency can coexist if there are clear decision-making processes and a consistent understanding of the intent of the law."

The new culture of oversight addresses the crucial concerns of the application of law, the humane handling of animals, and meat safety without further endangering the viability of small-scale abattoirs through shutdowns or recalls that are costly for small businesses. Small-scale operators depend heavily on a social licence granted them by their customers that is founded almost exclusively on quality product and reasonable prices. As Waltner-Toews (2009, 215) observes, "the real questions in food safety are questions of values and ethics. The technical questions, by comparison, are trivial." In short, safe and sustainable meat requires appropriate and context-specific regulatory oversight.

Sustainable meat also requires that *all* the edible parts of the animal are eaten, not just the ones that are popular. One of the challenges that faces sustainable meat producers is the fact that North Americans prefer certain cuts of meat. This poses significant hurdles for both producers of livestock and processors of meat to overcome in order to find ways to use the whole carcass. Our preference for chicken breasts means that the chicken marketing boards must find other outlets for the excess thighs and drumsticks. Our demand for steaks, roasts, and ribs forces creative marketing for the rest of the steer, lamb, or pig. As conscientious consumers, making use of the whole animal is about respect for an animal's life. If we, as a society, can come to terms with the reality that animals are killed for our meat, we will better support the integration, back into our communities, of the necessary infrastructure that enables sustainable livestock rearing and slaughter.

Sustainable meat requires that producers and processors receive reasonable payment and return on their expertise and investments. Most farmers are currently price-takers rather than price-makers – they must accept the price on offer whether or not it covers the cost of production, in conditions that mirror the Chicago Four and their manipulation and control of the prices paid for live animals. Eaters will have to pay higher prices for their food to enable farmers to be price-makers. This value should also extend to the butcher, adding them to the roster of respected trades and professions. The individual who works in a small to medium-sized, provincially licensed abattoir needs to know how to manage a live animal in the corral, how to humanely stun it, and how to perform all the tasks necessary to deliver a clean carcass into the cooler. These activities, and the skills necessary to perform them, are quite distinct from those of workers in large plants who perform repetitive, monotonous, single tasks in the large disassembly lines developed in Cincinnati and Chicago in the nineteenth century. Raising and killing animals compassionately are skills that are desperately needed. Revitalizing small-scale abattoirs is an opportunity to repopulate the trade with apprenticeships, training, and support.

Consumers seeking sustainable meat will most readily access it by supporting small and medium-scale provincially licensed abattoirs, or by doing the raising and slaughtering themselves. Setting aside the very real issue of hunger and poverty across the country, the fact that Canadians on average spend approximately 11 per cent of their disposable income on food means that there is surely some opportunity to address the abysmally low net farm incomes that have plagued farmers for decades (National Farmers Union 2011). As Margaret Visser (2010, 105) has rightly observed, "expenditure on food does not increase in the same ratio as income, but becomes relatively lower. People learn to expect that food will be cheap; money is for spending on other things." This will have to change if we truly want to eat sustainably and humanely produced meat.

Provincial abattoirs are generally structured so that they can accept "custom kill," processing a range of animals and species in response to the needs of their local farming community. In contrast, large federal plants are highly mechanized, requiring consistent and constant supply, in terms of species, size, shape, and volume. For instance, mechanical processing lines are designed for cornish-cross "meat birds." These lines are therefore less able to handle heritage breeds of chickens that vary in size. The inevitable variations in size and shape of other breeds may mean that they are not properly plucked, that limbs will be broken, and that skin will be torn. This then risks rejection of the carcass by the inspector, resulting in a loss to the farmer and the waste of an animal. Consumers will also need to shift their shopping habits and patronize the independent venues where provincially inspected meat is sold.

Sustainable food systems are coming to be understood more and more to mean that there is proximity between the sources of the food and the eater. Further, advocates of sustainable food systems are increasingly integrating other values and priorities into their food choices, such as ecologically sustainable practices; animals raised in environments that enable them to manifest their natural behaviours and are handled humanely throughout (including at slaughter); and safe working conditions and living wages for the humans involved in the production and supply chains. Cultural and policy shifts will be necessary in order to achieve these laudable goals. A truly sustainable meat regime is one that addresses social and economic concerns relating to livestock farmers, community health and resilience – not solely environmental well-being.

Summary Reflections on Abattoirs and Sustainable Meat

The intent of this chapter is to convey that there are alternatives to the two poles of veganism and industrial meat systems when it comes to the ethical choice about meat. However, consumers in search of sustainably and humanely raised meat have to realize their role in enabling its production, and the very real constraints experienced by the meat sector. Farmers and abattoir operators can only provide sustainable meat if they can cover their costs to produce it and receive a reasonable return for their time and investment.

The food systems of the twenty-first century are globally interconnected, and it is important to note that this integration is no accident. As Kneen (1993, 73) has explained, "to say simply that *industrialization* describes the transformation of farming and the food system in the latter half of the 20th century obscures the fact that ideology and special interests were the driving force of this industrialization. Equated with the notion of Progress, and therefore largely unchallenged, industrialization continues to be a major tool of distancing" humans from the sources of their food. This realization is an opportunity to reconnect to our place in the world and to the animals in it.

Animals and the people who care for them should be re-centred. This means that we will have to reverse how effectively we have "de-animalized" our meat. By dissociating that pink substance on white or black styrofoam from a living, breathing animal, we are excused from considering the ways in which it was raised and slaughtered. To treat animals with respect does not have to mean removing them from our diets. In fact, proponents of endangered breeds advocate for their place on our menus. The seeming paradox is true – in order to keep the rare breeds alive, we have to kill and eat them. This helps demonstrate the business case for raising them. This is also the case for sustainably and humanely raised livestock, no matter what their breed. As Wendell Berry (1996, 90) writes, "if animals are regarded as machines, they are confined in pens remote from the source of their food, where their excrement becomes, instead of a fertilizer, first a 'waste' and then a pollutant. Furthermore, because confinement feeding depends so largely on grains, grass is removed from the rotation of crops and more land is exposed to erosion." As noted in a number of previous chapters in this volume, sustainable meat and landscapes depend on ecological farmers raising biodiverse species and breeds. Ecological farmers are often very attentive to the needs of their animals up to and including at the point of their death, establishing systems to reduce the stress that the animals may experience en route and in strange surroundings at the abattoir. Those farmers, in turn, depend on small and medium-scale abattoirs in proximity to their operations, if not directly on their farms.

Livingston (1994) and others write about the problems that result from the domestication of the human – our alienation from nature. This may account for our ability to be so seemingly heartless about the fate of the millions of chickens de-beaked, of pigs with tails and teeth removed, all so that they can live out their lives in inhumanely small spaces for the sole purpose of producing meat for human consumption. We are far from the practices that Hugh Brody describes in *The Other Side of Eden* (2009, 244–5):

> Many Inuit would put a little fresh water in the mouth of a freshly killed seal or whale so that it, and all other seals and whales, would know that the hunter respected the willingness of the hunted to be killed and eaten. Gitxsan and Nisga'a would mark the harvest of the first salmon each season with statements of thanks to the salmon for agreeing to return to be harvested in the people's rivers. Algonquian hunters would place the bones of bears they had killed in trees, showing respect and appreciation to all bears. Bushmen of the southern Kalahari who gathered roots from deep in the desert sand would often place an offering in the hole they had dug before filling it in again, as a sign of respect and thanks to the plants. Failure to pay this kind of attention to creatures and plants risks causing them to stay away or to refuse to be found.

The care that Brody describes may not be practicable for most of us who consume meat. However, a greater attention to and respect for the beings whose flesh nourishes us may lead us to eat less and to consume more conscientiously.

Finally, if we are to truly commit to sustainable meat production, we will have to address the fact that meat production exists in North America as a result of the removal of the Indigenous people and their sovereign food systems from the landscape, food systems, and communities that had been sustained for millennia.

Notes

1 An introductory caveat is in order: this chapter takes as a founding assumption the idea that smaller-scale meat processing operations are more sustainable than large-scale industrial operations, for a number of reasons. For one, there is a direct link between the scale of meat processing operations and the method of management used to raise livestock (and as raised earlier in this book, the industrial model of meat production gives rise to a wide range of environmental problems). Second, while large-scale meat *processing* operations do indeed take significant efforts to reduce "waste" (which they see as potential losses in profit), their propensity for corporate consolidation leads to a range of other problems relating to sustainability, such as significantly further distances required to transport livestock and meat from farm to table, and the erosion of community relationships, food security, and farmer autonomy.

2 This does not mean that such parts went "unused" in a non-commercial sense, however. Hides could have been tanned, wool milled and spun, offal and offcuts used as feed for other animals or used as compost, lard rendered and used in baking, etc. The point is, without the additional processing power, smaller abattoirs were unable to include these parts of the animal within their profit streams.

3 There are many advantages to being able to slaughter and process animals on-site, ranging from not having to unduly stress the animals as a result of transport, to minimizing the chances for cross-contamination of pathogens from other farms, to increasing livestock producers' oversight of the treatment and processing of their product.

4 This waste is typically more than 50 per cent of the animal, for most species except poultry.

5 It must be stated that industry advisory groups to the federal government are often dominated if not exclusively made up of large-scale enterprises. For abattoirs in particular, small and medium-scale abattoirs will neither have the budget nor be able to release personnel to attend consultations or engage consistently in the work. See, for instance, the Beef Value Chain.

References

Azzam, Azzeddine M., and Dale G. Anderson. 1996. *Assessing Competition in Meatpacking: Economic History, Theory, and Evidence*. US Packers and Stockyards Programs and US Grain Inspection, Packers and Stockyards Administration. https://www.gipsa.usda.gov/psp/publication/con_tech%20report/rr96-6.pdf.

BC Centre for Disease Control. 2005. "Abattoirs: Plant Construction, Equipment and Operation Guidelines – To Qualify for Licensing under the British Columbia Meat Inspection Program." https://www2.gov.bc.ca/assets/gov/farming-natural-resources-and-industry/agriculture-and-seafood/food-safety/meat-inspection/abattoirsplantconstructequipoperation.pdf.

BC Ministry of Agriculture. 2018. "Agriculture in Brief: Regional District of Okanagan – Similkameen." https://www2.gov.bc.ca/assets/gov/farming-natural-resources-and-industry/agriculture-and-seafood/statistics/census/aginbrief_okanagan-similkameen.pdf.

Berry, Wendell. 1996. *The Unsettling of America: Culture and Agriculture*. San Francisco: Sierra Club Books.

Boucher, Christina. 2008. "Healthy Communities: The Impact of Provincial Health Policy on Rural Living – An Inquiry into Bella Coola and the Meat Inspection Regulations." Bella Coola, BC: Bella Coola General Hospital.

Brody, Hugh. 2009. *The Other Side of Eden: Hunters, Farmers and the Shaping of the World*. New York: North Point Press.

Cronon, William. 1992. *Nature's Metropolis: Chicago and the Great West*. New York: W.W. Norton.

D'Aliesio, Renata. 2013. "Feds Discussed Bailing Out XL Foods to Ease Fallout from Beef Recall." *Globe and Mail*, 15 October 2013. https://www.theglobeandmail.com/news/national/feds-discussed-aid-for-xl-foods-to-ease-fallout-from-beef-recall/article14864041/.

Food Safety News. 2016. "47 Million Pounds of Meat and Poultry Products Caught in Big Veggie Recall." Food Safety News.com. 12 May 2016. https://www.foodsafetynews.com/2016/05/47-million-pounds-of-meat-and-poultry-products-caught-in-big-veggie-recall/.

Gordon, David. 1984. "Swift & Co. v. United States: The Beef Trust and the Stream of Commerce Doctrine." *The American Journal of Legal History* 28 (3): 244–79. https://doi.org/10.2307/844700.

Johnson, Brigitt. 2008. "Impact of the Meat Inspection Regulation on Slaughter Capacity in the North Okanagan Regional District." https://www.socialplanning.ca/pdf/food_security/meat_inspection_final_report.pdf.

Kneen, Brewster. 1993. *From Land to Mouth: Understanding the Food System, Second Helping*. 2nd ed. Toronto: NC Press.

Libecap, Gary D. 1992. "The Rise of the Chicago Packers and the Origins of Meat Inspection and Antitrust." *Economic Inquiry* 30: 242–62.

Livingston, John A. 1994. *Rogue Primate: An Exploration of Human Domestication*. Lanham, MD: Roberts Rinehart Publishers.

Martin, Wanda, Erika Mundel, and Karen Rideout. 2016. "Finding Balance: Food Safety, Food Security, and Public Health." In *Conversations in Food Studies*, edited by Colin R. Anderson, Jennifer Brady, and Charles Z. Levkoe, 170–92. Winnipeg: University of Manitoba Press.

National Farmers Union. 2011. "The State of Canadian Agriculture by the Numbers." Saskatoon, SK: National Farmers Union. https://www.nfu.ca/wp-content/uploads/2018/05/farm_income_exports_imports.pdf.

Ostry, Alex S. 2006. *Nutrition Policy in Canada, 1870–1939*. Vancouver: University of British Columbia Press.

PBS. 2014. "Interview: Patrick Boyle." Frontline: Modern Meat. 2014. https://www.pbs.org/wgbh/pages/frontline/shows/meat/interviews/boyle.html.

Reichert, Patricia, and Margaret Thomson. 2010. "Salt Spring Island Livestock Production Study." http://www.communitycouncil.ca/sites/default/files/11j-livestock-production-study.pdf.

Skogstad, Grace. 2006. "Multilevel Regulatory Governance of Food Safety: A Work in Progress." In *Rules, Rules, Rules, Rules: Multi-Level Regulatory Governance*, edited by G. Bruce Doern and Robert Johnston, 157–79. Toronto: University of Toronto Press.

– 2008. *Internationalization and Canadian Agriculture: Policy and Governing Paradigms*. Toronto: University of Toronto Press.

Visser, Margaret. 2010. *Since Eve Ate Apples: Much Depends on Dinner*. Toronto: Harper Perennial Canada.

Walker, Francis. 1906. "The 'Beef Trust' and the United States Government." *The Economic Journal* 16 (64): 491–514. https://doi.org/10.2307/2221472.

Waltner-Toews, David. 2009. *Food, Sex and Salmonella: Why Our Food Is Making Us Sick*. Vancouver, BC: Greystone Books.

Which Way(s) Forward?

Ryan M. Katz-Rosene and Sarah J. Martin

If one thing is clear from the preceding chapters, it is that the path forward for "sustainable meat" is itself anything but clear. As some of our contributors have argued, sustainable practices in meat production and consumption are possible and indeed happening already. Holistic planned grazers and other agro-ecological farmers are working to supply local food chains with high-quality, humanely raised animal-sourced foods, produced in a regenerative manner; hunters, fishers, and trappers in First Nations and rural communities are acquiring meat in ways that conserve waterways, regional habitats, and traditional or cultural practices; and ethical eaters closely attuned to the production context, or their own roles as humans living amidst a multitude of complex human-animal relationships in the Anthropocene, are finding ways to practise meat-eating in ways that can be sustained. Other commentators (also including contributors herein) are more skeptical about the limitations of such greening. There is an evident problem of scale which all environmentally conscious meat-eaters ought to confront – meat's relative caloric and nutritional density is reflected in the significant natural resources that go into its production. In global terms, the growing human population, growing economies, and growing intensification of production have put meat on a path which the earth simply cannot sustain.

One of the obvious questions coming out of this space of contention is whether sustainable meat relations ultimately require the downscaling of meat production and consumption, and if so, what might this mean in practice: Does "green meat" mean less meat? Another central question revolves around the role of alternative forms of protein in diets around the world: Does "green meat" mean *redefining* meat (to include, for instance, non-animal-cultured meat analogues or other novel proteins from insects)? A third question involves how meat is being transformed by modern industrial processes like globalization, mechanization, and urbanization: Does "green meat" mean transforming agriculture and embracing a post-industrial food system? And underlying all these questions is the broader issue of governance: Does "green meat" mean reforming and transforming the governance of meat production and consumption? If so, who will determine the future of "green meat"?

In the following pages we try to draw out a broad set of answers to these questions from the preceding chapters, while making the case that when it comes to green meat we can "have it all," so long as (a) what we have is more reflective of human *needs* than of *desires*; (b) what we have is embedded in committed efforts to produce food in a truly ecological manner; and (c) the prescriptive solutions to making meat more sustainable are sensitive to the *unevenness* seen in different social and cultural spaces and agricultural contexts. This suggests that "green meat" is not so much a singular end goal as much as a multifaceted process continually in flux – and a process which appears to be travelling in multiple directions at once. Yet we also add an important caveat, upon which we elaborate below: just as there are limitations on the extent to which meat relations can be "greened," we suggest that there are similarly limitations on the extent to which traditional livestock can feasibly be *removed* from the food system. In short, it seems evident to us that animals occupy an essential role in the spheres of agricultural production, food consumption and nutrition, and many world cultures and cuisines. This is particularly evident in situations where animal-sourced food is embedded within biospheric, economic, and human-animal relations. So it is that we believe meat *can* play an important role in a sustainable future – economically, socially, and environmentally – while we acknowledge that much needs to change from currently dominant practices in meat consumption and production if that role is to be fulfilled. We build this case by expanding on the future "pathways" for sustainable meat outlined in the introduction. Different actors at varied scales (from international organizations to small self-organizing local groups), both inside and outside of the industrial meat complex, are pursuing varied "green meat" futures.

Madly Off in Three Directions

In the introductory chapter we briefly identified three categories of responses to present-day discussions on the meat-environment relationship. We would like to explore these in more detail here, and consider their respective strengths and weaknesses. As we noted at the outset, the future of meat is headed in at least three different directions at once; three "pathways" aiming at green meat production and consumption relations:

Modernizing Meat

The first pathway centres on the idea of "modernizing meat." This view is characterized by an emphasis on technological innovation and further intensification of meat production to improve efficiency. One of the key assumptions underlying the "modernizing meat" pathway is the idea that as the global population of humans increases, the demand for protein will inevitably grow, especially in emerging economies such as China and India. The modernist vision of environmentally responsible meat production is premised on the introduction of new technologies which reduce the use of water, land, and other inputs, or which recycle previously discarded materials and thus produce less waste and pollution (for instance, bio-digesters that capture methane released from manure and use this to generate energy).

Corporate ecological rhetoric regarding "sustainable meat" is a key example of the modernizing meat narrative. The "verifiable sustainable beef" pilot project from McDonald's,[1] for instance, champions technological tools like advanced hormones and targeted antibiotics because these tools support their definitions of "animal health" and "food safety," while at the same time ensuring "production efficiency." Take, for instance, the following quote about a recent corporate sustainable beef verification program in Canada: "McDonald's was not talking about producing beef with 'freedom from' (freedom from hormones and antibiotics). In fact, the project welcomed science and technology – [asking] what tools can modern beef production use that *increase efficiency*, reduce the environmental footprint, respect animal welfare yet yield a very healthy, safe food product?" (Hart 2016, emphasis added). Again, the aim is to increase the global food supply through "sustainable intensification" (Jowit 2012). Interestingly, part of the justification of this narrative arises from the admission that global livestock numbers must not increase. Rather, the actual animals themselves must become more productive without growing the global herd. In a film clip emphasizing the benefits of modern livestock production in this way, Mitloehner gives the comparative example of the typical dairy cow in California, Mexico, and India, noting that the "modernized" California cow can produce five times as much dairy as the Mexican one, and twenty times as much as the Indian one. This, notes Mitloehner, is because the US dairy industry embraces "advanced genetics," "advanced health care," and "optimal diets" (Angus TV 2012). The inclinations of this pathway are thus clearly modernist, and lead to the assertion that increasing industrialization will *reduce* the net impact of livestock production as the industry becomes more efficient. Thus, Mitloehner concludes, "in order for those growing populations in places like India and China to support their societal needs – nutritional needs – they will have to follow suit with what we have done here [in the US], which is producing livestock products with as small a herd as possible" (ibid.). By using animal genetics (to induce multiple births, for instance, or to sequence genomes to select for more productive and healthier animals), livestock producers aim to increase the amount of animal protein produced per unit of input required (see HLPE 2016).

This pathway aims to improve the efficiency of industrial agriculture and extends from the animals themselves to how and what they are fed, as well as the issue of "waste." Along with increased productivity of livestock, proposals under the theme of modernizing meat aim to reduce negative environmental externalities in the production of animal feeds, through improved plant breeding, reducing waste and by-products, and replacing feed grain with crop residues (which otherwise would be "wasted"). It thus appeals to eco-modernist imperatives on the need to improve performance through technological innovation and intensification (Asafu-Adjaye et al. 2015). As such, this pathway has a number of prominent backers, including global actors such as the Gates Foundation, USAID, some policy-makers at the FAO, and the Consultative Group on International Agricultural Research (CGIAR), all of whom generally agree with the premise that higher productivity leads to greater incomes and improved livelihoods (HLPE 2016). In addition to corporate giants like McDonald's and international institutions, several national-scale organizations support this pathway as well. For instance, the National Farmers Union in the UK has argued (in concert with the UK government) that mega-farms are a solution to the twin problems of resource constraints (e.g., arable land) and high demand for food products.

However, as the chapters in this volume have indicated, each of the three pathways outlined here has no shortage of established criticisms, and the "modernizing meat" camp is no exception. As Weis explains in chapter 2, the industrial-scale production of meat "exacerbates a series of intractable biological and physical problems" which are "never resolved but rather are overridden with continual applications of short-term fixes." Weis further identifies the embedded linkages between industrially produced livestock and a range of environmental problems associated with mono-culture feed production: soil erosion and degradation, vulnerabilities to pests and diseases, greater demand for expensive and energy-intensive inputs, and water overuse and contamination. As one report from the FAO (2015) has calculated, conventional methods of food production globally (which is to say contemporary industrial-dominated methods of food production) produce an environmental cost equivalent to $3 trillion per year. While it is true that those in the "modernizing meat" camp would use this premise as demonstrating the need to improve efficiencies and production practices, critics point out the potential folly of trying to fix industrial agriculture with neo-industrial agriculture. One of the fundamental challenges to this pathway is its dependence on using (industrially produced) grain as animal feed. In a world faced by arable land constraints and growing concerns about soil health, a system that grows tremendous amounts of grain only to be used as animal feed will appear inefficient, since more plant-based protein (in terms of net weight) could have been produced if such crops were consumed directly by humans, thereby using less inputs per gram of protein produced (Poore and Nemecek 2018). In sum, modernizing meat replicates the present industrial agricultural system, but emphasizes innovation and additional efficiencies rather than fundamental change.

Replacing Meat

In part because of this fundamental challenge, the second pathway – "replacing meat" – targets the consumption of meat itself, calling for alternative sources of protein to meet the expected growth in global demand. Proponents of this pathway advocate non-animal sources of protein and/or unconventional "livestock" (such as insects) or synthetically grown meat proteins (as discussed by Newman in chapter 9). There are a number of motivations for this way of thinking (including ethical concerns about the roles humans play in killing sentient beings for food), but ultimately the assertion that we consider for the purposes of this book is the pathway's underlying *environmental* claim: since less land and water is typically needed to produce a unit of vegetable protein than a similar quantity of animal protein, it is asserted that meeting the future protein needs of the world's growing population would be much more achievable if we removed traditional livestock from the equation (Oppenlander 2013; Kateman, Bittman, and Crocker 2017).

As Blue points out in chapter 8, this narrative *against* livestock has found considerable purchase in contemporary notions of "climate friendly diets" – many of which call for the removal or significant reduction of meat, in particular red meat, from Western diets. One notable example is found in the recent writings of renowned environmentalist and *Guardian* columnist George Monbiot, who has made the case that all forms of livestock rearing – even supposedly "sustainable grazing" operations – are wasteful and inefficient in producing protein: "Almost all forms of animal farming cause environmental damage, but none more so than keeping them outdoors. The reason is inefficiency. Grazing is not just slightly inefficient, it is stupendously wasteful. Roughly twice as much of the world's surface is used for grazing as for growing crops, yet animals fed entirely on pasture produce just one gram out of the 81g of protein consumed per person per day" (Monbiot 2017). By replacing animal proteins for plant-based proteins (from pulses, in particular), Monbiot and others in this camp argue that we could feed as many people using far less land, thereby allowing us to return a large portion of farmlands to nature for "re-wilding."

In addition to plant-based proteins, other travellers along the "replacing meat" pathway advocate for "lab-grown" cultured meat analogues, which despite remaining in a largely developmental phase, are benefitting from increasing interest and investments. For example, in 2017, China signed a $300 million deal with Israeli firms to purchase their lab-grown proteins (Roberts 2017); and major meat corporations including Maple Leaf Foods in Canada, and Tyson and Cargill in the US, are investing in meat analogues as well (Bloomberg 2018; Little 2018). One may question whether such synthetically produced meat analogues qualify as "meat," but arguably that is the intention of many of these producers. One key example is the burger made by the company Impossible Foods. Using soy products and genetically engineered yeast, the company has produced a substance that chemically behaves like the "heme" compound found in hemoglobin (the iron-containing protein in animal blood). It is founded on a range of highly complex engineering processes, including gas chromatography-mass spectrometry to isolate the compounds in real meat responsible for generating the compelling aroma, feel, and taste of meat. According to its creators, both genetically engineered and "fermentation-based" cellular meat analogues are more sustainable than meat derived from livestock, using only 5 per cent of the land required and 25 per cent of the water required to produce an equivalent amount of animal-based meat (all while emitting 12.5 per cent of the GHGs associated with animal-based meats) (Simon 2017).

Another dimension involved in the shift to alternative proteins is that of insect farming. While more than 2 billion people globally already consume insects within traditional diets, the idea of farming insects is relatively new in the West. The FAO has produced an extensive report into insect farming, noting a number of environmental benefits to be accrued from greater acceptance of entomophagy (insect consumption) in Western societies: "The environmental benefits of rearing insects for food and feed are founded on the high feed conversion efficiency of insects. Crickets, for example, require only 2 kilograms of feed for every 1 kilogram of bodyweight gain. In addition, insects can be reared on organic side-streams (including human and animal waste) and can help reduce environmental contamination. Insects are reported to emit fewer greenhouse gases and less ammonia than cattle or pigs, and they require significantly less land and water than cattle rearing" (van Huis et al. 2013, xiv).

While there are a great many "side roads" involved in this "replacing meat" pathway, we argue that this pathway often defaults to industrial practices, and thus shares some of the same eco-modernist assumptions as the "modernizing meat" pathway (with the key exception that conventional livestock animals are not involved). This is because feeding vast numbers of people with the equivalent protein quality as that promoted by the replacing meat crowd would inevitably require highly mechanized systems of crop production (of legumes and pulses, notably), which tend to emphasize genetic uniformity, genetic engineering, and other chemical inputs to control weeds and pests, advanced irrigation methods, and – given the lack of animal manure – a considerable reliance on energy-intensive synthetic fertilizers. Similarly, since lab meat is still in its infancy, it is too early to say what environmental impacts might relate to this form of food production. As Mattick (2018, 34) has pointed out, there is reason to be cautious about the per unit footprint claims of lab-based meats, because they typically do not incorporate the displacement of new forms of environmental externalities to other sectors and spaces (for instance, energy used in the laboratories, additional transport of the product, food-grade single-use plastics to hold cell cultures, etc.): "The absence of livestock would not necessarily translate into sustainable or efficient processes – particularly when it comes to energy requirements." While insect farming offers some environmental advantages over conventional livestock production in terms of land and water requirements, and waste conversion and GHG emissions, it poses some risks, in certain contexts, to humans, animals, plants, and biodiversity in general (van Huis and Oonincx 2017).

The environmental impacts of mono-cultured pulse crops, laboratory meat, and insect farming thus ironically form part of the basis for some of the leading criticisms of "replacing meat," although there are others. As we discuss in the introductory chapter, and as touched on by Thompson, Pritty, and Thapa in chapter 6, and Kenefick in chapter 7, another category of criticism relates to the culinary (cultural) and nutritional value of meat in the diets of various communities around the world. For reasons of cultural practice, culinary choice, and even nutritional benefit, animal-based meat is clearly a food of choice for people on every continent – even in India, where almost one-third of the population describes itself as vegetarian or vegan (Heinrich Böll Foundation and Friends of the Earth Europe 2014, 57). That is, rising income levels are equated just about everywhere on the planet with greater meat consumption (see figure 11.1; and Stoll-Kleemann and O'Riordan 2015). For proponents of the "replacing meat" pathway, this is of course no reasonable justification for continuing along what they see as a destructive path, but the point of raising this criticism is to encourage consideration of the problem in pragmatic terms, which requires thinking about the material limitations of the idea of completely phasing out animal agriculture (more on this below).

Restoring Meat

Some critics view both the "replacement" and "re-modernizing" approaches above as misguided, claiming that they have failed to see how it is precisely the creeping distance between people and their food that is ultimately at fault in driving unsustainable meat consumption practices (Fairlie 2010; Niman 2014; Dingman 2015; Keith 2009; Hayes and Hayes 2015). Industrial agriculture has changed animal diets (away from natural forages to grains, notably); laden foods with agro-chemicals, excess sugars, and synthetic fats; and has resulted in the concentration of wealth in the hands of very few corporate players who control the system through vertical integration and market control (while leaving the vast majority of small-scale producers broke and debt-ridden). Approaching the problem of meat unsustainability through a socio-ecological lens, such critics thus call for the "restoration" of meat by reasserting the essential role that animals play in many self-sustaining farm ecosystems. There are many different foundations from which those within the "restoring meat" camp arrive at the problem (and, as Frith indicates in chapter 5, there are a number of internal debates within this pathway, particularly over the benefit and impact of some forms of grazing over others, and whether the restoration of meat involves *greater* numbers of ruminants or *fewer* of them). Yet, whether under the name of "restoration agriculture" (Shepard 2013) or "holistic management" (Savory and Butterfield 1999), or other emerging community-supported agriculture projects (Salatin 2007), a range of unique approaches are coalescing into a new agro-ecological movement within which meat is recognized as playing an important part of a healthy, environmentally friendly, and just community-oriented diet.

The proponents of this pathway argue that animals offer a range of cultural, social, and ecological benefits that are largely irreplaceable with non-animal alternatives. In theory, a reduction in meat demand from *industrial* farms (concurrent with a shift to smaller, more diffuse and diverse mixed organic farms) could alleviate many of the ecological stresses involved in conventional agriculture by building up soil carbon, reducing soil erosion, and better protecting groundwater (all while producing great benefit to animal welfare). As an example, one proponent of holistic management explains how careful management of livestock can produce ecological benefits tied to soil, as well as the water and carbon cycles: "If done properly, the benefits of holistic land management are vast. Inputs can be reduced because the animals are increasing (and improving) their own food source by aeration and fertilization. The food source improves because the soil health increases. Healthier soil holds greater amounts of water, making the landscape increasingly immune to both drought and flooding. Healthier soil also packs in the carbon, turning an atmospheric liability into an agricultural asset" (Giebler 2016). Hence, the "restoring meat" pathway challenges mainstream narratives about climate change in two main ways. First, it attempts to offer a more holistic (one might say "eco-systemic") picture of both the benefits and drawbacks – or the inputs and outputs – of animal husbandry within the agricultural system and even the earth system; and second, it claims to offer a method of temporarily offsetting the rise in global GHG emissions by sequestering carbon in agricultural soils. Donovan (2013, 2) explains it this way: "Because soils hold more carbon than the atmosphere and vegetation combined, and can hold it longer, people are increasingly looking to soil carbon as an opportunity to both mitigate and adapt to climate change, along with its twin issue, ecosystem function. Grasslands are not just empty spaces for producing livestock, or flyover land between urban economies. They have a major influence on the composition of the atmosphere, with greater leverage than fossil fuels because they can accumulate carbon, not just release it to the atmosphere."

According to this line of thinking, livestock have an important role to play in the restoration of global grasslands, which comprise somewhere in the area of 40 per cent of the world's land surface (Suttie et al. 2005). If grazed on pasturelands and rangelands (and particularly lands less suitable to crop production), livestock can help to regenerate the land through (a) building up soil organic carbon and improving soil fertility; (b) reducing biodiversity loss; (c) reducing unnecessary water withdrawals; (d) reducing the amount of air and water pollution from agriculture; and (e) reducing soil erosion. Grazing livestock (compared to raising them in an industrial setting) can also help reduce the rate of methane and nitrous oxide emissions from livestock production, while also offsetting (if not negating) these emissions through the sequestration of carbon dioxide (Teague et al. 2016). There is no doubt that animal agriculture – like all human endeavours – influences its environment, yet many argue that managing livestock in an agro-ecological way qualifies as one of the most "sustainable" forms of human activity available, given the range of ecosystem services provided and the length of time that animal husbandry has thus far been practised. True, the attempt to embed this type of agriculture within the natural biogeochemical cycles of the earth means that it simply cannot be as "efficient" a producer of protein as "intensive" industrial systems, and that likely means that if we are going to eat "good meat," we will almost certainly have to eat *less* of it (particularly because the human population continues to grow so quickly). Yet as we conclude below, that's not to say there is no role for meat in the human diet.

Restoring meat is not just about ecological or environmental processes in relation to settler agriculture. As Thompson, Pritty, and Thapa show in chapter 6, the Garden Hill First Nation's food and territorial sovereignty is relational and shaped by its foodshed (and watershed). In turn, hunting, fishing, and gathering is not just a restoration of a type of consumption, but these practices are tightly woven into Indigenous sovereignty and traditional knowledge systems and values that shape the environment in unique ways. In order to restore meat there is no single model, but rather many practices aiming to restore human-animal and environmental relations more broadly.

Of course, as discussed above, and in a number of chapters herein, there is no shortage of criticisms of the "restoring meat" pathway, both from the modernizing crowd, which labels grazing as highly inefficient as compared to intensive grain-feeding operations, and the replacing meat crowd, which argues that all forms of conventional livestock production are overly taxing on the global environment.

What is interesting to note, however, is that all three pathways appear to be experiencing a robust expression in the world today. "Big Meat" is hard at work to market the idea of a turn toward sustainable practices while also investing large sums of capital into technological innovations that promote new variants of industrial-scale meat production (see Global Roundtable for Sustainable Beef 2016); engineering start-ups like Impossible Foods and civil society campaigns like Meatless Monday are pushing the idea of a transformation in global diets away from animal-based meats to alternative forms of protein; and all the while new local food movements, practitioners of agro-ecological production methods, and a range of small to medium-scale grazing operations are advocating for the re-embedding of meat within local human-influenced ecosystems (wherein animals and the meat they provide are recognized as providing important social, economic, and ecological benefits). All three of these pathways are in play at the same time. In the remainder of this chapter we contemplate how this multivalent and multi-directional system is being governed and regulated.

Governing "Green Meat": High-Level Proposals and Policies

As argued above, a range of actors and players globally have outlined distinct transformations in the way meat is defined and produced in order to achieve more sustainable methods of production. The second main question we address in this concluding chapter is one of global governance: How will the transformation to "green meat" be governed? To guide our discussion of the global governance of "green meat," we focus on a recent report published by the UN-based Committee on World Food Security's High-Level Panel of Experts (HLPE) on Food Security and Nutrition (FSN), which specifically examined the role(s) of livestock in achieving the twin goals of sustainable agricultural development, and food security and nutrition (HLPE 2016). The HLPE does the important legwork of targeting specific policies to different types of livestock rearing operations (smallholder mixed, commercial grazing, intensive, and pastoral), and further reflects the pathways we have discussed above, with emphasis on how livestock is a powerful "engine" for agricultural development and "a uniquely powerful entry-point for understanding agricultural development as a whole" (ibid., 10). That is, it ties the ideologies and objectives of the three green meat pathways we discuss above to scale-specific policies which address a complex range of issues involved in sustainability (including food security and environmental impacts).

The report, *Sustainable Agricultural Development for Food Security and Nutrition: What Roles for Livestock?* draws on the Right to Food, the Sustainable Development Goals (SDGs), and the Rome Declaration on Nutrition (Second International Conference on Nutrition 2014), which commits countries to increase investments in food systems to improve people's diets and nutrition. There is an urgency to support agricultural development for the 1.3 billion people who count on agriculture for their livelihoods, and often live in extreme poverty, and to address the "triple burden" of global hunger (affecting 792 million people), micro-nutrient deficiencies (affecting 2 billion people), and over-nutrition (which now exceeds global hunger levels) (HLPE 2016). The report recognizes the complex and heterogeneous character of human-animal relationships and it suggests that policy-makers change their focus from agricultural and livestock *specialization* to greater support of *diversification*. Inter-species synergies, including mixed crop and livestock operations that enhance environmental improvements such as soil quality, can provide a buffer against changing climate conditions and volatile markets (ibid., 100).

The HLPE's focus on livestock is timely because it outlines how changes in livestock production and consumption have reconfigured agriculture in recent decades in at least three ways. First, the growth of industrial livestock practices has had implications for agricultural markets and the livelihoods of millions of poor people who fully or partially depend on animal rearing for subsistence. Second, livestock production and consumption affects global environmental issues such as climate change, resource scarcity, and land use. Third, human health is linked to the uneven consumption patterns exemplified in the triple burdens noted above, which in turn are shaped by global agricultural trade, uneven consumption patterns, and corporate concentration (Clapp 2012).

Sustainable agricultural development, according to the HLPE, is built on the three pillars of resource efficiency, resilience, and social equity. Resource efficiency is often aligned with market solutions to improve productive capacity. Similarly, resilience is aligned with economic and production efficiencies, and improving ecological management such as diversifying livestock and landscapes and moving away from monocultures. "Social equity" is dependent on varied norms and practices that secure social, labour, and animal welfare and is site specific. To reflect the diversity of farming systems, the HLPE and the FAO use a typology of four broad livestock production systems: smallholder mixed, commercial grazing, intensive, and pastoral production systems.

Smallholder mixed farming represents producers who rely on both livestock and crops. These farms are found in all countries, but are primarily located in Africa and Asia, and while small in scale, the farms are estimated to produce up to 80 per cent of the food consumed in Asia and sub-Saharan Africa (HLPE 2016, 38). The report recognizes that the mixed farming systems are multi-functional, where the animals provide draught power, fuel, manure, safety nets, and food for local consumption. These systems provide social coherence and are less harmful to the environment. In addition, these are the most diverse of

the livestock systems, providing some resilience to climate change and
to price volatility (ibid.). Generalizing about millions of smallholders is
difficult and therefore there are some tensions inherent in the typology.
On the one hand, smallholders are generally considered poor. On the
other hand, the relationship to small, localized economies may protect
them from the volatility of global markets and offer other types of
non-monetary social benefits (ibid.).

The second type of livestock production system is *pastoralist*.
Pastoralism is associated with some of the globe's poorest areas and
oldest civilizations in Latin America, Asia, sub-Saharan Africa, and
Europe. The HLPE highlights the unique qualities of pastoral systems
that span a variety of land tenure and management practices. It is estimated that 25 per cent of the globe's land is pastoralist (de Jode 2014, 14).
Concepts of ownership are generally linked to animals rather than any
form of land tenure beyond common resources. As such, pastoralism is
associated with relatively high levels of animal diversity (HLPE 2016, 39).
The HLPE identifies key policy priorities such as land-tenure rights,
sustainable management, and social protection policies that include
both human and animal health. At the same time, it calls for recognition for common-owned land and resources, and transhumance – the
seasonal movement of people and animals between pastures.

The third type of system, *commercial grazing*, is distinguished from
pastoralist systems by secured access to land and land tenure, and it is
often linked to global or national-scale markets, rather than localized
and subsistence relations (ibid.). Commercial grazing takes place in most
parts of the world, but operations in Canada, Australia, New Zealand
and the western US are generally large scale in comparison to other
areas. Unlike pastoralism, labour is often used in commercial grazing
operations with secured access to large areas of pasture (ibid.). The scale
and intensity of the operations have different environmental effects.
The proposed solutions for this group largely focus on maintaining
and improving grasslands through pasture management, which will
contribute to mitigation and adaptation of climate change. The rationale
is that grassland-ruminant systems produce animal-sourced food with
minimum or perhaps positive environmental services (Teague et al.
2016). Other proposals include further developing crop, livestock and
forest integrative systems thereby protecting forests and biodiversity,
and supporting further carbon sequestration.

The fourth type is *intensive livestock*, which is distinguished by its
reliance on labour, external inputs (feed and fuel), and access to capital.
Productivity is measured with animal units per worker, or animal

productivity per worker in comparison to other systems (HLPE 2016, 40). Intensive livestock operations usually involve pigs and poultry, and can be found in many areas, but mostly in the Global North and increasingly in emerging economies. Intensive livestock operations have developed alongside global commodity markets, producing standardized and uniform products that meet sanitary and market regulations. As a result, production costs are affected by global feed and fuel markets as well as livestock markets. The margins are often very small, so resource efficiency is central to this model and includes developing animals and feed with high yields (ibid.). It is recognized that one of the key issues is that feed systems have been separated from the animals who are housed in industrial systems and are basically "landless" (ibid., 138). In addition, this "de-linking" has caused higher energy and fertilizer consumption, which is driven by cheap fossil fuels (UNCTAD 2013, 139). Under the sustainable agricultural development rubric of resource efficiency, intensive livestock operations score highly. But as discussed above, its environmental externalities are plenty. The HLPE suggests producers in this category should track the "technical efficiency" of individual animals by implementing precision technologies (HLPE 2016, 117). The sustainable intensity approach is replicated through improved management of manure, including exporting to other regions and integrating with crops. On the efficiency side, the HLPE report recommends more sustainable feed and *reducing* the use of antibiotics as prophylactics.

From the HLPE framework, then, we can see how and why the three pathways above are concomitantly occurring in practice, despite being somewhat contradictory in theory. One policy proposal that may be facilitating common ground between the green meat pathways (or at least certain elements of them) is the notion of a required scaled reduction in global meat consumption. As the HLPE report notes, "a number of organizations and experts have made the link between reduced consumption of [animal sourced food] and smaller environmental footprints, and reduced natural resource use and GHG emissions" (HLPE, 2016, 102), and while it may seem on the surface that this proposal would be opposed by those in the "modernizing meat" and "restoring meat" crowd, there are in fact ways in which these pathways could work commensurately with the notion of an overall reduction in meat. As noted above, many in the modernizing meat crowd accept that the number of livestock animals should not be allowed to grow, particularly as the trends over recent decades have been unsustainable: as the IPCC's regionally specific statistics note (see figure II.I), the number of livestock globally has indeed grown, particularly poultry (having nearly

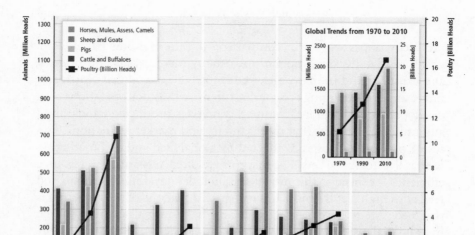

Figure II.I Global trends in livestock production, by economic region
Source: Reprinted, with permission, from Smith et al. (2014, 821).

quadrupled in number since 1970). The number of pigs, sheep, and goats has also grown globally, as has the number of cattle. Nevertheless, since 1970 the number of pigs and cattle have declined in both OECD countries and so-called Economies in Transition (EIT) countries, and in the latter nations the number of sheep and goats has also declined. Further, in some cases in industrialized nations (albeit rarely), the amount of meat consumption appears to have reached a peak.

While one might expect these developments to be causing consternation amongst the world's largest meat producers and their shareholders (and to be sure, this is occurring in part; see Begany 2015), one must remember that the main corporate players in the modernizing meat crowd are ultimately motivated by profits. This helps explain why some of them are increasingly open to the idea of diversifying the products they offer. In a post explaining why American meat consumption is declining, Shapiro offers a number of examples of interesting acquisitions and takeovers which seem to be broadening the idea of what types of proteins are included in the market for meat and its competitors: Hormel, a giant in the pork industry, recently purchased Skippy (a peanut butter brand, and a protein alternative); Kraft, which owns meat giant Oscar Mayer, has also purchased Boca Burgers (which makes vegan soy protein burgers); even Burger King has signed on to promote vegetarian alternatives through support for the Meatless Monday campaign (see Shapiro 2015).

Similarly, many elements within the "restoring meat" pathway are also content to see an overall reduction in meat consumption in industrial economies, because they believe that present levels of consumption cannot be matched by ecological forms of livestock production. That is, agro-ecological production recognizes that animals are *part of* an ecological system, not the entirety of it. The social practice of eating *less* meat (but making sure that whatever meat *is* consumed is produced in ecologically sound ways) is actually commensurate with the local food movement, improved health, and environmental sustainability.

From Policy to Practice: Some Obstacles

While some of the work advocated by the HLPE and various actors within the three "green meat" pathways is already being carried out, much remains to be done in order to convert policy to practice, particularly at the level of the state, and particularly in terms of recognizing the nuanced balance between supporting the ecological production of meat while simultaneously bringing about declining meat consumption in industrialized economies. For instance, the Global Agenda for Sustainable Livestock (GASL) – a multi-stakeholder platform for consultations that includes governments, academic researchers, the private sector, and civil society organizations – met in Panama City with the goal of inserting livestock into the UN Sustainable Development Goals (in what is called the "Panama Declaration"; GASL 2016); but, while it calls for a greening of meat production in various scales of production, it fails to address the problem of quantity. Signatories of the Panama Declaration agree to support a raft of initiatives including the SDGs themselves, integrating sustainable livestock programs and developing institutions. But it does not address the need to consider the scale and trajectory of livestock production, which is a problem.

Despite the extensive work of global institutions to set out a policy framework for sustainable meat, as well as material action taken by the corporate sector and growing networks of small-scale farmers and food security organizations, there remains much more work to be done. One jurisdiction that appears to be largely absent from pursuing green meat is the state. Mason and Lang (2017, 260) explain that there has been a rise of "neoliberal consumerist thinking" with the decline of state influence. In most industrialized countries, the state supports the production of industrial meat through policies that include subsidies and other supports (some less direct, such as nutritional guidelines). The state is generally sidelined in most accounts of meat production and consumption, and yet it plays a crucial role (as Brynne hints in chapter 10). The industrialization of livestock production is unjust, violent, and environmentally destructive, but it has also produced alternative new niche markets. The politics of local food are shaped by industrialization, and yet are being governed in new ways that are developing in these niche markets such as farmer's market regulations, or organic certification or labelling. Often these new markets for meat are based on direct connections, rather than the "distance" contemporary commodity chains sustain (Clapp 2012). The governance actors operate in new ways and now include the involvement of non-profits and other non-state actors. So, unlike the corporate-state bargain that facilitated the growth of the industrial model in the postwar years, this niche market relies on market relations, and almost exclusively voluntary principles. The model of governance today is more complex, operating at multiple scales and populated by multiple actors (Mason and Lang 2017, 260).

In sum, when it comes to the question of who will govern the greening of meat, we must cast the net wide and take a multi-scaled approach, including global governance from international institutions, state forms of regulation at both domestic and sub-national jurisdictions, self-governance from various producers (including both corporate and small-scale producers), and even to some extent market governance (with the support of various market tools like carbon pricing, to shape behaviour through shifting cost profiles of various foods and production methods). Global institutions must continue to gather data and frame the policy priorities using a planetary scope, since this is an issue touching on questions of development, human health, prosperity, and environment, among other global concerns. States need to enact smart policies and regulations which both facilitate the broad-based efforts to green meat (including producing alternative proteins) while signaling to producers that outdated, environmentally taxing methods of production will no longer be supported. As Mason and Lang have suggested (and we would agree), sustainable dietary guidelines should be married with the SDGs in the context of governance and policy. Producers themselves must self-govern – which in a corporate context may mean applying the principles of Corporate Social Responsibility wholeheartedly, and in a small-scale farmer/pastoralist sense means education, reflection, and openness to new methods of doing business. Finally, markets must be utilized, built, and/or regulated to ensure that greed, gluttony, waste, and degradation are not the recipients of financial gain, but rather the opposite. This wide cast approach is in part a necessity, given the rather heterogeneous (and to a certain extent conflicting) nature of the various pathways to meat being pursued by the range of actors and stakeholders in the debate.

Conclusion

We began this concluding chapter by raising four broad questions aiming to help define "green meat": (1) Does green meat mean *less* meat? (2) Does green meat require us to redefine meat to include other forms of protein? (3) Does green meat mean embracing a post-industrial food system? (4) Does green meat mean reforming and transforming the governance of meat production and consumption? As editors of this volume, we argue that, in many ways, "green meat" *does* mean eating less meat – particularly within industrialized economies. For one, we eat too much meat as is, with North Americans eating in the area of 100 kgs of meat per year, with obvious impacts on human health – from obesity and diabetes, according to the conventional (though increasingly contested) nutritional wisdom. Second, we argue that it means embracing modest dietary shifts to allow for some level of replacement of animal-based proteins with non-animal proteins in industrial societies (while in other national economic contexts allowing the opposite type of transformation for nutritional reasons). Third, green meat, in our view, does mean transitioning to a post-industrial food system, particularly as located in community and ecologically grounded production systems. And finally, green meat requires an embrace of a multi-modal and more complex system of governance via international organizations, the state, some market-based mechanisms, and even individual forms of "self-governance."

However, to this we add what we think is one final important corollary: the idea of reducing meat, *on its own*, is incomplete as a "solution" to the problem of unsustainability in food production, *unless* it is accompanied by more nuanced reflections regarding the qualitative aspects of how we nourish ourselves with protein. In other words, the problem of unsustainable food is not addressed merely by reducing the *quantity* of a particular kind of food. What good does it do to eat less meat if the remaining meat consumed is still produced using ecologically unsound practices? Similarly, what good does it do to replace meat with plant-based alternatives if those replacements are similarly grown in environmentally damaging ways? And what good comes from an agricultural system that banishes animals, if the end result is an unnatural agricultural system where inputs (fertilizers and pesticides, notably) are produced and used in ways that damage the soil and other natural environments and wildlife in the long term?

One of the most common rebuttals from vegans in addressing the value and essential role played by animals in regenerative agricultural systems is that having animals on a farm does not mean they have to be killed and eaten. This is a fair point, since on a technical level there is no reason why sheep, cows, pigs and fowl cannot continue to provide their ecosystemic services through to old age, so long as they remain healthy. And, of course, it should be pointed out that the dairy industry earns its keep from healthy *living* animals. But here lies an economic and ecological problem: How does the farmer afford to keep animals if they yield no value from them in return to cover the cost of their rearing? The age-old equation here, which arose out of the origins of sedentary human civilization, has been that the value of animal products covered the costs of maintaining those animals, with the eco-systemic services carried out as an *added bonus*. This may seem a crude calculus when we consider it is the lives of living beings we are talking about (and yes, a whole lot of ethical questions come up here which we leave to others; if you wish to immerse yourself in the debate, see Grandin 2010; Pollan 2006; Foer 2010). Nevertheless, this calculus has ultimately guided farmers and small-scale pastoralists alike since time immemorial.

In short, changes in the livestock production regime and meat consumption relations that aim to encourage *less* consumption of meat produced through organic, regenerative practices could offer social and ecological benefits. Further, a policy of supporting changes to the production and consumption relations of meat (in order to promote organic and regenerative livestock management and a reduction in meat consumption) will ensure that the sector's mitigation targets are being addressed while continuing to provide known benefits to society. As noted above, the social practice of eating *less* meat and eating *good* meat – or wasting less meat and treating meat as a special, high-quality form of occasional protein – is actually commensurate with the local food movement, improved health, and environmental sustainability. Ultimately, we would encourage everyone to take the time to consider the social and ecological "hoofprint" of the meat (and meat alternatives) they personally consume. By learning about from where (and how far) one's food has come, discovering what types of resources and inputs were used to make it and by whom, and by considering who (or what entities) benefitted from the money spent on it, we can begin to situate our food in our local and global communities, and help inform more sustainable dietary choices.

Note

1   Incidentally, McDonald's reportedly serves about 2 per cent of all beef
    produced in the world!

References

Angus TV. 2012. *Frank Mitloehner and the Benefits of Modern Livestock
    Production*. https://www.youtube.com/watch?time_continue=4&v=NDC
    b6jioPTw.
Asafu-Adjaye, J., L. Blomquist, S. Brand, B.W. Brook, R. Defries, E. Ellis,
    C. Foreman, et al. 2015. "An Ecomodernist Manifesto." http://ecite.utas.
    edu.au/107149.
Begany, Tim. 2015. "How the 'Death Of Meat' Could Impact Your Portfolio."
    StreetAuthority.com (blog). 2015. https://www.streetauthority.com/active-
    trading/how-death-meat-could-impact-your-portfolio-30502646.
Bloomberg. 2018. "How Peas, Bugs and Shrimp Play a Role in
    Diversifying Cargill's Business." https://www.bloomberg.com/news/
    videos/2018-10-12/how-peas-bugs-shrimp-play-a-role-in-diversifying-
    cargill-s-business-video.
Clapp, Jennifer. 2012. *Food*. Malden, MA: Polity.
Dingman, Brad. 2015. *Reclamation: A Tale of Blood, Betrayal, and Bioregional
    Meat*. Ithaca, NY: Feral Visions.
Donovan, Peter. 2013. "Measuring Soil Carbon Change: A Flexible, Practical,
    Local Method." Soil Carbon Coalition. http://soilcarboncoalition.org/files/
    MeasuringSoilCarbonChange.pdf.
Fairlie, Simon. 2010. *Meat: A Benign Extravagance*. White River Junction, VT:
    Chelsea Green.
Foer, Jonathan Safran. 2010. *Eating Animals*. New York: Little, Brown.
GASL. 2016. "Panama Declaration: The Global Agenda for Sustainable
    Livestock Contributing to the UN 2030 Sustainable Development
    Agenda." Global Agenda for Sustainable Livestock and the Food and
    Agriculture Organization of the UN.
Giebler, Bill. 2016. "Meat, the Unlikely Climate Hero?" New Hope Network.
    3 November 2016. http://www.newhope.com/news/meat-unlikely-
    climate-hero.
Global Roundtable for Sustainable Beef. 2016. "Global Roundtable for
    Sustainable Beef: What Is Sustainable Beef?" 2016. https://grsbeef.org/
    WhatIsSustainableBeef.
Grandin, Temple. 2010. "Auditing Animal Welfare at Slaughter Plants." *Meat
    Science* 86 (1): 56–65. https://doi.org/10.1016/j.meatsci.2010.04.022.

Hart, Lee. 2016. "Sustainable Beef Is within Our Grasp: McDonald's Restaurant Project Set the Tone for Canadian Beef Industry." *Canadian Cattlemen* (blog). 15 August 2016. https://www.canadiancattlemen.ca/2016/08/15/sustainable-beef-within-our-grasp/.

Hayes, Denis, and Gail Boyer Hayes. 2015. *Cowed: The Hidden Impact of 93 Million Cows on America's Health, Economy, Politics, Culture, and Environment*. New York: W.W. Norton.

Heinrich Böll Foundation, and Friends of the Earth Europe. 2014. *Meat Atlas: Facts and Figures about the Animals We Eat*. Berlin: Heinrich. http://www.boell.de/sites/default/files/meat_atlas2014.pdf.

HLPE. 2016. *Sustainable Agricultural Development for Food Security and Nutrition: What Roles for Livestock? A Report by the High Level Panel of Experts on Food Security and Nutrition of the Committee on World Food Security*. HLPE Report 10. Rome, Italy: High Level Panel of Experts on Food Security and Nutrition. http://www.fao.org/3/a-i5795e.pdf.

Huis, Arnold van, and Dennis G.A.B. Oonincx. 2017. "The Environmental Sustainability of Insects as Food and Feed. A Review." *Agronomy for Sustainable Development* 37 (5, article 43): 1–14. https://doi.org/10.1007/s13593-017-0452-8.

Huis, Arnold van, Joost Van Itterbeeck, Harmke Klunder, Afton Halloran, and Guilia Muir. 2013. *Edible Insects: Future Prospects for Food and Feed Security*. FAO Forestry Paper 171. Rome: Food and Agriculture Organization of the United Nations.

Jode, Helen de. 2014. "The Green Quarter: A Decade of Progress across the World in Sustainable Pastoralism." Nairobi: IUCN. https://portals.iucn.org/library/sites/library/files/documents/2014-047.pdf.

Jowit, Juliette. 2012. "Super Farms Are Needed in UK, Says Leader of National Farmers Union." *The Guardian*, 5 June 2012. https://www.theguardian.com/environment/2012/jun/05/uk-needs-super-farms-says-nfu.

Kateman, Brian, Mark Bittman, and Pat Crocker. 2017. *The Reducetarian Solution: How the Surprisingly Simple Act of Reducing the Amount of Meat in Your Diet Can Transform Your Health and the Planet*. New York: TarcherPerigee.

Keith, Lierre. 2009. *The Vegetarian Myth: Food, Justice, and Sustainability*. 1st ed. Crescent City, CA: PM Press.

Little, Amanda. 2018. "Tyson's Quest to Be Your One-Stop Protein Shop." Bloomberg.com, 15 August 2018. https://www.bloomberg.com/news/features/2018-08-15/tyson-s-quest-to-be-your-one-stop-protein-shop.

Mason, Pamela, and Tim Lang. 2017. *Sustainable Diets: How Ecological Nutrition Can Transform Consumption and the Food System*. London and New York: Routledge.

Mattick, Carolyn S. 2018. "Cellular Agriculture: The Coming Revolution in Food Production." *Bulletin of the Atomic Scientists* 74 (1): 32–5. https://doi.org/10.1080/00963402.2017.1413059.

Monbiot, George. 2017. "Goodbye – and Good Riddance – to Livestock Farming." *The Guardian*, 4 October 2017. https://www.theguardian.com/commentisfree/2017/oct/04/livestock-farming-artificial-meat-industry-animals.

Niman, Nicolette Hahn. 2014. *Defending Beef*. White River Junction, VT: Chelsea Green.

Oppenlander, Richard A. 2013. *Food Choice and Sustainability: Why Buying Local, Eating Less Meat, and Taking Baby Steps Won't Work*. Minneapolis, MN: Langdon Street Press.

Pollan, Michael. 2006. *The Omnivore's Dilemma: A Natural History of Four Meals*. New York: Penguin.

Poore, J., and T. Nemecek. 2018. "Reducing Food's Environmental Impacts through Producers and Consumers." *Science* 360 (6392): 987–92. https://doi.org/10.1126/science.aaq0216.

Roberts, Rachel. 2017. "China Signs $300m to Buy Lab-Grown Meat from Israel." *The Independent*, 16 September 2017. http://www.independent.co.uk/news/world/asia/china-israel-trade-deal-lab-grown-meat-veganism-vegetarianism-a7950901.html.

Salatin, Joel. 2007. *Everything I Want to Do Is Illegal*. Swope, VA: Polyface.

Savory, Allan, and Jody Butterfield. 1999. *Holistic Management: A New Framework for Decision Making*. Washington, DC: Island Press.

Shapiro, Paul. 2015. "Americans Are Eating Less and Less Meat Every Year. Why?" Forks Over Knives (blog). 22 September 2015. https://www.forksoverknives.com/americans-are-eating-less-and-less-meat-every-year-why/.

Shepard, Mark. 2013. *Restoration Agriculture: Real World Permaculture for Farmers*. Austin, TX: Acres USA.

Simon, Matt. 2017. "Inside the Strange Science of the Fake Meat That 'Bleeds.'" *Wired*. 20 September 2017. https://www.wired.com/story/the-impossible-burger/.

Smith, P., H. Bustamente, H. Clark, H. Dong, E.A. Elsiddig, H. Haberl, R. Harper, et al. 2014. "Agriculture, Forestry and Other Land Use (AFOLU)." In *Climate Change 2014: Mitigation of Climate Change. Contribution of Working Group III to the IPCC Fifth Assessment Report*, edited by O. Edenhofer, R. Pichs-Madruga, Y. Sokona, E Farahani, S. Kadner, K. Seyboth, A. Adler, et al., 811–922. Cambridge: Cambridge University Press.

Stoll-Kleemann, Susanne, and Tim O'Riordan. 2015. "The Sustainability Challenges of Our Meat and Dairy Diets." *Environment: Science and Policy*

for Sustainable Development 57 (3): 34–48. https://doi.org/10.1080/0013915
7.2015.1025644.

Suttie, J.M., Stephen G. Reynolds, Caterina Batello, and Food and
Agriculture Organization of the United Nations. 2005. *Grasslands of the
World.* Rome: Food and Agricultural Organization of the United Nations.

Teague, W.R., S. Apfelbaum, R. Lal, U.P. Kreuter, J. Rowntree, C.A. Davies,
R. Conser, et al. 2016. "The Role of Ruminants in Reducing Agriculture's
Carbon Footprint in North America." *Journal of Soil and Water
Conservation* 71 (2): 156–64. https://doi.org/10.2489/jswc.71.2.156.

UNCTAD. 2013. *Trade and Environment Review 2013: Wake Up before It Is Too
Late: Make Agriculture Truly Sustainable Now for Food Security in a Changing
Climate.* Geneva, Switzerland: United Nations Conference on Trade
and Development.

Contributors

GWENDOLYN BLUE is an associate professor in the Department of Geography at the University of Calgary. Formally trained in cultural studies, her research interests centre on public engagement with environmental and health issues. She was the lead researcher on a Social Sciences and Humanities Research Council–funded project on Global Public Participation and Climate Change, and is currently a collaborator on two SSHRC-funded projects examining public participation and climate policy. Other research interests lie with post-humanist approaches to publics, public engagement, and environmental politics.

ABRA BRYNNE is a nationally respected food systems advocate who has worked closely with farmers and the food industry for almost thirty years. Her longstanding interest in the regulatory systems that impact food production found a practical application working closely with abattoir proponents and farmers for six years, assisting them to understand and meet the various government requirements of licensing. She continues to analyze legislation and works to ameliorate the regulatory environment for small-scale producers wherever possible. Her passion for food policy is applied across diverse contracts and work relationships with local governments, NGOs, academics, food processors, and farmers.

SHELDON FRITH is a holistic management supervisor and consultant at the Northern Farm Training Institute in Hay River, Northwest Territories. He is the author of *Letter to a Vegetarian Nation* (2016), and frequently blogs at RegenerateLand.com.

RYAN M. KATZ-ROSENE is an assistant professor at the University of Ottawa's School of Political Studies, where he studies climate policy and environmental debates, with specialties in the global political economy of energy, transportation, and agriculture. His most recent book, co-authored with Matthew Paterson, is *Thinking Ecologically about the Global Political Economy* (Routledge 2018). Ryan currently serves as president of the Environmental Studies Association of Canada. Aside from his life as an academic, Ryan co-owns and helps to manage Rock's End Farm – his family's small-scale organic farm near Wakefield, Quebec.

ALEXANDRA KENEFICK is a PhD candidate researching meat consumption and sustainability at Concordia University, in Montreal. Her work focuses on the ways in which contemporary production and consumption patterns have created a self-perpetuating distanciation and obfuscation in the relationship between eaters and the meat they consume. The aim of her research is to observe and develop opportunities for direct consumer engagement with meat animals and practices in order to reconnect eaters and meat consumption, and to reveal hidden externalities of the industrial agricultural complex.

SARAH J. MARTIN is an assistant professor at the Department of Political Science, Memorial University, in St John's, Newfoundland. Sarah's scholarly interests have always been centred around the global political economy of food, with a particular interest in the interactions between finance, markets, and agriculture. Her present research is focused on the environmental impact of the global production and trade of animal feed.

LENORE NEWMAN holds a Canada Research Chair in Food Security and Environment at the University of the Fraser Valley, where she is an associate professor in the Department of Geography and the Environment. She runs a research program focused on Canadian regional cuisines, local food sovereignty, culturally preferred foods, and agricultural land use. She has written extensively on the resurgence of farmers' markets in Canada, and is a strong advocate for fresh, local food.

PEPPER PRITTY is a registered nurse and practises in the area of Indigenous health and environmental health. She is a doctoral student in the Natural Resources Institute at the University of Manitoba studying food and medicine systems of Indigenous-built and social environments. She is passionate about chronic disease prevention and promoting land-based teachings as a source of health and healing.

CAITLIN M. SCOTT is a professor at George Brown College in Toronto. Her research explores the challenges of governing for sustainable diets, focusing on ideational debates and power. She is interested specifically in food at the intersection of health and environmental issues. Her work places emphasis on the role that Big Food corporations are playing in framing sustainability strategies, and investigates how processed products fit into conceptions of sustainable food consumption.

KESHAB THAPA is a doctoral student at the Natural Resources Institute of the University of Manitoba. He has worked in Nepal in community-based biodiversity management and climate change adaptation. His research and learning areas are related to Indigenous sovereignty, land-based reconciliation, community-based climate change adaptation, and art-based research methodologies.

SHIRLEY THOMPSON conducts participatory action research in the area of food security and community development in Canada's remote First Nation communities. She is an associate professor in the Natural Resources Institute at the University of Manitoba.

TONY WEIS is an associate professor in the Department of Geography, Western University. His research interests are broadly located in the field of political ecology, with a focus on agriculture and rural development. His most recent book is *The Ecological Hoofprint: The Global Burden of Industrial Livestock* (Zed, 2013).

Index

abattoir, 186, 192–3, 201; provincially licensed, 194–7, 200; small and medium-scale, 189–91, 198–9, 202, 203n5. *See also* slaughterhouse

adaptive multi-paddock grazing, 90, 96, 102. *See also* holistic planned grazing (HPG)

ADM, 32

agriculture, 32, 36, 53, 56n4, 94; community-supported, 213; conventional, 94, 178, 214; industrial, 11, 33, 209–10, 213; organic, 12, 59n35; regenerative, 12, 22, 59n35; settler, 22, 215. *See also* agro-ecology; animal agriculture; cellular agriculture; farming

agro-ecology, 14–15, 34, 38n7, 221; benefits, 213–15; and livestock production, 51–2, 55

amino acids. *See* protein

animal agriculture, 12–13, 16, 43–6, 48–50; brutality, 176; corporate lobbying, 177; and corporations, 74–5, 177; cultural aspects of, 16–17; environmental consequences of, 3, 22, 43–4, 171, 215; forms

and scale of, 4; and GHGs, 46, 49–50, 54, 57n15; replacement of, 6, 20, 45, 169, 213. *See also* animal husbandry

animal husbandry, 15, 18, 169–71, 215. *See also* livestock

animal welfare, 5–6, 140–1, 174; humane, 200–1

antibiotic, 35, 208, 219; antibiotic-free, 5

Barilla Center for Food and Nutrition Foundation, 69

Bayer-Monsanto, 32. *See also* Chicago Four

Beyond Meat, 22n1, 74–5, 175

biodiversity, 93, 97, 139, 180; decline, 10, 36–7, 214

Brundtland Report, 6, 110

Bunge, 32

Burger King, 32, 220

CAFOS. *See* Concentrated Animal Feeding Operations

Canada, 156–9, 200; Indigenous peoples in, 107–8, 112, 115; and family farms, 9; livestock in, 58n29; meat consumption in, 8,